THE ORIGIN
OF TRAGEDY

βαρύτιμοι
χθόνιοι θήκας κατέχοντες.
AESCH. *Suppl.* 24—5.

THE ORIGIN

OF TRAGEDY

with special reference
to the
Greek Tragedians

William Ridgeway, Sc.D., F.B.A.

BENJAMIN BLOM  New York/London

First published by
Cambridge University Press, 1910
Reissued 1966, by
Benjamin Blom, Inc., Bronx, N. Y. 10452
L. C. Cat. Card No. 65-19621

Printed in U.S.A. by
NOBLE OFFSET PRINTERS, INC.
NEW YORK 3, N. Y.

ROBERTO YELVERTON TYRRELL

ΤΡΟΦΕΙΑ

PREFACE

AS I had long been dissatisfied with the theory of the Origin of Tragedy universally accepted, I have tried to obtain the true solution of the problem by approaching it from the anthropological standpoint.

The general theory here advanced—that Tragedy originated in the worship of the dead—was first put forward in a lecture before the Society for the Promotion of Hellenic Studies in 1904, summaries of which were printed in the *Proceedings* of that Society and in the *Athenæum* (1904, p. 660). It also appeared in a fuller form in the *Quarterly Review* (Oct. 1908). The first section of Chapter I. in the present work is an expansion of that article, and for permission to use this I have to thank Mr John Murray and Mr G. W. Prothero. The section on the *Eumenides* in Chapter IV. was published in the *Classical Review* (1907, pp. 163–8), whilst that on the *Supplices* of Aeschylus was printed in the Cambridge *Greek Praelections* (1906), but each of these has been altered in various details. The subject-matter of the whole work formed the material for a course of lectures which I delivered in my capacity as Brereton Reader in Classics in the Lent Term, 1908.

It only remains for me to offer my best thanks to those who have aided me in various ways. I am indebted to my friends Dr and Mrs Seligmann for permission to print their account of a Vedda dramatic performance and for the photograph reproduced in Fig. 12 (p. 103); to Mr A. J. B. Wace, M.A., Fellow of Pembroke College, Cambridge, for his account of the Carnival Play in Northern Greece; to Mr W. Aldis Wright,

D.C.L., LL.D., Litt.D., Vice-Master of Trinity College, Cambridge, to Mr John Harrower, M.A., LL.D., Professor of Greek in the University of Aberdeen, to Mr Harold Littledale, M.A., Litt.D., Professor of English Literature in University College, Cardiff, and to Mr H. M. Chadwick, M.A., Fellow of Clare College, Cambridge, for useful references; to Mr A. B. Cook, M.A., Reader in Classical Archaeology, and Fellow of Queens' College, Cambridge, for the photograph from which Fig. 9 is reproduced; to the Council of the Society for the Promotion of Hellenic Studies and to Mr R. M. Dawkins, M.A., Fellow of Emmanuel College, Cambridge, and Director of the British School at Athens, for permission to use the illustrations shown in my Figs. 7 and 8; to Mr J. E. Sandys, Litt.D., F.B.A., Public Orator in the University of Cambridge, for sanctioning the use of two blocks from his *Bacchae* for my Figs. 10 and 13, and to Miss J. E. Harrison for a similar sanction of the use of a block from her *Prolegomena to the Study of Greek Religion* for my Fig. 5.

WILLIAM RIDGEWAY.

FLENDYSHE,
    FEN DITTON,
        August 6th, 1910.

TABLE OF CONTENTS

CHAPTER I

THE ORIGIN OF TRAGEDY

CHAPTER II

THE RISE OF ATTIC TRAGEDY

CHAPTER III

PRIMITIVE DRAMAS AMONG ASIATIC PEOPLES

CHAPTER IV

SURVIVALS OF THE PRIMITIVE TYPE IN EXTANT GREEK TRAGEDIES

CHAPTER V

THE EXPANSION OF TRAGEDY

LIST OF ILLUSTRATIONS

CHAPTER I

THE ORIGIN OF TRAGEDY

οἱ δ' ἐπεὶ εἰσάγαγον κλυτὰ δώματα, τὸν μὲν ἔπειτα
τρητοῖς ἐν λεχέεσσι θέσαν, παρὰ δ' εἷσαν ἀοιδοὺς
θρήνων ἐξάρχους, οἵ τε στονόεσσαν ἀοιδὴν
οἱ μὲν δὴ θρήνεον, ἐπὶ δὲ στενάχοντο γυναῖκες,
τῇσιν δ' Ἀνδρομάχη λευκώλενος ἦρχε γόοιο,
Ἕκτορος ἀνδροφόνοιο κάρη μετὰ χερσὶν ἔχουσα.
Il. xxiv, 719-24.

No branch of Literature and Art has been more popular
amongst civilised and semi-civilised peoples than the Drama,
nor has any exercised a more powerful influence on national
thought and sentiment, especially that side of it known as
Tragedy. It is therefore not surprising that no department
of Literature or Art has had more attraction for the historian
and the critic from ancient times down to our own day. But
innumerable as have been the writers on this theme, they have
without exception confined their attention to the rise of the
Greek drama, to its imitation in Rome, to the Mysteries and
Miracles of medieval Christianity, to the revival of the classical
form, and to its splendid development in the plays of Marlowe,
Shakespeare, Calderon, Corneille, and Racine. Moreover all
writers instead of seeking for the origin of the Drama by a
rigid application of the historical and comparative methods
have approached its study from the *a priori* standpoint of pure
Aesthetics. This was but natural, as students had their eyes
fixed almost exclusively on the Golden Age of the Attic drama,
and they regarded the creations of the tragic poets as but one
phase of that marvellous outburst of Art which has marked out
from all others the age of Pericles. Even now all study of Art

1

is almost invariably based on *a priori* assumptions, no regard being taken of the Anthropological method, and it could hardly have been expected that writers on the drama would have followed other lines.

No matter how widely writers on Greek Tragedy may differ from each other in details, they are all agreed that although its beginnings are shrouded in the mists of antiquity, certain main facts respecting its early stages are firmly established: (1) That it was the invention of the Dorians in certain districts of Peloponnesus, (2) that it arose wholly out of the worship of Dionysus, (3) that the Satyric Drama likewise grew up in the same Dorian States out of rustic and jovial dithyrambs common among the lower classes in the same districts as those in which Tragedy is supposed to have had its birth, (4) that the Satyric Drama was a kind of comic relief to the tragedy or tragedies to which it was an adjunct and of which in early times it seems to have been the inseparable concomitant, (5) that the *Thymele* was from the first the altar of Dionysus, and (6) that Thespis was the first to establish Tragedy on a proper basis, some holding that his grand step consisted merely in separating the leader from the rest of the Chorus and making him interrupt the choral parts with some sort of Epic recitation, whilst others think that he was the first to apply to moral purposes the sufferings, often undeserved, of heroes. A closer examination of the available data, scanty as they are, may perhaps show that most of these common beliefs have no foundation in fact, and that it may be necessary to remodel completely our views concerning the first beginnings and development of the Tragic art.

The Claim of the Dorians.

It has been universally assumed that the Dorians were the inventors of Tragedy on the grounds that (1) Aristotle said so, and (2) that the Chorus in the Attic tragedies are all in the Doric dialect. But Aristotle makes no such statement in the *Poetics*[1], for he merely remarks that some of the Dorians lay claim to both Tragedy and Comedy on etymological grounds,

---

[1] III, 4.

maintaining that the word *drama* is Doric because they (the Dorians) use δρᾶν where the Athenians say πράττειν, though he himself in no wise endorses their pretension. The Dorians' argument has just as little value and has been just as misleading as many other arguments both ancient and modern which, like it, are based solely on etymology.

Dialect of the Chorus. The second argument on which scholars rely has no better foundation in fact. It has been assumed that certain linguistic forms found in the choruses of the Attic tragedies are in the Doric dialect and that to it likewise belong certain forms used also in the dialogue in which ᾱ appears instead of η[1]. The present writer has long since

---

[1] e.g. ἕκατι, δαρόν, Ἀθάνα, λοχαγός, κυναγός, ποδαγός, ὀπαδός. Brugmann [*Grundriss*, Band I (2nd ed.) pp. 166-7] says that the change from ᾱ into η had already taken place in what he calls the Attic-Ionic period (in der Zeit der Ion.-Att. Urgemeinschaft). He holds that in such words as χώρα, πράττω, καρδία, ἰάσομαι, γενεά, σικύα, = Ionic χώρη, πρήσσω, κραδίη, ἰήσομαι, γενεή, σικύη, etc., there has been a change back from η to ᾱ. But he gives no evidence and only assumes that Attic had once gone as far as Ionic in modifying ᾱ into η. Nor does he give any proof that χώρη had changed back into χώρα. He assumes that ρ, ι, ε, and ν, had the power of changing η back into ᾱ, but why should not these sounds have had the power of keeping original ᾱ from being changed into η? So far from his being able to show any tendency in Attic for η to revert to ᾱ, he himself points out that there were many exceptions "durch Neubildung." Thus in the fourth cent. B.C. ὑγιῆ, ἐνδεῆ, εὐφυῆ supplanted ὑγιᾶ, ἐνδεᾶ, εὐφυᾶ, etc. The only instance to the contrary cited by Brugmann is ὑφάναι instead of ὑφῆναι. But as the only instance of this aorist given by Veitch (*Greek Verbs*) is in *Anthol.* VI, 265, an epigram to Lacinian Hera wholly composed in *Doric*, the form can hardly be used to prove that there was at any time a tendency in *Attic* to replace η by ᾱ. Brugmann's contention that Attic went the whole way with Ionic and then turned back is just as unreasonable as if any one were to maintain that, because certain phonetic tendencies especially marked in the dialect of the Americans of New England are also found in a less degree in the dialect of Lincolnshire in England, whence many of the first settlers in New England came, therefore the dialect of Lincolnshire had once had all the phonetic peculiarities of the modern Yankees, but that it had at a later period turned back. The obvious explanation—that certain tendencies of the Lincolnshire dialect brought by the settlers to America had there later on further developed under new conditions, whilst the Lincolnshire did not advance so quickly or so far—applies equally well to the relation between Attic and Ionic. Certain tendencies already existing before the emigrants from Attica settled in Ionia were fully developed by the latter, whilst their brethren who had remained in Greece did not advance at all so far or so quickly. For the full discussion cf. my *Early Age of Greece*, vol. I, pp. 668-9.

shown[1] that certain other forms found in Attic tragedy and
supposed to have been borrowed from the Ionic dialect, e.g.
Third Plurals in -οιατο, -αιατο, are really good old Attic; he
has also pointed out[2] that as no other characteristic of the
Doric dialect except ā is found either in the Choruses or in
the dialogues of Tragedy, these forms are in no wise Doric,
but merely old Attic forms which naturally survived in sacred
hymns and ancient ballads, ever the last refuge of archaic
words and forms.   It is moreover difficult to believe that the
Athenians would have borrowed the diction of their sacred
songs from the hated Dorians, whom they would not permit
even to enter their sanctuaries and share with them the worship
of their gods, no exception being made even in the case of
royalty itself.   Thus when the Spartans occupied Athens in
B.C. 509, and Cleomenes their king sought to enter the temple
of Athena, the priestess withstood him on the ground that it
was not lawful for Dorians to do so[3].

The Dithyramb.   Aristotle states[4] that "Tragedy at first
was mere improvisation like Comedy: the one originated with
the leaders of the dithyramb, the other with those of the phallic
songs which are still in use in many of our cities.   It was not
till late that the short plot was discarded for one of greater
compass and the grotesque diction of the earlier Satyric for the
stately manner of Tragedy."   From this passage the exponents
of the orthodox view have universally assumed that the
Dithyramb was Doric in origin.   Yet we have explicit historical
information to the contrary.   Herodotus[5] tells us that Arion
the famous harper "was the first of all men of whom we have
any knowledge to compose a dithyramb, to give it that name,
and to teach it to a chorus," whilst we know from the same

---

[1] *Early Age of Greece*, vol. I, pp. 670–1; *Transactions of Cambridge
Philological Society*, vol. II (1881–2), pp. 186–7.

[2] *Early Age of Greece*, vol. I, p. 670.

[3] Herod. v, 72 : ἡ δὲ ἱρείη ἐξαναστᾶσα ἐκ τοῦ θρόνου πρὶν ἢ τὰς θύρας αὐτὸν
ἀμεῖψαι εἶπε· Ὦ ξεῖνε Λακεδαιμόνιε, πάλιν χώρει μηδὲ ἔσιθι ἐς τὸ ἱρόν· οὐ γὰρ
θεμιτὸν Δωριεῦσι παριέναι ἐνθαῦτα.

[4] *Poetics*, 4 : ἀπὸ τῶν ἐξαρχόντων τὸν διθύραμβον κτλ.

[5] I, 23 : ᾿Αρίονα τὸν Μηθυμναῖον...ἐόντα κιθαρῳδὸν τῶν τότε ἐόντων οὐδενὸς
δεύτερον, καὶ διθύραμβον πρῶτον ἀνθρώπων τῶν ἡμεῖς ἴδμεν, ποιήσαντά τε καὶ
οὐνομάσαντα καὶ διδάξαντα ἐν Κορίνθῳ.

passage that Arion was a native of Methymna in Lesbos. But although Herodotus is probably right in ascribing to Arion the full development into a distinct artistic form, the name had long before been in use for some ruder form of song, since it is mentioned by Archilochus[1] of Paros, who flourished about B.C. 670, and therefore preceded Arion by more than half a century. Thus neither the fully developed dithyramb nor even its ruder form can be ascribed to the Dorians, but must be regarded as the invention of the older population of Greece to which Arion and Archilochus belonged. Arion taught his dithyramb to a chorus of fifty at Corinth in the reign of Periander (B.C. 625—585). According to Suidas[2] he introduced Satyrs speaking in metre and the same writer describes him as the "inventor of the tragic style[3]." It is quite clear from the language of Aristotle that the beginnings of the dithyramb already existed in rude improvisations, or scarcely less rude hymns, long before Arion had given to these untutored utterances of primitive men artistic form and the name of dithyramb.

It must also at once be pointed out that though Aristotle implies a close connection between the " earlier satyric " and the dithyramb, neither he nor Herodotus in his account of the invention of the dithyramb by Arion, state that the newly invented or rather improved form of literature was confined solely to the ritual of Dionysus. But to Aristotle's statement we shall presently return. True, Pindar[4] in a famous passage when alluding to the production of Arion's dithyramb at Corinth, exclaims: "Whence were revealed the new charms of Dionysus, with the accompaniment of the ox-driving dithyramb? Who made new means of guidance in the harness of steeds, or set the twin king of birds on the temples of the gods?" Yet we are not justified in inferring from this passage that the dithyramb was confined to the worship of the Thracian god. On the contrary we have every reason for believing that, certainly

---

[1] *Fragm.* 79 : ὡς Διωνύσοι' ἄνακτος καλὸν ἐξάρξαι μέλος
οἶδα διθύραμβον, οἴνῳ συγκεραυνωθεὶς φρένας.

[2] s.v. *Arion* : Σατύρους εἰσενεγκεῖν ἔμμετρα λέγοντας.

[3] τραγικοῦ τρόπου εὑρετής.

[4] *Ol.* XIII, 18-9: ταὶ Διωνύσου πόθεν ἐξέφανεν σὺν βοηλάτᾳ χάριτες διθυράμβῳ;

in Pindar's own time, and probably from its first rude beginnings,
the dithyramb was used in commemoration of heroes. Thus
his own contemporary and great rival, Simonides[1] of Ceos
(B.C. 556—467), a composer of many dithyrambs, wrote one called
Memnon, in praise of that ill-fated hero. The epithet "ox-driving"
used by Pindar differentiates from others the peculiar character
of the dithyramb sung in honour of Dionysus. As it has been
commonly held that Tragedy got its name from the he-goat
(τράγος), said to have been the prize in such competitions,
so the epithet "ox-driving" has been supposed to mean that
in the case of dithyrambic contests the prize was an ox. In
later times, at Athens at least, though we have no evidence
that Attic practice means general use in Greece, in musical
contests an ox was the first prize, an *amphoreus* the second,
and a he-goat the third[2]. These contests, like others in the
great festivals of Greece, may have undergone modifications
in later times.

But the true explanation may rather be found in a
passage of Pausanias[3]. Speaking of the Cynaetheans, an
Arcadian community, he says: "What is most worthy of note
is that there is a sanctuary of Dionysus here, and that they
hold a festival in winter, at which men, their bodies greased
with oil, pick out a bull from a herd (whichever bull the god
puts it into their head to take), lift it up, and carry it to the
sanctuary. Such is their mode of sacrifice." It would thus
seem not unlikely that in Dionysiac ritual the bull to be
sacrificed was driven or dragged along by the chorus of
celebrants.

But although the dithyramb may have thus been used in
the worship of Dionysus, it does not at all follow that it was
confined to his ritual. From the statement of Aristotle that it
was not till late that the grotesque diction of the earlier Satyric
was discarded for the stately manner of Tragedy it might at
first sight be maintained that Tragedy had arisen solely out of

---

[1] Strabo, 619, 43 (Didot): ταφῆναι δὲ λέγεται Μέμνων περὶ Πάλτον τῆς Συρίας
παρὰ Βαδᾶν ποταμόν, ὡς εἴρηκε Σιμωνίδης ἐν Μέμνονι διθυράμβῳ τῶν Δηλιακῶν.

[2] Schol. Plato, *Rep.*, 394 c: τῶν δὲ ποιητῶν τῷ μὲν πρώτῳ βοῦς ἔπαθλον
ἦν, τῷ δὲ δευτέρῳ ἀμφορεύς, τῷ δὲ τρίτῳ τράγος, ὃν τρυγὶ κεχρισμένον ἀπῆγον.

[3] VII, 19, 1 (Frazer's trans.).

the cult of Dionysus and his Satyrs. But a fuller statement in
the same famous passage shows clearly that he regarded Tragedy
as the outcome of the Epic: "As in the serious style Homer is
pre-eminent among poets, for he alone combined dramatic form
with excellence of imitation, so too he first laid down the main
lines of Comedy by dramatising the ludicrous instead of writing
personal satire. His *Margites* bears the same relation to
Comedy that the *Iliad* and the *Odyssey* bear to Tragedy. But
when Tragedy and Comedy came to light the two classes of
poets still followed their natural bent: the lampooners became
writers of Comedy, and the Epic poets were succeeded by
tragedians, since the drama was a larger and higher form of
art [1]."

As the Epic poets sung of the exploits and sorrows of heroes
and not merely of the adventures or sufferings of Dionysus,
Aristotle cannot have regarded the dithyrambs, out of which he
says Tragedy arose, as restricted to the worship of the Thracian
god. Now as he holds the tragedians to have been the
successors of the Epic poets who followed the serious style, and
certainly did not use "the grotesque Satyric diction," the tragic
writers must from the first have used the serious diction of the
Epic and not the grotesque language of the Satyric drama.

That Aristotle is partly right in holding Tragedy to be the
lineal descendant of the Epic is confirmed by a fact familiar to all
scholars. The speeches of messengers in tragedies come nearest
to Epic narrative, and in these it is not uncommon to find forms
of verbs used without the augment, just as in the epic poems.
On the other hand the Choral odes did not arise out of the
Epic, for their origin was really in that Lyric poetry, which,
though hitherto regarded as a later stage in literary development than the Epic, must really be held prior. Joy and
exultation after victory in battle or success in the chase, the
outpourings of the anguished heart, and the transports of the
lover, are, and have ever been, not expressed in set heroic
measure, but in lyrical outbursts. Such are the rude songs out
of which arose the ancient Irish epics, and such also are those
embedded in the Icelandic Sagas. So too when Achilles sang

[1] *Poet.* 4 (Butcher's trans.).

to his harp the "glories of heroes[1]," he was not chaunting heroic lays, like a rhapsodist, but rather singing rude songs about the deeds of doughty men, and of such the Odes of Pindar are the lineal descendants. These wild lyric utterances not only preceded, but were concurrent with and formed the material for the fully developed Epic with its uniform hexameter metre, and though hushed for a season, in the fullness of time their stirring and sweet strains burst forth once more, this time from the lips of Tyrtaeus, Sappho and Alcaeus.

It must be confessed that Aristotle's account of the origin of Tragedy is confused and apparently self-contradictory. The fact is that from his standpoint he was chiefly interested in the fully developed Tragedy as a great form of art, and as we shall see later (p. 57), he cared little about its first beginnings.

Finally it may be pointed out that as Tragedy in the main arose from the Epic, and as the great epics were certainly not composed in the Doric dialect, we have thus a further reason for rejecting the claim of the Dorians.

Lasus. The establishment at Athens of contests in which dithyrambs were performed by Cyclic choruses is ascribed to Lasus, son of Charbinus, born about B.C. 548 at Hermione, a town of Argolis. This place was not settled by the Dorians but, as we are expressly told by Herodotus[2], its inhabitants were Dryopians, one of the aboriginal Pelasgian tribes of Greece. It is therefore very unlikely that Lasus was a Dorian. He settled at Athens and lived there under the Pisistratidae and probably under Pisistratus himself. Herodotus[3] relates how he had detected and exposed Onomacritus, the renowned oracle-monger and editor of Musaeus, for having made an interpolation in an oracle of that poet respecting certain islands off Lemnos. We know from Aelian[4] that Lasus composed dithyrambs, and from Athenaeus[5] that he wrote a hymn, in which the letter Sigma did not occur, in honour of the Demeter of his native place Hermione and that he was famous for playing on words. But his claim to fame rests

---

[1] *Il.* ix, 186.   [2] viii, 43.   [3] vii, 6.

[4] *Nat. An.* viii, 47 : ἐν γοῦν τοῖς Λάσου λεγομένοις διθυράμβοις κτλ.

[5] 455 c and d : ὕμνος ἄσιγμός ἐστιν (citing a treatise on Music by Heraclides Ponticus); 338 b. Hesychius refers to his word-plays (λασίσματα) s.v.

chiefly on his development of the dithyramb¹, the part that he
took in the establishment of musical contests at Athens, and
the remarkable influence that he exercised upon the history
of Greek music.

According to Suidas² he wrote a work on Music, whilst
we learn from Plutarch³ that he modified greatly the music
of the day by adapting the rhythms to the dithyrambic style,
by making more use of the varied notes of the flute, and by
a greater range of sounds. The date of the first musical
contest at Athens is placed by the Parian Chronicle in Ol. 68, 1
(B.C. 508). The prize however did not fall to Lasus himself,
but to one Hypodicus of Chalcis. Aristophanes⁴ refers to a
contest between Lasus and Simonides in which the former again
suffered defeat. We have no reason for supposing that Lasus
in his dithyrambs any more than his rival restricted himself to
purely Dionysiac themes, and like the latter he may well have
sung the sorrows of heroes. It is certain at least that Cyclic
choruses were not confined to the worship of Dionysus, for a
Cyclic chorus danced round the altar of the Twelve gods at
Athens on the occasion of the Great Dionysia. We may therefore conclude that the dithyramb was not the invention of the
Dorians, and that at no time was it confined solely to the cult
of the Thracian god.

The claims of the Dorians to the invention of Tragedy may
therefore be safely rejected, since (1) Aristotle certainly does
not endorse their pretensions; (2) the supposed Doric forms
in Tragedy are simply old Attic; and (3) neither Arion nor
Archilochus were Dorians.

---

¹ Schol., Ar. *Av.* 1403: τὸν κυκλιοδιδάσκαλον : 'Αντὶ τοῦ διθυραμβοποιόν,
εἴρηται γὰρ ὅτι ἐγκύκλια διδάσκουσιν. 'Αντίπατρος δὲ καὶ Εὐφρόνιος ἐν τοῖς
ὑπομνήμασι φασὶ τοὺς κυκλίους χοροὺς στῆσαι πρῶτον Λᾶσον τὸν Ἑρμιονέα, οἱ δὲ
ἀρχαιότεροι Ἑλλάνικος καὶ Δικαίαρχος, 'Αρίονα τὸν Μηθυμναῖον, Δικαίαρχος μὲν ἐν
τῷ περὶ Διονυσιακῶν ἀγώνων, Ἑλλάνικος δὲ ἐν τοῖς Κραναικοῖς.

² s.v. *Lasus*: πρῶτος δὲ οὗτος περὶ μουσικῆς λόγον ἔγραψε, καὶ διθύραμβον εἰς
ἀγῶνα εἰσήγαγε, καὶ τοὺς ἐριστικοὺς εἰσηγήσατο λόγους.

³ Plut. *de musica*, 29: εἰς τὴν διθυραμβικὴν ἀγωγὴν μεταστήσας τοὺς ῥυθμοὺς
καὶ τῇ τῶν αὐλῶν πολυφωνίᾳ κατακολουθήσαι πλείοσί τε φθόγγοις καὶ διερριμμένοις
χρησάμενος εἰς μετάθεσιν τὴν προϋπάρχουσαν ἤγαγε μουσικήν.

⁴ *Vesp.* 1410.

The Worship of Dionysus.

Let us next examine the belief that Tragedy arose solely from the worship of Dionysus. Aristotle himself has shown once for all that the Drama like every other form of Art springs from that love of imitation, which man possesses in a far higher degree than any other animal, and from the love of rhythm likewise implanted in him. But he assumed, on insufficient grounds as we have just seen, that "the stately manner of Tragedy" arose out of "the grotesque diction of the earlier Satyric." If it can be shown that in districts of Greece, where

Fig. 1. Thracian coin showing Ox-cart.

mimetic dances were performed long before the Dorian invasion or the introduction of the worship of Dionysus into that country, there were dramatic performances and solemn festivals held not in honour of the Thracian wine-god but of very different personages, we shall be forced to the conclusion that Greek Tragedy did not arise from the cult of Dionysus and his Satyrs.

Let us first trace briefly the origin of that worship and its spread in Greece. Homer indeed knows of Dionysus, but only as a Thracian deity. Lycurgus, an ancient Thracian chief, scourged Dionysus and his attendant women so severely with his ox-whip that the god of wine had to take to water and seek an asylum with Thetis in the depths of the sea[1]. The Birth-story of Dionysus at Thebes is also alluded to in the *Iliad*[2], whilst we are told in the *Odyssey*[3] that Artemis slew Ariadne in Naxos "on the witness of Dionysus." Herodotus states that the three chief Thracian divinities were Ares, Dionysus, and Artemis (i.e. Bendis).

The oldest and most famous seat of the cult of Dionysus was not amongst the red-haired Thracians of the Danubian region, such as the Getae, who did not even worship him, but had separate divinities of their own[4]. His home was amongst

[1] *Il.* vi, 132 *sqq.*   [2] xiv, 325.   [3] *Od.* xi, 325.   [4] Herod. iv, 94–6.

the aboriginal dark-haired Thracians of the Pangaean range. On one of the loftiest of its peaks lay his great ancient oracle. The tribe of the Satrae dwelt around and the oracle was in charge of the Satrian clan of the Bessi[1].

The Thracians of this region were closely akin to the

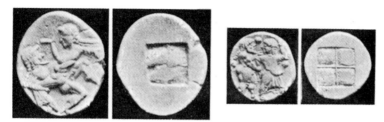

Fig. 2.   Silenus with a woman: Lete[2].   Fig. 3.   Silenus carrying off a woman: Lete.

indigenous population of Greece. They were no rude savages, as generally believed, for they were skilled in metal-work, striking coins of singular beauty and originality of types (Fig. 1) from the early part of the sixth century B.C. No less skilful were they in music and literature than in the material arts. From them had come Thamyris, and Orpheus and Linus, the

Fig. 4.   Sileni or Centaurs carrying off women: Orrescii.

master of Orpheus: from thence too had sprung Eumolpus who established the Mysteries at Eleusis. Almost all the aboriginal Thracian tribes had been conquered by the fair-haired race from the Danube and beyond, or else they had had to seek new homes in Asia, as was the case with the Dardanians, Phrygians and Mysians. But Herodotus[3] tells us that the mountaineers of Pangaeum, who in his own day defied the

---

[1] Herod. vii, 111.

[2] Figs. 2 and 3 are from coins in the Leake Collection, Fitzwilliam Museum, Cambridge.   [3] Herod. vii, 111.

arms of Xerxes, had at no time been conquered but had preserved their liberty secure in their snow-clad mountain fastnesses.
There can therefore be no reasonable doubt that in the oracle
of Dionysus served by the Bessi we have an original cult of
these indigenous Thracians. These tribes differed in many
respects from the so-called Thracians, such as the Getae, who
were really Celts. The former invariably tattooed themselves
and traced descent through women, differing in these particulars
as well as in others from their Celtic neighbours and oppressors,
whilst in their morals they were exceedingly lax, the girls up
to marriage being allowed complete licence. This circumstance
probably gave rise to a general belief amongst the neighbours
of the Satrae that they were addicted to all sorts of wild

Fig. 5.   Dionysus and his Satyrs (from the Würzburg cylix).

orgiastic rites, as is evidenced by the coins of that region on which
Satyrs or Sileni are seen carrying off women (Figs. 2, 3 and 4).
Colonel Leake long ago suggested that from the name of the great
tribe of the Satrae, amongst whom was the chief sanctuary of
Dionysus, arose the name of the Satyri, the constant attendants
of Dionysus in his wild rout (Fig. 5). This explanation seems
highly probable. Aristotle[1] has told us that just as we make our
gods in our own likeness, so do we also represent their lives as
like our own. Dionysus accordingly reflected the life of his own
worshippers. The Satyrs are simply his own Satrian tribesmen,
and the Bacchants (Fig. 6) are merely the young women of
the tribe allowed to range at will.

[1] *Pol.* I, 7 : ὥσπερ δὲ καὶ τὰ εἴδη ἑαυτοῖς ἀφομοιοῦσιν οἱ ἄνθρωποι, οὕτω καὶ τοὺς
βίους τῶν θεῶν.

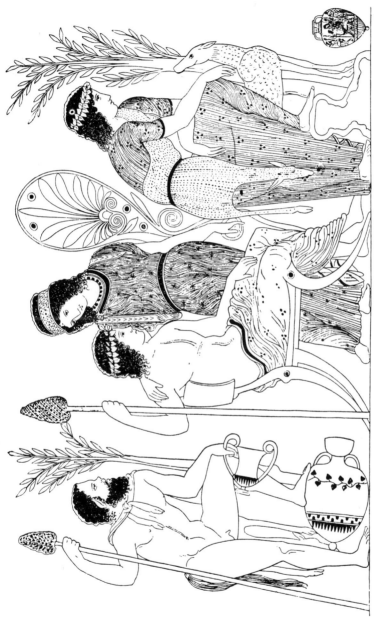

Fig. 6. Dionysus and Ariadne between a Satyr and a Bacchant.

It will be convenient at this point to treat at greater length of the Sileni and their relations to the Satyrs. It is difficult to find any explanation of their name or to discover the region in which it originated, but it is not improbable that it, like that of the Satyrs, was once the name of some tribe or clan. On several points however we can be quite certain. They cannot be separated from the Satyrs, since not only is Silenus regarded as the chief of the Satyrs, but Pausanias[1] gives us explicit information on this point. When speaking of a stone at Athens "of no great size but big enough for a little man to sit on, and on which, so said the folk, Silenus had rested when he came into the country along with Dionysus," he mentions "that elderly Satyrs are called Sileni." In another passage he states[2] that there was at Elis a temple dedicated to Silenus alone and not to him jointly with Dionysus. Methe ("Drunkenness") was represented handing to him a wine-cup, and the traveller remarks that the Sileni are a mortal race, as may be inferred especially from their graves. This identification of the Sileni with the Satyrs is thoroughly corroborated by two very important glosses in Hesychius[3]. In one of these we are told that according to Amerias the Sileni were called *Sauadae* by the Macedonians, whilst from the other we learn that amongst the Illyrians the Satyri were called *Deuadae*. Now there can be no doubt that in *Deuadae* and *Sauadae* we have only dialectic forms of the same name, as in the case of a well-known Illyrian or Macedonian tribe, which was termed both Dasaretii and Sesarethii[4]. In another gloss Hesychius[5] identifies the Sileni with the Satyri, whilst in yet another he calls them *Hermeni*.

From these various passages it is fairly certain that there was no essential difference between Sileni and Satyri, and also that neither Illyrians nor Macedonians used the name Sileni, but had a different term of their own for the creatures whom we see on the Thracian coins[6] either as naked men (Figs. 2 and 3)

---

[1] ɪ, 23, 5.   [2] vɪ, 24, 8.

[3] s.v. Σανάδαι· Σαῦδοι· Ἀμερίας τοὺς Σειληνοὺς οὕτω καλεῖσθαί φησιν ὑπὸ Μακεδόνων. s.v. Δευάδαι· οἱ Σάτυροι παρὰ Ἰλλυρίοις.

[4] Ridgeway, "Who were the Dorians?" *Anthropological Essays in honour of Tylor*, p. 308.

[5] s.vv. Σειληνοί and Ἑρμηνοί.

[6] Head, *Historia Numorum*, pp. 174, 176–7.

with horse's feet, ears, and tail (as at Lete), or as fully developed
into Centaurs (Fig. 4), as on those of the Orrescii, who, as I have
elsewhere pointed out, are probably no other than the Orestae,
reckoned as a Macedonian tribe by Strabo. In another place[1]
I have shown that the Centaurs of Thessaly were simply a
mountain tribe, living on Pelion, and that it was only at a late
period that their neighbours imputed to them every brutal
passion and represented them as semi-equine in order to typify
their bestial lust. In the men with the tails, ears, and feet of
horses on the Thracian coins we have the first step towards the
Centaurs on those of the Orrescii.

In the names Sileni, Deuadae or Sauadae, and Hermenoi,
we have probably old tribal or clan names, as in the case of
the Centauri of Thessaly. In literature the name Sileni first
occurs in the Homeric Hymn to Aphrodite[2], in which the
Sileni and Hermes are represented as consorting with the
nymphs in the recesses of the pleasant grots of Mount Ida.
A passage of Pindar cited by Pausanias[3] represents Silenus as
born at Malea and as having come from thence to Pyrrhichus,
an inland town of Laconia. The name Silenus seems not to be
old in Greece, and therefore may be regarded as imported either
from northern Greece and Thrace, or possibly from north-west
Asia Minor, whither of course it may well have passed with
Thracian immigrants or with the cult of Dionysus. One fact
of considerable importance comes out clearly,—Sileni or Satyrs
are not represented in goat form on the archaic Thracian coins,
but with equine attributes. There can be no doubt that the
semi-equine representations of the Satyrs or Sileni in the act
of carrying off women or nymphs refer to a wild and gross cult.

It must be borne in mind that orgiastic and licentious rites
have at all times and in many places been considered of great
importance for fertilising the earth in seed-time, and accordingly Dionysus and his ribald company may be but part and
parcel of a cult intimately connected with the fertilisation of the
earth. Since the present writer first put forward this view,
confirmatory evidence of a very important kind has come
to hand not only from Thrace itself but also from Northern

[1] Ridgeway, *The Early Age of Greece*, vol. i, 173–5.
[2] 261.   [3] iii, 25, 2.

Greece. There seems to be no doubt that a ceremony still used in Thrace with a view to securing an abundant harvest, is a distinct survival of Dionysiac rites. **The Modern Carnival in Thrace.** My friend Mr R. M. Dawkins, Fellow of Emmanuel College, Cambridge, and Director of the British School at Athens, has described[1] what seems to be an undoubted survival of such ceremonies. It is the Carnival festival held in the district about Viza (ancient $Bιζύη$) in Thrace, which was witnessed by Mr Dawkins in 1906. The ceremony had been previously described by G. M. Vizyenos, a native of Viza. His statements, based on personal knowledge dating back for forty years, Mr Dawkins was able to confirm from his own observations. Viza lies some eight hours by road north of the station of Tcherkesskeui on the railway between Constantinople and Adrianople, and nine hours from Midheia (Salmydessus) on the Black Sea.

"In all the knot of Christian villages, of which Viza is the centre, the festival in question is celebrated annually on Cheese Monday ($Τυρινὴ$ $Δευτέρα$). This day begins the last week of Carnival, which culminates on the following Sunday ($Κυριακὴ$ $τοῦ Τυροφάγου$). Lent then begins with Pure Monday ($Καθαρὰ$ $Δευτέρα$), when not only meat, as during Carnival, but also all kinds of animal food except bloodless molluscs are forbidden. The masquerade of this day was, even when Vizyenos saw it, no longer kept up in its fullness at Viza itself, but only in the neighbouring villages, of which he takes Haghios Gheorghios (Turkish, Evrenlu) as an example." Mr Dawkins spent "Cheese Monday" at this village and during his stay of a week in the district was able to supplement his notes by inquiries about the observances in other places. The list of masqueraders is as follows:

I. "Two $καλογέροι$ (Fig. 7), who play the principal parts. Their disguise consists of a headdress formed of an entire goatskin without the horns, stuffed out with hay so as to rise like a great shako at least a foot or eighteen inches above the head, and adorned at the top with a piece of red ribbon. The skin falls over the face and neck, forming thus a mask, with holes cut

[1] *Jour. Hell. Stud.*, 1906, pp. 191—206, Figs. 1—8, "The Modern Carnival in Thrace and the Cult of Dionysus."

out for the eyes and mouth. Round the waist three or four
sheep-bells are tied, and their hands are blackened. Their
shoulders are monstrously padded with hay to protect them
from blows, which, from Vizyenos' account, they used to receive
more freely than at present. He adds that the head-dress may
be made of the skin of a fox or wolf and that fawnskins were
worn on the shoulders, and upon the leg goatskins. The
essential and indispensable elements, he says, are the mask and
bells. It would seem from this that the resemblance of the
actor to an animal was formerly a good deal more marked than
at present. A little boy whom I saw on the Tuesday at Viza
acting as *kalogheros*, the only part there surviving, wore a tall
conical fur cap, and bells at his waist. He had no mask, but
his face as well as his hands were blackened. In one of the
villages the *kalogheroi* do not wear skins at all on their heads, but
beehives. One of the *kalogheroi* at Haghios Gheorghios carries
a wooden phallus and the other a mock bow. This bow (δοξάρι)
is in general appearance rather like a crossbow, but is made
only to scatter ashes or powder." Vizyenos adds that the carrier
of the bow is the leader of the two, and the other his servant
and follower, a view endorsed by Mr Dawkins himself. In the
drama with which the play closes it is the carrier of the bow
who shoots the other, and in this point Vizyenos agrees with
Mr Dawkins' observations.

II. "Two boys dressed as girls (Κορίτσια), called also in
some other villages, according to Vizyenos, νύφες, brides. These
wear a white skirt and apron, a peasant woman's bodice open
in front, and kerchiefs binding the chin and the brow. A third
kerchief hangs down behind, and from beneath it escapes a
corded black fringe like finely plaited hair. They check any
liberties with knotted handkerchiefs weighted with a few
bullets. It is to be noted that the *kalogheroi* at Haghios
Gheorghios must be married men, and the *koritsia* unmarried.
Vizyenos tells us also that these four actors are chosen for
periods of four years and that during this time a *koritsi* may
be betrothed, but must remain unmarried, a father being
able to refuse to allow his son to take this part on the ground
that he is thinking of getting married...."

III. Next comes a third female character, the Babo, a word in general use meaning an old woman. This personage was not represented in the play seen by Mr Dawkins, but her place was taken by the *katsivela*. The Babo herself still appears at other villages, and until quite recently was seen at Viza, where she has now been forbidden by the authorities. She is described by Vizyenos as a man dressed as an old woman carrying on her arm a basket containing "some absurd object or piece of wood swaddled in rags," which she treats as a baby. Of this child she is the *kapsomana*, and the child (*liknites*) is a seven-months child born out of lawful wedlock of a father whose name she does not know. Mr Dawkins was told at Viza that the Babo's child was always regarded as a bastard. *Kapsomana*, he was given to understand, meant nurse or foster-mother, but Vizyenos says that the Babo regards the child as her own, and kindred words make it almost certain that the real meaning is unmarried mother, mother of an illegitimate child. The word *likni* survives in the district meaning a cradle, made as usual of wood and shaped like a trough, and *liknites* is the local word for a baby in the cradle. "Nowhere else in Greece," writes Mr Dawkins, "have I found any evidence for these words used of baskets or cradles."

IV. The *katsiveloi*, or Gipsies, dressed like the Babo in miserable rags. Vizyenos says that there were three or four, apparently all male, though elsewhere he incidentally mentions a female *katsivela*. Mr Dawkins saw two only, a man and his wife. They carried a sapling some ten or twelve feet long, and their faces and hands were blackened. The man had no other disguise, but his wife wore a woman's coat and on the head a kerchief and a little false hair.

V. The Policemen. These are two or three young men carrying swords and whips, with embroidered kerchiefs tied round their fezzes. One of them carried also a length of chain for making captures. Lastly there is a man playing a bagpipe.

"The masqueraders spend the day in visiting each house in the village, receiving everywhere bread, eggs or money. The two *kalogheroi* lead the crowd, knocking loudly at the doors with the bow and phallus, and with the *koritsia* generally dance a little hand-in-hand, before the housewife brings out her contribution. They are followed by the *katsivelos* and *katsivela*, who are especially privileged to scare fowls and rob nests. In general anything lying about may be seized as a pledge to be redeemed, and the *koritsia* especially carry off babies with this object, and occasionally capture a man with their handkerchiefs. A recurring feature is an obscene pantomime between the *katsivelos* and his wife on the straw-heaps in front of the houses."

"By the afternoon no house was left unvisited, and everybody, men and women, gathered round the open space in front of the church. Here the drama proper is enacted. It began with a hand in hand dance of all the characters, the Policemen brandishing their drawn swords. The *kalogheroi* then withdrew, leaving the field to the Gipsy smiths, the *katsivelos* and his wife. These sat on the ground facing each other, and the *katsivelos* pounded on the ground with a stone, whilst the *katsivela* lifted her skirts up and down. This is understood to be a pantomimic representation of the forging of a plough-share, the man hammering like a blacksmith, whilst the fanning with the skirts represents the action of a pair of bellows. At this point, the Babo's child begins to get too big for the cradle, and, together with a huge appetite for meat and drink, he begins to demand a wife. This according to Vizyenos was followed by the chief *kalogheros* pursuing one of the *koritsia* and the celebration between them of a mock marriage, parodying the Greek rite of the bride and bridegroom. The first *kalogheros* is then seen sauntering about or standing the phallus upright on the ground and sitting upon it. Meanwhile his comrade stalks him from behind, and shoots him with the bow, whereupon the other falls down dead. After making sure that he is dead the slayer pretends to flay him. Whilst the *kalogheros* is thus lying dead his wife laments for him with loud cries, throwing herself across his prostrate body (Fig. 7). In this lament according to Vizyenos the slayer and the rest of the actors join, making a regular parody of a Christian funeral, burning dung as incense and pretending to sing the service, finally lifting up the corpse to carry it away."

The slain man then suddenly comes to life. Next follows

the serious part of the ceremony. There is another forging of
the ploughshare, and this time it is a real share. At about this
point all the implements used were thrown into the air with
cries, καὶ τοῦ χρόνου ("Next year also!"). The share being
supposed to be finished, a real plough was brought and the
mockery seemed to cease. Instead of oxen, the *koritsia* were
yoked and dragged it round the village square twice contrary
to the way of the sun. One of the *kalogheroi* was at the tail
of the plough and the other guided it in front, whilst a man
walked behind scattering seeds from a basket. Whilst the
plough is being drawn, they cry, "May wheat be ten piastres
the bushel! Rye five piastres the bushel! Barley three piastres
the bushel! Amen, O God, that the poor may eat! Yea, O God,
that poor folk be filled." Mr Dawkins has kindly presented to
the Cambridge Anthropological Museum the implements used
in the play that he witnessed.

There can be little doubt that we have in this local festival
a survival of a coarse and orgiastic rite performed by the ancient
Thracians in order to ensure fertility. It will be observed that
the fox-skin, and the fawn-skin which are so prominent in the
ancient Dionysiac rites here also survived, though now the
goat-skin, probably because of its greater cheapness, seems to
have replaced the skins of the wild animals used in the ancient
cult. As the fox-skin and the fawn-skin both formed part of
the ancient Thracian dress, and as the goat-skin was the most
common form of dress in ancient Greece, we need not indulge
in any speculations as to whether, in the modern Thracian play,
we have evidence of the worship of a goat-god or a fox-god
or a fawn-god.

Epiphany Carnival in Thessaly. But such rude
dramas are not confined to modern Thrace, for there is now
evidence of their survival in Northern Greece. My friend
Mr A. J. B. Wace, M.A., Fellow of Pembroke College, Cambridge,
has given me the following account of such a performance, which
has lately come within his own cognizance, when engaged in
making his important excavations in the prehistoric mounds of
Thessaly. He first heard of it at Almyro in Phthiotis.

On the eve of the Epiphany a kind of Satyric festival

takes place. Men dressed in goat-skins dance and sing round the bonfires, and a kind of play is acted. "This carnival

FIG. 7. The Modern Thracian Dionysiac Play.

dance, which takes place on Epiphany eve and in many cases on Epiphany day itself, occurs in Phthiotis, the Thessalian

plains, on Ossa, and in southern Macedonia, where Christians
of other nationality than Greek (i.e. Albanian and Bulgarian)
also celebrate it. The young men form bands about twelve
strong, four of these act and the rest dance and sing in two semi-
choruses. The four actors are the bridegroom (γαμβρός) clad
in a sheep- or goat-skin cloak with a mask of the same material
wearing bells and carrying a rusty sword, the bride (νύφη) a boy
dressed in a bride's costume, the Arab (Ἀράπης) wearing a
fustanella, a fez and with his face blacked, and the doctor
(ἰατρός), a part sometimes doubled by the one who takes the part
of the Arab. The thing opens with a dance of all, and a song
relating to Epiphany that suggests a rain charm. Then while
the other eight sing other songs of good luck relating to
different members of the community the four actors dance.
Presently the Arab molests the bride, then a quarrel ensues
between him and the bridegroom, this usually ends in the
latter being struck and falling down as though dead. The
bride throws herself on his body and laments him, and entreats
the doctor to restore him. The doctor comes, comforts the
bride, examines the bridegroom with some horseplay, and finally
revives him. The bridegroom then jumps up, and all dance
joyfully, and the proceedings end with an obscene pantomime
between the bridegroom and the bride. Nowadays the play
is not acted as fully as this. Usually the actors are only two,
the bride and the bridegroom, who is now compounded with
the Arab. But the full play has been acted till quite recently,
and when we saw the festival at Platanos in Phthiotis this
January we saw some survivals of the older custom. This is
the main outline of what is done. In addition the whole band
go round the villages singing at each house and demanding
presents in money or kind. In return they sing songs wishing
the householder good luck, if however he refuses to give, they
sing songs wishing him ill. The songs of course vary according
to the occupation or profession of the householder and his
family.

"A full account of the festival with some of the songs sung
I hope to publish shortly in the *Journal of Hellenic Studies*, as
there are several other minor points of some interest. Also

I hope to see this year a similar festival said to take place on Pelion on May 1st."

The Skyros Carnival. At Skyros a Carnival custom described by Mr J. C. Lawson, M.A., Fellow of Pembroke

FIG. 8. Skyros Masquerader.

College, Cambridge, and also by Mr R. M. Dawkins[1], seems

---

[1] R. M. Dawkins, *op. cit.*, pp. 202–3, Fig. 9 (from which my illustration (as well as Fig. 7) is taken by his kind permission).

closely allied to those of which we have spoken, though much
less of it is left. "There is no drama, but only the going about
the town of sets of three masqueraders, the Old Man (Fig. 8)
with bells and skin mask, and, according to Mr Lawson, with
skin cape also, who answers to the leading *kalogheros* of Thrace,
the Frank, not dressed in skins and probably corresponding to
the second *kalogheros*, and the *koritsi*, a boy dressed as a girl."

Abundant evidence will be given later on to show that
goat-skins were the most common dress of the ancient inhabitants of Greece, and that there is no more reason to suppose
the worship of Dionysus to be that of an ancient goat-god than
there is for believing that Athena and Zeus were both goat-
deities because the former is always represented with her *aegis*
(goat-skin), and the Father of gods and men is regularly styled
"goat-skin-wearer" in Homer.

Dionysus in Greece. But to return to Thrace. From of
old that region had been famous for its wine. Was not Maroneia
the home of priest Maron, who gave Odysseus that potent
vintage with which the hero ultimately beguiled Polyphemus
to his bane? The god who could make the corn grow, could
also load the vine with goodly bunches, and as the juice of the
grape had strange effects on men and women, it was naturally
inferred that it was the god himself who was in the wine, and
that he had taken possession of those who had drunk deeply of
his gift.

Nor is there wanting support for the view that the Bacchants
were really the Thracian girls. They are regularly termed
Bassaricae in allusion to the fox-skin ($\beta a\sigma\sigma a\rho i s$) which they
wore, whilst the fawn-skin ($\nu\epsilon\beta\rho i s$) formed normally a part of
their costume (Fig. 6) as well as of that of the god himself. Now
both fox-skins and fawn-skins were a characteristic feature in the
dress of the indigenous Thracians, as is shown by Herodotus[1],
for the Thracians in the army of Xerxes wore head-dresses of
fox-skin and moccasins of fawn-skin, standing alone in these
respects from all the other nationalities in that motley host.

There is further evidence that Dionysus was not a native
Greek divinity, but an immigrant from Thrace, for where his

[1] VII, 75.

worship appears in the former country, it is always spoken of as imported from Thrace and that at no remote period. Thus at Thebes the chief seat of his worship in Greece, Dionysus is found along with Ares, the other great Thracian male divinity, according to Homer and the later writers. But all the early legends declare that Thebes had been occupied by the Phlegyans, a great Thracian tribe, who appear in Homer in company with Ares. These Phlegyans also attacked Delphi, and though repulsed from that sacred spot, a remnant of them settled near Parnassus. Down to the time of Christ the people of Panopeus in Phocis declared that they were Thracians, and Pausanias[1] draws special attention to the un-Greek character of their town and its dwellings. It is also noteworthy that the only oracle of Dionysus of which we hear in Greece was at Amphicleia in Phocis.

The evidence of Homer is amply confirmed by later traditions, all of which declare unequivocally that Dionysus was a comparatively late comer into Greece. Thus the Athenians themselves believed that this cult, so far from being indigenous, was first introduced into their city by their king Amphictyon, and that it was a certain Pegasus of Eleutherae, an Attic township, who had first brought the god into Attica, and introduced him to the notice of king Amphictyon. Moreover, there is no ancient shrine of Dionysus on the Acropolis of Athens, as might naturally have been expected, if he were one of the ancient divinities of the land, like Athena and Poseidon. Nor was it only at Athens that he was regarded as of foreign origin, for Plutarch tells us that Dionysus had supplanted the worship of Poseidon in Naxos. From these legends it seems clear that the Greeks of classical times regarded the cult of Dionysus as adventitious, and as having replaced in some localities at least, as in Naxos, older forms of worship.

Mimetic dances. Were there no mimetic dances either grave or gay in Attica or Peloponnesus before the coming of the Thracian reveller with his Satyrs and Bacchants? Certainly in Attica in historical times there was the famous Bear dance at Brauron in which every Athenian girl had to participate

[1] x, 33. 11.

dressed as a bear, when she came to nubile years, or else no man would marry her[1]. Some have seen a survival of Totemism in this ceremony, but it is far more likely to have been some form of initiatory rite accompanied by a mimetic dance, such as those known amongst many modern savages. It is hard therefore to believe that this dance and others like it only arose after the arrival of the worship of Dionysus, with which it had at no time any connection, especially in view of the Athenian belief that the worship of Dionysus was not indigenous.

Let us now pass into Argolis, the seat of the great dynasties in both pre-Achean and pre-Dorian days. The monuments of Mycenae disclose representations of sacred dances, in which the performers apparently wear masks formed of the skins of animals. These have been well compared by Mr A. B. Cook[2] and others to certain animal dances among savage peoples of our own day. But as dancing of some kind or other is universal amongst even the lowest races of mankind, it will hardly be maintained by anyone that dancing was totally unknown in Greece until Dionysus came from Thrace. But the tradition in Homer[3] that Daedalus the Athenian artificer made a famous "Dance" or "Dancing-ground" for Ariadne at Cnossus in Crete, combined with the representations of mimetic dances on relics of the Bronze Age of Mycenae and the survival of similar dances in Attica down to a late period, prove that both dancing and mimetic dancing were familiar in Greece before the incoming of the Thracian cult.

Let us next turn to one of the old Pelasgian towns of Argolis in which the aboriginal inhabitants not only continued to form the great mass of the population, but were strong enough to expel their Dorian lords. In the ancient town of Sicyon, so famous by its connection with Bellerophon, one of the chief heroes of the pre-Homeric days of Greece, a native by name Orthagoras headed his fellow-townsmen, and in B.C. 676 overthrew the Dorian oligarchy and made himself master of

[1] Ar. *Lys.* 645.

[2] "Animal Worship in the Mycenaean Age," *Jour. Hell. Stud.* vol. xiv (1894) pp. 81—119.

[3] *Il.* xviii, 592.

the state. He and his descendants held the sovereignty for
nearly a century, and that too by resting on the support of
the democracy. Now whom did this Sicyonian democracy
especially honour and worship? No fact in Greek city life is
more familiar than the practice of burying the occist or founder
of the town or some great chief in the market-place, in order
that his spirit might keep watch and ward over his people, and
that his bones might be kept as safely as possible for fear lest
they, and consequently his spirit, might fall into the hands of an
enemy, as had happened (so said the legend) in the case of the
bones of Orestes[1]. So at Cyrene, Battus the founder was buried
in the Agora: "There at the end of the market-place in death
he lieth apart. Blest was he when he dwelt among men, and
since his death the people worship him as their hero[2]." This
was no exceptional case, for an examination of Pausanias will
convince anyone that there was not a town or a village in
Greece which had not its own hero or heroine. So was it
at Sicyon. In the very market-place stood the Heroum of
Adrastus[3], who alone of the Seven Champions that fought
against Thebes returned alive to his home. Cleisthenes was
the last descendant of Orthagoras who reigned at Sicyon, for
he had no son but an only daughter Agariste, who married
Megacles the Athenian and became the mother of Cleisthenes,
the Athenian lawgiver. In the reign of Cleisthenes (from
before B.C. 595 to about 560) war broke out between Sicyon
and Argos, and the despot stopped the rhapsodists from con-
tending in Epic recitations at Sicyon "because Argos and the
Argives formed the chief theme of Homer." But his hatred of
everything Argive did not stop at this. "There is," says
Herodotus[4], "in the very market-place of the Sicyonians the
heroum of Adrastus the son of Talaus. Now Cleisthenes wished
to cast him out of the country, inasmuch as he was an Argive.
So he went to Delphi and asked the oracle if he might evict
Adrastus (doubtless by casting his bones out of the country),
but the Pythian prophetess replied that 'Adrastus was the
king of Sicyon, whilst he (Cleisthenes) was only a stone-breaker.'

[1] Herod. ɪ, 67–8.   [2] Pind. *Pyth.* ɪv, 87.
[3] Herod. v, 67–8.   [4] v, 67–8.

When the god thus would not permit him to work his will,
he went home and bethought himself of a device by which
Adrastus of his own accord would betake himself off. He went
to Thebes in Boeotia and said that he wished to bring
Melanippus, the son of Astacus, to Sicyon. Having fetched
the bones of Melanippus, Cleisthenes assigned him a sacred
enclosure in the Prytaneum itself and planted him there in the
strongest part of it. He brought in Melanippus, because of all
men he was most odious to Adrastus, inasmuch as he had killed
Mecisteus and Tydeus, the brother and son-in-law of that hero.
When Cleisthenes had appointed Melanippus his sacred
enclosure, he took away the sacrifices and festivals from
Adrastus, and gave them to Melanippus. Now the Sicyonians
had been accustomed to honour Adrastus magnificently, for
Sicyon had been the land of Polybus, and Adrastus was
daughter's son to Polybus, and the latter gave the kingdom
to Adrastus. The Sicyonians honoured Adrastus, not only in
other respects, but with ' tragic dances alluding to his sorrows,'
not honouring Dionysus, but rather Adrastus. Cleisthenes
assigned the dances to Dionysus, but the sacrifice to Melanippus[1]."

It is clear from this that the cult of Dionysus was not
indigenous at Sicyon. It had been introduced there, as into
Attica and Naxos, and superimposed on the cult of the ancient
guardian hero of the land. We have thus proof not only of the
existence of mimetic dances in Peloponnesus, but also of "tragic

[1] Herod. v, 67: τά τε δὴ ἄλλα οἱ Σικυώνιοι ἐτίμων τὸν Ἄδρηστον καὶ δὴ
πρὸς τὰ πάθεα αὐτοῦ τραγικοῖσι χοροῖσι ἐγέραιρον, τὸν μὲν Διόνυσον οὐ τιμῶντες, τὸν
δὲ Ἄδρηστον. Κλεισθένης δὲ χοροὺς μὲν τῷ Διονύσῳ ἀπέδωκε, τὴν δὲ ἄλλην θυσίην
Μελανίππῳ.

Scholars with one accord have translated ἀπέδωκε "restored," assuming
that the tragic dances must have always belonged to Dionysus, and that
Cleisthenes simply gave back to that god what had been taken from him
by the Sicyonians and given to Adrastus at a very recent date. But as
Cleisthenes certainly did not "restore" the sacrifice to Melanippus, they are
constrained to resort to a "zeugma" and translate ἀπέδωκε "assigned" in the
second place. This of course is to strain the language to bolster up a false
assumption, whilst it overlooks the fact that the regular meaning of ἀποδίδωμι
in all Greek dialects is to "assign," and that when Herodotus uses it in the
sense of "restore" he adds ὀπίσω; cf. I, 13 : ἀποδοῦναι ὀπίσω ἐς Ἡρακλείδας τὴν
ἀρχήν.

dances" representing a hero's sufferings before the worship of
Dionysus was ever established there.

What is the meaning of such "tragic dances," and why did
the Sicyonians especially honour Adrastus, one of the ancient
kings of their race? Simply for the same reasons for which
ancestors, heroes and saints have been, and still are being,
worshipped almost everywhere under the sun. A good king in
life was deemed to bring prosperity to his people. Thus the
disguised Odysseus spake to Penelope: "Lady, no one of mortal
men in the wide world could find fault with thee, for thy fame
goes up to the wide heaven, as doth the fame of a blameless
king, one that fears the gods, and reigns among many men and
mighty, maintaining right, and the black earth bears wheat
and barley, and the trees are laden with fruit, and the sheep
bring forth and fail not, and the sea gives stores of fish, and all
out of his good guidance, and the people prosper under him[1]."
Nor was this doctrine confined to Greece. It was held strongly
also by peoples in Northern Europe. Although the doctrine of
cremation passed upwards into Scandinavia with the cult of
Odin, cremation never superseded inhumation. The masses
held to the older custom. Why they did so is made plain by
the following account of the death and burial of Freyr, the old
Swedish king. "Freyr (Fro) fell sick and when the sickness
came upon him men sought counsel and allowed few men to
approach him, and they built a great howe, and put a door and
three windows on to it, and when Freyr was dead, they carried
him secretly into the howe and told the Swedes that he was
alive. And they kept him there three years[2]. When all the
Swedes knew that Freyr was dead, but plenty and peace continued, then they believed that it would so be as long as Freyr
was in Sweden. So they would not burn him. And they called
him the god of the world and have sacrificed greatly to him ever
since for plenty and peace[3]."

When a great warrior dies and the arm that once brought
victory to his people can no longer lift spear or sword, and
though a great barrow be reared over his bones, all is not over:

"E'en in our ashes live their wonted fires,"

[1] *Od.* xix, 107 *sqq.*   [2] *Ynglinga Saga,* c. 12.   [3] *ibid.,* c. 13.

and the spirit of the dead man within is held to have the same passions and feelings in death that animated him in life. Thus in the Homeric Unseen World, that lay far away by the stream of Ocean in the West, Odysseus saw the phantom of Orion pursuing the spectral forms of the beasts that in life he had hunted over the lonely hills. The old chief within his grave-howe still thinks of his family and his people, and if they in their turn still think of him and nourish his spirit with offerings, and keep his vital element strengthened with libations of freshly-shed blood, then will he help them in the hour of peril, and he will use his kindly influence with Earth beneath to make her yield her increase and to make fruitful the herds and flocks and women of his tribe. Hence at Mycenae the older tombs of the royal house lay just within the gate; at Babylon the tomb of an ancient queen Nitocris[1] was over the gateway; Phalanthus, the founder of Tarentum, lay in the Agora of that city; whilst Brasidas, the brave Lacedaemonian general, was buried in the market-place at Amphipolis (B.C. 422) and worshipped as a hero. "At Tronis near Daulis there was a shrine of the hero-founder. Some say that this hero is Xanthippus, a famous warrior; but others say that he is Phocus, the son of Ornytion, son of Sisyphus. However that may be, he is worshipped every day, and the Phocians bring victims, and the blood they pour through a hole into the grave, but the flesh it is their custom to consume on the spot[2]."

Such a permanent opening into the grave to be used for offerings was discovered in the great barrow on the peninsula of Taman in South Russia near the village of Steblejevka. It was the burial place of a rich Greek family who lived there in the fourth century B.C. When the barrow was opened in 1864, there came to light two sepulchral chambers and a funnel-shaped aperture covered with a stone and leading down to a place enclosed with tiles on which a meal had evidently been offered to the dead[3]. Similar arrangements have been discovered in two Roman cemeteries near Carthage.

---

[1] Herod. I, 187.   [2] Paus. x, 4. 10.

[3] Stephani, *Compte-Rendu* (St Petersburg), 1865, pp. 5 *sqq.*; Frazer, *ad* Paus. x, 4. 10.

The tombs, which are numerous, are built of masonry and are square in shape, about five feet high by two or three broad. Each tomb enclosed one or more urns containing calcined bones. Each urn was covered with a saucer (patera) in the middle of which there was a hole, communicating with the exterior of the tomb by means of an earthenware tube placed either upright so as to come out at the top of the tomb or slanting so as to come out at one of the sides. Thus libations poured into the tube ran down into the urn and after wetting the bones of the dead escaped by a hole into a lower cavity of the tomb[1]. I have noticed in the museum at Colchester a Roman coffin made of lead. From the lid projects slantwise a long leaden pipe, which evidently extended from the exterior of the tomb into the interior of the coffin. A similar coffin is said to be preserved at Seville. When Canon Greenwell excavated a large barrow on the Yorkshire moors, he found a curious aperture extending from the surface to the inside of the cairn. It contained the remains of a piece of wood which had evidently once been used to close it. I have suggested that this opening served the same purpose as the others just mentioned.

Nor are we without proof that the same practice was carried out at the Shaft graves of Mycenae. A large stone pierced with a hole, discovered over these graves near which were found not only animal but also human bones, tells its ghastly tale of the sacrifices rendered periodically to the spirits of the ancient lords of Mycenae. The large stone with a cavity in the inner court of the palace at Tiryns, commonly called the altar of Zeus Herkeios, is probably a similar *bothros,* or sacrificial pit, into which offerings to the spirits of the dead were poured. But this practice was not confined to the earliest stratum of population in Peloponnesus. Pindar[2], when celebrating the glories of Olympia and her founder Pelops, tells how that hero

---

[1] A. L. Delattre, "Fouilles d'un cimetière romain à Carthage en 1888," *Revue Arch.* 3ème série, 12 (1888), p. 151 *sqq.* (cited by Frazer, *loc. cit.*).

[2] *Ol.* i, 91 *sqq.*: νῦν δ' ἐν αἱμακουρίαις
ἀγλααῖσι μέμικται,
'Αλφεοῦ πόρῳ κλιθείς,
τύμβον ἀμφίπολον ἔχων πολυξενωτάτῳ παρὰ βωμῷ.

" shares in the honours of blood-offerings where he lies buried
by Alpheus' stream, and has a barrow accessible on all sides
near a much-visited altar" (i.e. the altar of Zeus on the Cronion
hill).

As far then as the offerings of sacrifices to Adrastus are
concerned we have an ample explanation in the instances here
cited. But why should his sorrows be represented in mimetic
dances? We impute our own feelings to the dead and to our
gods, and the Greeks of the old days believed, as countless races
still believe, that what a man or a woman loved in life they
love in the grave, and in the world beyond the grave. When
a soldier dies, we give him a soldier's funeral and volleys of
musketry are fired over his grave. In the case of an officer his
charger is led after the funeral car, a survival of the time not
long past when the horse would have been slain at the grave, in
order that his master might ride him in the world of Spirits.

> " They buried the dark chief—they freed
> Beside the grave his battle-steed ;
> And swift an arrow cleaved its way
> To his stern heart ! one piercing neigh
> Arose,—and on the dead man's plain
> The rider grasps his steed again[1]."

So with the ancients and many barbarians of to-day. At the
closing scene jousts and contests of manly prowess are held
to please the spirit of the dead brave. Let us turn to Homer.
On that dread day when Achilles and his Acheans went back
to the hollow ships after the slaying of Hector, he suffered not
his Myrmidons to unyoke their chariots but said, " First let us
draw nigh and bewail Patrocles, and then shall we sup[2]." So
he and his Myrmidons thrice drove their chariots round the
spot where Patrocles' body lay, because the dead hero had
loved horsemanship in life and his spirit would be gladdened
by the sight of his chariot-driving comrades, who had not
forgotten him. Then, when the day came for burning the body,

---

[1] Thus as late as 1781 at the funeral of Frederic Casimir, Commander of
Lorraine, a horse was killed and buried with his master. For this and similar
instances, see Ridgeway, *The Origin and Influence of the Thoroughbred Horse*,
p. 128.

[2] *Il.* xxiii, 4—10.

Achilles held his great tournament which included every form of manly feat, that thus the soul of his lost friend might rejoice in knowing that he was not forgotten[1].

The oldest surviving poem in the English tongue, the *Lay of Beowulf*[2], furnishes us not only with a fine example of the same custom in our own race, but also demonstrates the desire of the hero to be had in remembrance and the care of his people to carry out his wish. As the brave old chieftain lay a dying he gave his final orders to the last surviving one of his kinsmen : " I speak in words my thanks to the Ruler of all, the King of Glory, the Everlasting Lord, for the treasures which I here gaze upon, for that I have been able to win such things for my people ere my death-day. Now that for the hoard of treasure I have sold the laying-down of my old life, fulfil ye now the people's need ; here can I be no more. Bid the warlike brave raise a mound, bright with funeral fire, at the headland of the sea ; it shall tower high on Whale's Ness as a memorial for my people, so that seafarers who drive tall ships from afar over the mists of ocean may call it in after time, Beowulf's Mound.... Then he took off his gold ring from his neck, gave to the thane his gold-adorned helm, his ring and coat-of-mail, and bade him use them well, saying to him : ' Thou art the last remnant of our race of the Waegmundings. Fate has swept away all my kinsmen, earls in valour, to the appointed doom. I must after them.' That was the old king's last word from the thoughts of his breast ere he sought the funeral pile, the hot, destroying flames. His soul departed from his bosom to seek the doom of the righteous."

When the day came for his burial, " For him then the people of the Goths prepared on the ground a firm funeral pyre, hung with helms, war-shields, bright coats-of-mail, as he had asked. Then in the midst the warriors, the heroes laid the great prince, their beloved lord, lamenting. The warrior then began to kindle on the hill the greatest of funeral pyres ; the wood reek mounted up black above the burning pile, the roaring flame mingled with the sound of weeping when the tumult of

[1] *Il.* xxɪɪɪ, 257 *sqq.*
[2] Huyshe's translation, pp. 170–71, 179–80.

the wind ceased until, glowing within, it had destroyed the corpse. Sad at heart, care-laden in mind, they mourned their liege lord's death. [Six mutilated lines follow, of which, however, enough remains to reconstruct the meaning as follows :—] Likewise the wife of aforetime, with hair bound up, sang a mournful lay for Beowulf, often said that she sorely feared the evil days for herself, much slaughter, terror of warriors, humiliation and captivity. Heaven swallowed up the smoke; then the people of the Weders made a Mound on the cliff; high it was and broad, seen far and wide by seafarers, and for ten days they built the war-hero's beacon. The remains of the burning they surrounded with a wall as skilled men could most worthily devise. In the mound they placed rings and jewels, all such adornments as the war-minded men had before taken from the hoard. They left the treasure of earls to the earth to hold the gold in the ground where now it yet remains, as useless to men as it was before.

" Then around the funeral Mound rode twelve battle-brave Athelings, sons of earls ; they would lament their (loss), mourn their king, utter the word-lay, and speak of the hero. They praised his nobleness and greatly extolled his heroic deed.

" So is it meet that man should praise his friend and lord with words, love him in heart, when he must fare forth from the fleeting body.

" Thus did the people of the Goths, companions of his hearth, mourn the fall of their lord; said that he was a world-king, mildest of men and kindest ; to his people most gracious, and of praise most desirous."

Similar rites and laments attended the obsequies of the Hunnish kings. Jordanes[1] has preserved an account of some of the ceremonies carried out at the funeral of the mighty Attila, who had died on the night of his marriage with the beautiful Ildico. The body was placed in a silken pavilion, and then followed a strange spectacle. Horsemen, the flower of the Huns, riding round the spot where the king lay, uttering funeral laments, and recalling his exploits ; how Attila, foremost of the Huns, son of Mundzuccus, was the lord of most valiant nations ;

---

[1] *De Getarum sive Gothorum Origine et Rebus gestis*, XLIX.

how with power unheard of before his day he became sole
master of the kingdoms of Scythia and Germany; how by
capturing cities he had struck terror into the Eastern and
Western Empires, how he had yielded to their entreaties and
had consented to receive an annual tribute in lieu of plundering
them completely; how after he had accomplished all this with
unchequered good fortune, he had fallen not by the enemy's
sword, nor by the treachery of his followers, but when his
people were in full enjoyment of peace and prosperity, in the
very midst of pleasure, he had met a painless death. Who
would call this death! When they had thus bewailed and
lamented him to the full, they held over his grave-mound a
funeral feast, termed in their tongue a *strava*, in which pleasure
and grief were strangely commingled. Secretly in the silence of
the night they laid his body in the earth. His coffin was
furnished with gold, silver and iron, the iron typifying the
sword with which he had subdued the nations, the gold and
the silver the treasures won by his conquests. There were
besides the weapons captured in his great victories, trappings
adorned with precious stones and the various kinds of imperial
insignia. To ensure the safety of these immense treasures, the
slaves who carried out the work received a ghastly guerdon, for
instant death sent the buriers to join the buried.

In the funeral of Beowulf and Attila we have celebrations
at the time of death and burial. But there is no lack of evidence
that in many places periodic festivals were held at the graves of
departed heroes. In a lonely spot in county Cork there is a little
ancient Irish *liss* or fort with a single circular rampart in perfect
preservation; just outside the entrance stands a barrow known
through endless generations as the "Hillock of the Fair." Here
until some forty years ago there was an annual gathering of
the country folk for a fair, and foot-races were run alongside
of the mound. Then the landlord had the fair transferred to
a village some four miles distant, but, though the fair was moved
to a thriving village from a desolate spot, it has practically
died out. Then came a road-contractor who thought that
the barrow, which was made of pieces of the local limestone,
would supply good cheap material for the roads. He laid

ruthless hands on the ancient mound and soon brought to light
a fine cromlech composed of four upright stones, supporting
as usual a great flat capstone. In the cist thus formed were
found a bronze sword, human bones and other objects. Now it
is clear why the footraces had been held there year by year from
the Bronze Age down to our own time. The old chief delighted
in manhood when in life, so in death his spirit was honoured
by the enactment of manly feats as the seasons revolved.

Nor is there any lack of evidence that such periodic celebrations in honour of heroes were held in classical Greece.
Pindar[1] declares that "the tomb of Iolaus" was "a just witness"
to the honour won by Epharmostus of Opus in Locris. This of
course refers to the Iolaea, the famous games held at Thebes,
sometimes called the Heraclea, to commemorate Heracles and
his faithful comrade Iolaus. It is clear that the contests were
held beside the tomb in order doubtless to please the spirit of
the dead man within. The prize was a bronze tripod[2]. Besides
this festival there were likewise others in Boeotia[2] in honour of
old worthies, such as the Trophonia at Lebadea and the
Amphiaraea at Oropus, in honour of Trophonius and Amphiaraus
respectively.

Moreover the victor in such games on his return to his
native town sought to please the spirit of its chief hero by
placing a wreath upon his shrine. Thus Pindar[3] proclaims that
Epharmostus, the Opuntian athlete, " by being victorious hath
crowned at the feast the altar of Ajax Oileus," the great hero
of the Locrians, who regularly represented him on their coins[4].

But it is not only the ghosts of those who have enjoyed pros-
perous and happy lives who love to be remembered. The souls of
those who have suffered much and have had great catastrophes
are especially supposed to take a melancholy pleasure in the
remembrance of their woes. So in *Hamlet*[5] the ghost says:

> " Hamlet, remember me,"

and Hamlet replies,

---

[1] *Ol.* IX, 98–9.   [2] Schol. Pind. *Ol.* VII, 154.   [3] *Ol.* IX, 112.
[4] So at Gela tragedians sacrificed at the tomb of Aeschylus as to a hero and
rehearsed their plays on it (Vit. Aesch.).
[5] I. v.

"Remember thee, ay, thou poor ghost,
While memory holds her seat in this distracted globe"

(placing his hand on his head).

That the ghosts of those who have been murdered or have been done to death unjustly, like to have their sorrows kept in remembrance is no mere modern or mediaeval idea, but can be amply illustrated from ancient Greece itself. At Tegea in Arcadia[1] there was a curious annual ceremony, which throws some light on the origin of Tragedy and also shows how the worship of a god (and that god not necessarily Dionysus) may become connected with, or superimposed upon, that of a local personage. The people of Tegea held that Apollo was not an indigenous god in their land, although there were in their town certain images known as Apollo Agyieus. The Tegeans said that they had set these up for the following reason. Artemis and Apollo went to every country and took vengeance on all the men who had refused hospitality to their mother Leto as she wandered homeless in her pregnancy. When in their vengeful progress the twin deities arrived at Tegea, Scephrus, son of Tegeates the king, went up to Apollo and talked with him apart. Thereupon Limon his brother suspecting that what Scephrus was saying reflected on himself, ran at his brother and slew him. Punishment at once overtook the fratricide, for Artemis shot him. Tegeates and Maera his wife sacrificed to Apollo and Artemis at the time, but afterwards a great barrenness fell upon the land and an oracle was sent from Delphi that they should bewail Scephrus. "So at the festival of Apollo they perform various ceremonies in honour of Scephrus, and in particular the priestess of Artemis pursues a man, feigning that she is Artemis and he Limon."

That those who had been slain unjustly, more especially by those of kindred blood or race were supposed to be able to produce barrenness and bring blight on the crops and various ills upon both man and beast, is rendered certain by a famous story in Herodotus[2]: "The Phoceans, captured in the great sea-fight at Alalia by the Etruscans and Carthaginians (B.C. 546), were brought to Agylla or Caere in Etruria. There their

---

[1] Paus. VIII, 53. 2.   [2] I, 167.

captors divided the spoil and in the distribution by lot most
of them seem to have fallen to the Etruscans. They led them
forth and stoned them to death. After that it came to pass
that everything belonging to the Agyllaeans that passed by
the spot where the stoned Phoceans lay in death, whether
cattle, beasts of burden, or human beings, became distorted,
maimed or paralysed. The Agyllaeans accordingly sent to
Delphi in their desire to atone for their sin and to obtain
a respite from their punishment. The Pythian prophetess
bade them do as they do unto this day—they make great
offerings to them as heroes and hold contests of athletes and
horses."

It is now clear that athletic feats, contests of horsemanship,
and tragic dances are all part of the same principle—the
honouring and appeasing of the dead. More than one writer
on Tragedy has felt the difficulty in explaining why it is that
the earliest dithyrambs of which we hear were grave and
solemn hymns rather than rude licentious vintage songs. This
difficulty disappears as soon as we realise that they were
composed to be sung round the graves of the mighty dead.
At the great Dionysia a Cyclic chorus danced round the altar
of the twelve gods at Athens, and there is little doubt that the
Tragic chorus which honoured Adrastus danced round his tomb
in the Agora at Sicyon, and we may be sure that the mimetic
performance with which the ghost of Scephrus was placated at
Tegea, was held close by his tomb. We have seen that in
sacrificing to a hero no fire was employed, for the blood or the
pelanos was poured into a *bothros* or hole beside or in the grave,
or even as at Tronis, through an aperture reaching right down
to the dead inside. But in the case of a god the offering was
burned in order that its essence might thus ascend to heaven.
When a hero was promoted to godhead, as was Heracles, the
chief factor in his apotheosis was that henceforth he was
honoured with fire offerings burned upon an altar instead of
with a fireless *pelanos* poured into a hole in the grave. Adrastus
must have been honoured at Sicyon in the latter way, but
when the tragic chorus was taken from him and transferred
to Dionysus, the tomb round which the chorus danced now

became the altar of Dionysus and fire was kindled upon it, the tomb thus passing into a fire-altar. Thus arose the *thymele* of Dionysus. Curiously enough Sicyon itself supplies us with the classical instance of a shrine which was both a heroum and also a fire-altar. The Sicyonians had continued to worship Heracles as a hero, until Phaestus came and insisted on sacrificing to him as to a deity. The Sicyonians, wishing to make sure of doing what was right, continued both forms of ritual: "To this day," says Pausanias[1], "the Sicyonians after slaying a lamb and burning the thighs on the altar, eat part of the flesh as of a regular sacrificial victim, and offer part of the flesh as to a hero," doubtless placing the flesh without fire in a *bothros*, in or at the base of the altar or on a table in front of the altar.

In every town and village throughout Greece there was the shrine of the local hero or heroine, whose cult in later days in many cases had superimposed upon it that of some of the great divinities, such as Zeus, Apollo, Poseidon, Hermes, Artemis, Athena, or Dionysus. Hence we meet such combinations as Zeus Amphiaraus, Zeus Trophonius, Zeus Agamemnon, Hermes Aepytus, Artemis Orthia, Athena Alea, whilst Poseidon was worshipped in the Erechtheum on the same altar as Erechtheus, the tomb of the hero-king having become the fire-altar of the god; similarly at Tegea the cult of Scephrus seems to have merged into that of Apollo.

The Thymele.

Can we now get a clue to the true origin of the *thymele* which appears in the history of Tragedy as an inseparable concomitant of the chorus? The word *thymele* does not occur in Homer, but it is frequent, as might be expected, in the Attic tragedians. It is by no means confined to the altar of Dionysus, for it is commonly used of the altars of all the gods[2]. But from a fragment of Eupolis it seems also to have meant a cake, used in offerings, made of barley meal

---

[1] II, 10. 1.

[2] Aesch. *Suppl.* 667; Eur. *Ion* 114 (τὰν Φοίβου θυμέλαν), *Suppl.* 65 (δεξιπύρους θεῶν θυμέλας), etc.

and oil, from which it appears to be the same as the *pelanos*, the mixture of barley meal, honey and oil, which was offered not merely to gods, but also to the dead. The name *thymele* was likewise further extended to the whole shrine wherein stood the altar[1]. But here we are especially concerned with its use in the theatre.

Let us first hear what the ancients themselves have to say on the matter. Pollux[2], when enumerating the parts of a theatre, says: "The *skene* was appropriated to the actors, the *orchestra* to the chorus. In the *orchestra* was the *thymele*, whether it was a *bema* (a step or platform) or a *bomos* (an altar or a tomb). On the stage was a *bomos* of the kind that stands in streets in front of house doors, and a table bearing cakes was termed the *theoris* or *thyoris*. The *eleos* was an old-fashioned table on which in the days before Thespis someone mounted and held a dialogue with the members of the Chorus[3]." In the *Etymologicum Magnum* we have the following important statement on the word θυμέλη[4]. "The *thymele* of the theatre bears down to the present day a name derived from the circumstance that upon it the sacrifices are cut up, i.e. the sacrificial victims. It was on a table that they stood and sang in the country parts before Tragedy had taken proper shape."

From these two passages we learn the following facts: (1) that on the *skene* stood a *bomos* (altar or tomb) of the kind customary in streets in front of the house door; (2) that beside this stood a sacred table bearing cakes; (3) that this table was not called *thymele*, but *theoris* or *thyoris*; (4) that in the *orchestra* stood the *thymele*, either in the form of a *bema* (step, platform) or of a *bomos* (altar, tomb); (5) that in the days before Thespis a table called *eleos* (a common table for cutting up

---

[1] Eur. *El.* 713 : θυμέλαι δ' ἐπίτναντο χρυσήλατοι.

[2] IV, 123 : καὶ σκηνὴ μὲν ὑποκριτῶν ἴδιον, ἡ δὲ ὀρχήστρα τοῦ χοροῦ, ἐν ᾗ καὶ ἡ θυμέλη, εἴτε βῆμά τι οὖσα εἴτε βωμός.

[3] IV, 123 : ἐπὶ δὲ τῆς σκηνῆς καὶ ἀγυιεὺς ἔκειτο βωμὸς ὁ πρὸ τῶν θυρῶν, καὶ τράπεζα πέμματα ἔχουσα, ἡ θεωρὶς ὠνομάζετο ἢ θυωρίς. ἐλεὸς δ' ἦν τράπεζα ἀρχαία, ἐφ' ἧν πρὸ Θέσπιδος εἶς τις ἀναβὰς τοῖς χορευταῖς ἀπεκρίνατο.

[4] ἡ τοῦ θεάτρου μέχρι νῦν ἀπὸ τῆς τραπέζης ὠνόμασται, παρὰ τὸ ἐπ' αὐτῆς τὰ θύη μερίζεσθαι, τουτέστι, τὰ θυόμενα ἱερεῖα. τράπεζα δὲ ἦν, ἐφ' ἧς ἐν τοῖς ἀγροῖς ᾖδον, μήπω τάξιν λαβούσης τραγῳδίας.

meat, etc.), of an old-fashioned type, was used as an extemporised stage on which someone, the poet or leader, mounted and held a dialogue with the other members of the Chorus. This shows that Thespis was not the first to introduce dialogue between some kind of actor and the chorus. The table on which the actor stood had nothing sacred about it. This statement of Pollux is amply confirmed by the second passage which declares that in old days in the country parts before Tragedy had taken its full shape, the singers stood and sang upon a table (*trapeza*). We must therefore be careful not to confuse the sacred table (*theoris*), on which offerings were laid in front of the *bomos*, with the ordinary table extemporised into a stage. The derivation of *thymele* given above is virtually that still generally accepted, i.e. from $\theta\acute{v}\epsilon\iota\nu$, "to sacrifice," lit. "to raise a smoke," that is, to offer burnt sacrifice. It is the term regularly used of sacrificing to gods, whilst the term $\dot{\epsilon}\nu\alpha\gamma\acute{\iota}\zeta\epsilon\iota\nu$ is used of the "fireless offerings" made to the dead. Thus the offerings cut up on the *thymele* (according to the *Etymologicum Magnum*) were those to be offered with fire and therefore to a god, but at the same time it is quite possible that the term *thyos, thysia*, came to be used generally of all sorts of sacrifice.

Pollux plainly had doubts whether the *thymele* was a *bema* (step or platform), or a *bomos* (altar or tomb), but it is very probable that the two coincided. A raised altar or tomb with or without a step or steps was nothing else than a *bema* (cf. Fig. 9, p. 45). By the time when Pollux was writing, the term *thymele* had come to be generally used of a raised platform. This too is certainly the sense in which it is employed by Plutarch where it is contrasted with the *skene*. Plutarch[1] uses it in several passages as a platform from which people spoke or sang, though at the same time he speaks of it as something distinct from the stage (*skene*). The scholiast on Aristophanes, *Equites* 516, uses it apparently in a like sense, for he represents the comic poet as coming forward to the *thymele* to recite

---

[1] III, 119, 2 (Reiske): Sulla, in celebration of his victory at Thebes, caused a *thymele* to be erected near the fountain of Oedipus; I, 447, 11: Alexander borne along with his companions on a lofty *thymele* drawn by eight horses; VIII, 456, 7: $\sigma\kappa\eta\nu\dot{\eta}\nu$ $\kappa\alpha\grave{\iota}$ $\theta\upsilon\mu\acute{\epsilon}\lambda\eta\nu$.

the *Parabasis*. On the strength of the latter passage and of
one of those from Plutarch, to which I have just referred,
Liddell and Scott (s.v.) explain the *thymele* as "an altar-shaped
platform in the middle of the orchestra, on the steps of which
stood the leader of the Chorus (anciently the poet himself) to
direct its movements."

Mr Haigh[1], adopting the view set forth by my friend Mr A. B.
Cook[2], Reader in Classical Archaeology in the University of
Cambridge, says that "the first innovation was the introduction
of a dialogue between the coryphaeus and the choreutae in the
intervals of the choral ode. For the purpose of carrying on this
dialogue the coryphaeus used to mount upon the sacrificial
table, which stood beside the altar in the centre of the orchestra.
Such sacrificial tables are often found in ancient vase paintings
by the side of the regular altar, and were used for cutting up
the victims or for receiving various bloodless offerings, such
as cakes and vegetables. Both the table and the altar were
called by the same name, *thymele*. This table on which the
coryphaeus took his stand, surrounded by the choristers, was
the prototype of the stage in the later Greek theatre." But
the reader will notice (1) that there is not a single word in the
ancient sources (on which Mr Cook and Mr Haigh relied) to
show that a table was ever called a *thymele*, and (2) to show
that the sacred table which stood, not in the *orchestra* beside
the *thymele*, but on the stage (*skene*), bearing on it sacred cakes,
was identical with the ordinary common table used by rustics
as a temporary platform on which they stood and sang.

Let us turn to the material evidence. Various ancient
theatres have been excavated in Greece in modern times, but
only in one of them, that at Priene, have the remains of an
altar been discovered. In this theatre some fifteen years ago
the altar was found standing in its original position. It is
placed just in front of the first row of seats, exactly opposite
the centre of the stage[3]. Mr Haigh doubts whether this was

---

[1] *The Attic Theatre* (2nd ed., 1898), p. 106.

[2] "On the Thymele in Greek Theatres," *Class. Review* (1895), vol. IX,
pp. 370–8.

[3] Haigh, *The Attic Theatre* (2nd ed.), p. 137.

the usual position of the altar in a Greek theatre. "In the earliest period (writes he), when the drama was still a purely lyrical performance, the altar stood in the centre of the orchestra and the chorus danced round about it. The evidence supplied by the remains at Athens and Epidaurus rather favours the view that in these theatres it still occupied the same position." "In the middle of the theatre at Epidaurus there is a round stone, 28 inches in diameter, let into the ground, so as to be on the same level with the surrounding surface. In the middle of the stone is a circular hole. A similar hole is found in the later Athenian orchestra." The purpose of this stone cannot be determined with certainty. It has been suggested that these holes were meant for the reception of small stone altars. At Athens the surface of the fifth and fourth century orchestra has not been preserved, but the Roman pavement has survived, which may retain vestiges of the original design. There is no trace of an altar, but in the centre is a large rhombus-shaped figure bounded by two strips of marble. The interior of the figure is paved with small slabs of marble also rhombus-shaped and of different colours. In the middle of the figure is a block of Pentelic marble 41 inches long and 17½ inches broad. The centre of the block has a shallow circular depression, which may have been intended to receive an altar of Dionysus. At the Piraeus the centre of the orchestra was marked by a small pit. The excavations at Megalopolis failed to find any remains of the *thymele* or altar, which doubtless stood in the centre of the orchestra[1].

It may be that in the depressions in the centre of the stone found in the middle of the orchestra at Athens we have really a hollow to receive offerings, and that the circular hole in the stone in the middle of the orchestra at Epidaurus, as also the pit found in the centre of the orchestra at Piraeus, may both have served a like purpose. These hollows may well represent the *bothros* into which offerings to dead heroes were placed. It was quite easy to place over these stones a temporary platform, such as the *thymele* had certainly become in Hellenistic and Roman times.

[1] Haigh and Cook, *loc. cit.*

Mr Cook in his paper already cited has shown that the statements of Pollux and the *Etymologicum Magnum* are amply corroborated by the evidence of extant monuments. He points out that the table (*trapeza* or *eleos*) was a usual concomitant of a *bomos* (altar or tomb), and that it was employed to hold the objects to be offered on the *bomos*. But he seems wrong (*a*) in assuming that the *trapeza* or *eleos* on which the singers stood, was identical with the sacred table (*theoris*), which stood beside the *bomos* on the stage (and not in the orchestra), and (*b*) in deducing from thence one form of *thymele*. In support of this he cites a Pan-Athenaic vase in the British Museum (B. 141), showing a musical contest between two persons confronted on a kind of platform. The platform is a horizontal table-top supported on legs, one showing at each end, the lower part of which is roughly carved to represent animal paws. In this he rightly recognizes the *trapeza* referred to by Pollux and the *Etymologicum Magnum*. Its shape, he thinks, accords precisely with that of a *trapeza* placed before the cultus statues of Dionysus Dendrites. But it does not follow that because a table used for holding offerings is in the same archaic form as the tables used for ordinary domestic purposes any singer would have ventured to stand upon and use as a platform the table dedicated to a god or hero.

Another vase in the same collection (B. 188) shows an apparently solid *bema*, the *motif* being repeated twice with a slight variation: (*a*) a musical contest with a *bema* of three steps, on which stand two youths confronted, and (*b*) a *bema* of one step on which stand two youths side by side. There is thus archaeological evidence for the statement of Pollux and the *Etymologicum Magnum* that tables were used as extemporary platforms by the rustics, though there is none to show that such tables were in any sense *thymelae*, whilst there is also proof that the *thymele* was a *bema* or platform of one or more steps. But such is the form of the tomb of Agamemnon (Fig. 14, p. 121). Moreover the tomb of Agamemnon in the *Choephorae* (p. 119) and that of Proteus in the *Helena* (p. 139) are compared to a *bomos*. Such *bema* can be seen in the illustration (Fig. 9), which I am enabled to show by the kindness of

Fig. 9. Theban Scyphos showing a Bema or Thymele.

Mr Cook[1]. It is from a Theban black-figured *scyphos* in the
British Museum (B. 78). It is thus described by Mr H. B.
Walters: "Flute-player to left, with puffed out cheeks,
wearing a beaded fillet and himation; in front of him, two
grotesque nude figures to left, the first slightly bearded,
holding up a *tympanon* (?); the other beardless, with a wreath
in his hand and another on his head, standing on a *thymele* (?).
On the left a branch." A very interesting discovery made in
Athens in an ancient Dionysiac precinct near the Areopagus
does not prove that the table was the *thymele* itself, for it may
have been meant to bear offerings for the object of adoration. In
the middle of the precinct " are the remains of an altar in the
form of a table resting on four legs and beside this in the basis
of the altar is a sinking for a stela."[2] It may be that we must
not recognize, as has been done, a *thymele* in this table. Possibly
it was a table for offerings presented to the *stele* or the object
of veneration represented by that *stele*, whether Dionysus, or
some ancient hero upon whose cult that of Dionysus may have
been placed. Not only, as already said, were *trapezai* the regular
accessories of altars, as on the Lycaean Mount in Arcadia, but
even of much'smaller objects of adoration.

Thus at Chaeronea the supposed spear or sceptre of Aga-
mcmnon was held in great sanctity, and a table stood beside it[3].
"The god whom the Chaeroneans honour most is the sceptre
which Homer says Hephaestus made for Zeus. This sceptre
they worship naming it a spear, and that there is something divine
about it is proved by the distinction that it confers on its
owners. There is no public temple built for it, but the man
who acts as priest keeps the sceptre in his own house for a year
and sacrifices are offered to it daily and a table is set beside it
covered with all sorts of flesh and cakes."

Here we have the sacred table of offerings corresponding
with its cakes to the sacred table with cakes called *theoris*
or *thyoris*, which stood on the ancient *skene* (stage) beside the
bomos.

The facts here set forth show that there were two forms of
worship in the Greek theatre:

[1] *op. cit.*, p. 374, with figure.   [2] Cook, *op. cit.*, p. 370.   [3] Paus. IX, 4. 11–12.

I. The *bomos* on the stage with its table of offerings. This *bomos* was like the conical pillars which stood in the streets before house doors, and called in later times Apollo Agyieus, but which were more probably the grave-stones of ancient worthies. The offerings to this *bomos* were cakes, such as those commonly offered to the dead.

II. In the *orchestra* stood the *thymele*, a true altar for offering burnt sacrifices to the gods. This may also have had its table and have stood over a *bothros*. Here sacrifice was offered to Dionysus before the performance began.

To this *thymele* came forward ($\pi\alpha\rho\alpha\beta\acute{a}\varsigma$) the comic poet, or in his name the *coryphaeus*, to deliver the *Parabasis*, a term which derived its name from this circumstance. But as Comedy borrowed largely the practices established by Tragedy, it is not unreasonable to suppose that the leader of the solemn hymns or dithyrambs from which Tragedy arose also took his stand on the steps of the *thymele* or on some object near it, in later times a temporary platform.

The Skene. But quite distinct from the table for offerings near the *bomos* on the stage, and possibly from the other one beside the *thymele* in the *orchestra*, there was the ordinary table used as a temporary stage in early times before Tragedy had taken its proper shape. It was out of such table-stages that the *skene* eventually grew and not from a sacred table for offerings.

THE INTRODUCTION OF THE CULT OF DIONYSUS.

As there were two altars in the theatre, there were undoubtedly survivals of two distinct cults. Can we explain this hitherto neglected point? The superimposition of the cults of Dionysus upon that of an old hero gives us exactly the explanation needed for the facts.

At Sicyon the tomb of Adrastus stood right in the market-place and round it the tragic chorus that represented his sorrows danced their solemn measure and sang their solemn hymn. When Cleisthenes handed over to Dionysus the tragic choruses of Adrastus, the dance would still be held in the same place and the tomb of Adrastus would either become the fire-altar of Dionysus (*thymele*) or else a separate altar of Dionysus would be set up beside it or close by. Thus in the embryo of the Tragic theatre there were two centres of adoration, the tomb of the hero and the fire-altar of Dionysus, and at the sacred spot where before only the ritual of a hero was performed, there were now two cults; the one in honour of the old dead hero, the other with burnt sacrifice in honour of the god Dionysus. The shrine henceforth played a double part like that of Heracles close by (p. 38).

But the religious principles that led to this double cult at Sicyon were at work all over Greece. In very many places the tomb of the old hero or heroine, in whose honour mimetic dances had been held from of old, was incorporated into the worship of some more potent divinity. If the new cult was that of Dionysus, the tomb either became the *thymele* of that god, or a fire altar was erected beside the tomb of the hero. But it does not follow that in every case where such super-imposition took place, Dionysus was the god who overshadowed the worship of the local hero. Thus we have seen that at Tegea in Arcadia the dramatic performance in honour of Scephrus did not form a part of the cult of the Thracian god, but was associated with that of Apollo. In a later section it will be shown at length that in the extant Greek tragedies the tombs of heroes play a very prominent part. At this stage it will suffice to cite one of the most striking instances. In the *Choephori* the tomb of Agamemnon forms the centre of the opening scene. To it approach from the palace the chorus of handmaids in attendance on Electra, their purpose being to offer at the command of Clytemnestra propitiatory offerings to the murdered king and husband. The connection of the worship of Dionysus with festivals in which the cult of the dead bore a very important part, has recently been placed beyond doubt in the case of the chief Attic festivals with which the name of that god is associated. These were (1) the *Country Dionysia* (τὰ κατ᾽ ἀγρούς) held in the country villages in the month of December, (2) the *Lenaea*, held at Athens in the second half of January (in the month anciently termed Lenaion from this very festival, but later Gamelion), (3) the *Anthesteria* held in Athens in March,

(4) the *Great* or *City Dionysia* (τὰ ἐν ἄστει) held in the first part of April. It is obvious that all four festivals fall at seasons of the year when there is no vintage.

Now as each Attic month bore a name[1] derived from the chief festival held at that season, we might naturally expect to find a month named after Dionysus, if the City Dionysia had been of great antiquity, or if the festival held at that time of year had had that god's name associated with it from a distant past. But the fact that such is not the case is exactly in accordance with its history. Plays were practically only to be seen at that festival and at the Lenaea, but there were also certain acting contests at the Anthesteria, whilst there were dramatic exhibitions in the various country townships during the Rural Dionysia, though in Athens itself there were apparently no performances at this season. Yet the dramatic performances at the Great Dionysia were only of a comparatively recent date. It was the principal time for the exhibition of tragedies, and it was at this festival that the earliest public competitions in Tragedy were established. The first contest was held in B.C. 535, when Thespis, now an old man, took part in the performances and won the crown of victory. It was but a short time before that date that Pisistratus had returned once more from exile and had begun his third and final tyranny. The regulations of the tragic contests must therefore have been carried out under his auspices. As the festival, at least in its more splendid form, is known to have been of a comparatively late date, critics have been led to conjecture that the entire festival was first instituted by that despot. But it seems more probable that like the other three

---

[1] I have shown (*Proc. Cambridge Philological Society* (1907)), pp. 2, 3, that the termination -ων of the names of the Attic months (e.g. Ποσειδεών, -ῶνος, Βοηδρομιών, Γαμηλιών, etc.) is simply the genitive plural of the name of the festival held in the particular month, Ποσειδεῖα, Ποσειδείων, Βοηδρόμια, Βοηδρομίων, Γαμήλια, Γαμηλίων, with the change of accent for differentiation of sense. The same explanation holds good for the nom. term. ών, e.g. πιθών from πίθων, gen. plur. of πίθος; πυλών from gen. plur. πύλων (πύλη) etc. The month would be called μὴν Γαμηλιών etc., and from such phrases as ἐπὶ μηνὸς Γαμηλίων etc. the gen. would come to be regarded as a nom. sing. and be declined accordingly. Cf. Lat. *sestertium*, from *sestertiorum*, *sestertium*, gen. plur. of *sestertius*.

festivals with which the name and worship of Dionysus became connected, it too was already in existence from an early date and was merely reorganised by Pisistratus under a new name with the addition of a new cult and the institution of elaborate dramatic contests.

The villages of Attica had each their own local hero and to these local festivals of the dead the worship of Dionysus became attached, as it did to that of Adrastus at Sicyon. The Anthesteria was a great festival of the dead, as has been proved by Miss Harrison[1]. Its purpose, probably like that of the other festivals, was to ensure that the earth should yield her increase. On the third day, called the *Chytrae*, " pots " of cooked vegetables were offered to the gods and to the dead, and there were Cyclic choruses. Of course it may be urged that these choruses were Dionysiac, but on the first day of the City Dionysia Cyclic choruses danced round the altar of the Twelve gods in the Agora, which plainly shows that such Cyclic dances were by no means confined at Athens to Dionysus. There can be no doubt that choruses were pre-Dionysiac in Attica as well as in other parts of Greece. If then such dramatic choruses were employed at a festival, mainly and originally that of the dead, for the dead were worshipped long before Dionysus was introduced, if through all times their cult continued, and if in older Attica there were men like Simonides, who composed such hymns or laments in honour of the dead, we are justified in considering that choruses at the Anthesteria were far older than the introduction of the cult of Dionysus into Athens.

THE SATYRIC DRAMA.

It is commonly held that in the early days of Tragedy the Satyric Drama invariably represented the sufferings or adventures of Dionysus and his attendant Satyrs, who, as we have seen, were probably merely his own Satrian tribesmen, just as the Bacchants represented the young women of that tribe. We have also had occasion to note that the cult in its native land was apparently a gross licentious ritual supposed, like those witnessed by Mr Dawkins in Thrace and by Mr Wace in

---

[1] *Prolegomena to the Study of Greek Religion*, p. 34 sqq.

Northern Greece, to have a potent effect on the fertility of women, flocks and fields. An examination of the evidence will convince the reader that the cult of Dionysus which entered Attica and Peloponnesus and the rest of Greece was of the same unclean character. According to the Attic tradition the worship of Dionysus was first introduced into Athens by king Amphictyon, to whose notice it had been brought by one Pegasus of Eleutherae, a town on the borders of Attica and Boeotia. Here Dionysus was worshipped, as also at Hermione in Argolis, the birthplace of Lasus, under the name of *Melanaigis*, "Wearer of the Black Goatskin." In a building near the precincts of the temple of Dionysus at Athens, Pausanias[1] saw "images of clay representing Amphictyon, king of Athens, feasting Dionysus and other gods. Here too is Pegasus of Eleutherae, who introduced the god to the Athenians by the aid of the Delphic oracle, which reminded the Athenians that in the days of Icarius the god had once sojourned in the land." At Hermione, says Pausanias[2], they held annually a musical contest and a regatta in the god's honour at which prizes were given. The nature of the cult introduced by Pegasus we know well from the scholiast on Aristophanes (*Acharnians*, 243): "Pegasus of Eleutherae, a town in Boeotia, took the image of Dionysus and went into Attica. But the Athenians did not receive the god with honour. The god was wroth, and accordingly a certain disease attacked them, which proved incurable. Now as the malady would not yield to magic or skill, in despair they despatched envoys in all haste (to Delphi). On their return they declared that the only means of curing the disease was to fetch the god with all honour. In obedience to these commands the Athenians, both privately and publicly, prepared *phalloi* and honoured the god with them, in perpetual memory of their affliction, also perhaps because the god is the cause

---

[1] I, 2. 5.

[2] II, 35. 1. This passage (first pointed out by me, *Jour. Hell. Stud.* 1881, p. 315) is almost our only direct evidence from ancient writers for boat-racing amongst the ancient Greeks, though (as Hirschfeld has shown) the Attic Ephebic inscriptions prove that boat-racing was practised by the Athenian youths. There is probably a reference in a still earlier passage (Pindar, *Isth.* IV, 5) ναες ἐν πόντῳ καὶ ἐν ἅρμασιν ἵπποι διὰ τεάν, ὦ 'νασσα, τιμὰν ὠκυδινάτοις ἐν ἀμίλλαισι θαυμασταὶ πέλονται.

of the procreation of children, for drunkenness excites pleasure and acts as an aphrodisiac." No wonder then that Lycurgus the old Thracian king scourged Dionysus and his attendant women, and no wonder too that in B.C. 186 old Cato, then Censor, induced the Roman Senate to pass the famous decree *de Bacchanalibus* in his attempt to stamp out, or stem the advance of, those accursed rites.

But one thing at least is certain. Our extant tragedies are singularly free from all impurity, and do not seem to have been fit instruments for celebrating the obscene ceremonies of the Dionysus of Eleutherae. But as the cult of Dionysus which entered Athens and the rest of Greece was a gross ritual, like its modern survivals in Thrace and Northern Greece (p. 16), that element ought to be found in the branch of Tragedy which was specially consecrated to Dionysus. Of this the *Cyclops*[1] of Euripides, the only extant Satyric drama, supplies the most indisputable evidence, for there is in it at least one passage meet to do honour to the god of Eleutherae after the manner prescribed for the Athenians on the introduction of his cult, and which forms a fit commentary on the representations of the Sileni or Satyrs seen on the coins of Thrace (Figs. 2—4). The speaker is none other than Silenus himself who is haranguing the Chorus of Satyrs in praise of wine and lechery.

It is agreed by all that the Satyric Drama stood perfectly apart from Comedy (which as we are told by Aristotle arose out of the local phallic songs). Indeed the Satyric drama was termed by the ancients "Tragedy at play" ($\pi a i \zeta o v \sigma a$ $\tau \rho a \gamma \omega \delta i a$)[2]. As we have said above, it has been generally supposed to have grown out of rude licentious dithyrambs of the Dorians. But there is no evidence for the existence of such licentious dithyrambs, and as neither the dithyramb nor Tragedy itself can be held to be Dorian in origin, we must look for some other explanation of the Satyric drama. Now when the Chorus, which

---

[1] 169–72 : ἵν' ἔστι τουτί τ' ὀρθὸν ἐξανιστάναι
μαστοῦ τε δραγμὸς καὶ παρεσκευασμένου
ψαῦσαι χεροῖν λειμῶνος, ὀρχηστύς θ' ἅμα
κακῶν τε λῇστις.

[2] Demetrius, *de elocut.* § 169.

had for generations danced in honour of Adrastus, was transferred
to Dionysus, some element of that god's own cult must have been
added to the ritual round the heroum in the Agora at Sicyon.
In the early days of Tragedy the Satyric dramas invariably consisted of the adventures of Dionysus and his attendant Satyrs,
his own Satrian tribesmen. But as it has just been shown
that Tragedy arose from the worship of native Greek heroes long
before Dionysus came from his ancient seat on Mount Pangaeum,
it may be that the only true Dionysiac element in the tragic
performances at Athens and probably elsewhere was the Satyric
drama. This would be in complete harmony with the view of
the ancients themselves who evidently regarded the Satyric
drama as having an origin distinct from that of Tragedy
proper, though both primarily arose out of choruses[1]. The
Satyrs and Bacchants are certainly Thracian in their mytho-
logical origin, and there can be no doubt that the foxskins and
fawnskins of the latter were part of the ancient Thracian dress
(p. 24). In the light of the facts obtained by Mr Dawkins and
Mr Wace that the chief actors in the gross dramatic performances
of modern Thrace and Thessaly not only now wear goatskins,
but formerly used those of the fox and fawn (p. 17), we are led
to the conclusion that the Satyric Drama, with its grossness and
obscenity, its Sileni and its Satyrs, came down into Greece
from Thrace along with the worship of Dionysus.

This hypothesis completely accounts for the clear separa-
tion in origin between it and Attic Comedy proper, though
each arose out of gross performances, and also for the prominence of this class of play in the early days of the Drama.
Thus Pratinas of Phlius, who, as we shall see, introduced this
form of drama into Attica towards the end of the 5th century B.C.,
is said to have composed no less than thirty-two Satyric dramas
and fifty tragedies, whilst Choerilus was so famous for his
productions in the same field that it gave rise to the proverb,
"when Choerilus was king among the Satyrs." As time went
on the Satyric dramas dealt less and less with the adventures
of Dionysus until finally, as in the *Cyclops* of Euripides, the

---

[1] Athen. 630 c : συνέστηκε δὲ καὶ σατυρικὴ πᾶσα ποίησις τὸ παλαιὸν ἐκ χορῶν ὡς
καὶ ἡ τότε τραγῳδία.

only extant example, the leading character is not Dionysus, but some hero or other, in this case Odysseus, who fell in with Silenus and a rout of Satyrs. It was almost certainly this departure from the original strictly Dionysiac character that gave rise to the criticism of old-fashioned people "not a word about Dionysus" (οὐδὲν πρὸς Διόνυσον). Thus even that which had once been the true Dionysiac element faded before the national instincts of the Athenians, and with the invention of melodrama by Euripides and the rise of true Comedy it finally disappeared altogether.

Thus the *Alcestis*—the earliest extant work of Euripides, took the place of a regular Satyric drama in the tetralogy with which the poet obtained the second prize in B.C. 438, Sophocles being first. The other three works were the *Cressae*, the *Alcmaeon*, and the *Telephus*. The Greek argument describes the play as "somewhat comic[1]," probably in allusion to the refusals of his father and all his friends to die instead of Admetus when that selfish egoist requests them to be his substitute, and also because of the boisterous behaviour of Heracles before he hears of the death of the heroine. The argument also terms it as "rather Satyric[1]" because it has a happy ending. Such a drama gave to the audience the relief necessary after three tragedies, whilst the desire of the Athenians for obscene buffoonery was now gratified to the full by the writers of the Old Comedy. Thus the Dionysiac grossness was finally purged out of Tragedy and the triumph of the native heroic element was complete.

The time indeed was to come when Euripides, in his later years now resident at the court of Archelaus, was to glorify the invincible power of the great god of Thrace. Yet this was not to be in that coarse Satyric drama, which had its birth in Thrace, but in the great tragedy commonly known as the *Bacchae*, but more accurately styled *Pentheus* by the best ancient authorities. On this same theme of the Theban king Aeschylus had composed his play of the *Pentheus*, whilst Thespis was said to have dramatised it long before Pratinas

---

[1] κωμικωτέραν ἔχει τὴν κατασκευήν . . . τὸ δὲ δρᾶμά ἐστι σατυρικώτερον ὅτι εἰς χαρὰν καὶ ἡδονὴν καταστρέφει.

ever introduced his Satyric drama into Athens. Thus in this play in which Euripides upheld the resistless power of Dionysus, he employs as his instrument not that dramatic type which had passed with the god down into Greece, but that lofty and noble form evolved on Greek soil from the worship of the heroic dead.

Of course it has been said that the Satyric drama gave the comic relief to the tragedies which are supposed rightly or wrongly always to have preceded it. But it is clear that, though gross and obscene, it was distinctly an inherent part of the cult of the Thracian god of vegetation and fertility. In this it differs completely from the rustic buffoonery out of which, according to Aristotle, Comedy undoubtedly sprang. Although the origin of the latter is well known, it had no early history, for "it was only late that the Archon granted a Comic chorus." The reason of this becomes obvious from what we have just seen. The Tragedy, which was the lineal descendant of the tragic dance and solemn hymn round the tomb of the old hero, was of real importance to the community, since it was essentially a religious rite, the omission of which might be fraught with dread consequences to the land. The State therefore naturally furnished the cost of the exhibition of tragedies. The Satyric drama was the worship of the new god from Thrace who performed the same functions for vegetation as the old heroes of the land, but in a higher degree, and as it was grafted on the old ritual the State of necessity likewise defrayed the expenses of this act of worship. But Comedy, which grew out of mere rustic buffoonery, had no claim to respect as a religious ceremony, and accordingly the State did not take it up until after Tragedy had been developed into a distinct *genre* of literature, and until Comedy, which had been developed on the lines of Tragedy, was also recognised as a legitimate form of the Drama.

CHAPTER II

THE RISE OF ATTIC TRAGEDY

Ignotum tragicae genus inuenisse Camenae
Dicitur et plaustris uexisse poemata Thespis.
Hor. *Ars Poet.* 275–6.

Rude dramatic performances representing the sufferings of heroes had long been performed at Sicyon as we have seen, and probably in numerous other places, both in Peloponnesus and in Greece north of the Isthmus. Thus, as already shown (p. 40), in the days before Thespis the poet or coryphaeus stood on a table and held a dialogue with the chorus. But it could not be said that Tragic art had taken full shape, or that there were professional actors. Doubtless there were not a few poets and leaders of tragic dances (for the poet in early times was the leader of his own chorus) who each in their day and generation made some attempt at a more elaborate performance, though naturally for the most part their efforts were abortive. In the early stages of all arts and sciences the story is always the same. There are many pioneers, often regarded by their contemporaries as failures, if not as foolish and even wicked, as was the fate of the alchemists. Greek Philosophy itself has the same history. The Ionic Hylacists took each a single element, Thales water, Heraclitus fire, and Anaximenes air, out of which each supposed everything in Nature was formed. Empedocles, embracing all three and adding to them earth, formulated for the first time the doctrine of the Four Elements. Yet these great minds did not altogether escape contempt, for Aristotle when speaking of their successor, Anaxagoras of Clazomenae, and his doctrine of a Mind which arranged the amorphous elements into a well ordered Kosmos, declares that he appeared as "one sober amongst men full of wine." It is not then surprising that Aristotle[1] in his account of the origin of Tragedy wholly ignores all those who made the first steps in its evolution, not even making mention of Thespis himself or yet of so notable a man as Phrynichus. "Tragedy," says he, "advanced by slow degrees; each new element that showed itself was in turn developed. Having passed through many changes, it found its natural form, and there it stopped. Aeschylus first introduced a second actor; he diminished the importance of the chorus and assigned the leading part to the dialogue. Sophocles raised the number of actors to three and added scene-painting. Moreover, it was not till late that the short plot was discarded for one of greater compass, and the grotesque diction of the earlier Satyric form for the stately manner of Tragedy. The iambic measure then replaced the trochaic tetrameter, which was originally employed when poetry was of the Satyric order and had greater affinities with dancing." To this last point we shall refer later on. The fact is that Aristotle was only interested in Tragedy as a fully developed art, and paid little heed to its early history. It was probably this disregard for its early stages that led him to the doctrine that Tragedy had arisen out of the grotesqueness of the Satyric drama. Yet this seems contrary to his own penetrating statement that "when Tragedy and Comedy came to light, the two classes of poets still followed their natural bent; the lampooners became writers of Comedy, and the Epic poets were succeeded by Tragedians, since the drama was a larger and higher form of art." He likewise states that the *Iliad* and *Odyssey* bear the same relation to Tragedy, that the *Margites* does to Comedy. In this case he certainly does not derive Tragedy from the "grotesque diction" of the Satyric, but from the lofty epic diction in which the glories and sorrows of heroes were sung. A brief examination of the history of Tragedy will show that the latter view is the true one.

Thus we know that before the time of Thespis there were some fifteen writers of Tragedy[2], probably for the most part in Peloponnesus. It is not without significance that the first and

---

[1] *Poetics* iv.   [2] Suidas s.v. *Thespis.*

most distinguished of these, Epigenes, was a native of that
very town of Sicyon, where long before the introduction of the
cult of Dionysus there had been mimetic dances in honour of
king Adrastus.   It is not then a matter for surprise that
ancient writers regarded the Sicyonians as the founders of
Tragedy[1] or that Suidas[2] expressly dates the beginning of the
Tragic art from Epigenes and Thespis.   What advance, if any,
Epigenes may have made we know not, for we have only a few
vague statements respecting him.   From one of these[3] we learn
that he certainly did not confine himself to Dionysiac subjects.

Thespis.   The first beginnings of Tragedy in Attica are
inseparably bound up by tradition with the name of Thespis,
although before his time there were rude dramatic performances
in which "someone mounted a table and held a dialogue with
the members of the Chorus" (p. 40).   This famous man was
born at Icaria[4], a deme or village of Attica, not far from the
border of the Megarid, some time in the early part of the
sixth century B.C.   There can be no doubt that the performances which he gave in Athens were entirely of a new
character.   No better proof of this can be found than the
anger which he excited in Solon, as is told by Plutarch[5]:
"When Thespis and his companions began to make innovations
in tragedy, the novelty of the thing attracted general attention,
though as yet no public competition had been established.   Solon,
who was naturally fond of listening and learning, and who to a
still greater degree in his old age indulged himself with leisure
and amusement, and even with convivial drinking parties and
music, went to see Thespis, who was himself acting, as was the
custom in old times.   When the play was over, Solon asked
him if he were not ashamed to utter and act such lies in the
presence of so great a company.   On Thespis saying that there
was no harm in speaking and acting thus 'for sport,' Solon
smote the ground vehemently with his staff and said, ' If we go

[1] Themistius, *or.* xxvii, p. 406 (Dindorf).

[2] s.v. *Thespis.*   [3] Zenob. v, 4; Suidas s.v. οὐδὲν πρὸς Διόνυσον.

[4] Athen. 40 B : ἀπὸ μέθης καὶ ἡ τῆς κωμῳδίας καὶ ἡ τῆς τραγῳδίας εὕρεσις ἐν
Ἰκαρίᾳ τῆς Ἀττικῆς.

[5] *Solon* 29.

on praising and honouring this kind of sport, we shall soon find it at work in the serious affairs of life.'"

Thespis and his company had as yet no rivals and no competitors, for dramatic contests were not established until many years later. Mimetic dances had indeed been part of the ritual worship of heroes for untold generations, but there had been no contests between rival choruses or actors. Thespis was an old man by the time there was a prize for which to strive. Shortly before the 61st Olympiad (B.C. 536–5) Pisistratus, already twice despot of Athens and twice expelled, returned once more from exile and began his third reign, which was only to be terminated by death in B.C. 527. In B.C. 535 he founded the Great or City Dionysia in honour of the Thracian god and instituted as a most important, if not the most important, feature of the festival, a prize for tragic competition¹. In this the aged Thespis took part, and had the good fortune, not always vouchsafed to pioneers or inventors, to receive the crown of victory. Unhappily, Tradition has not left us the name of the play with which he won this first dramatic contest, but the titles of several of his tragedies have been preserved for us by Suidas²: Ἆθλα Πελίου ἢ Φόρβας, Ἱερεῖς, Ἠίθεοι, Πενθεύς. But scholars have questioned the reliability of this statement on the ground that Aristoxenus³ relates that Heraclides Ponticus composed tragedies and inscribed them with the name of Thespis. To these names we shall presently return. But though it was only in B.C. 535 that he entered for his first contest, his life had been devoted to the calling of both playwright and actor, for we have ample testimony that the early dramatists, as in our own Elizabethan age, acted in their own plays. We are not only told by Aristotle⁴ that "in the early days

---

¹ *Marmor Par.* ep. 43 : ἀφ' οὗ Θέσπις ὁ ποιητὴς [ἐφάνη], πρῶτος ὃς ἐδίδαξε [δρ]ᾶ[μα ἐν ἄ]στ[ει, καὶ ἐ]τέθη ὁ [τ]ράγος [ἆθλον], ἔτη....The date unfortunately is lost, but must have fallen between B.C. 542 and B.C. 520, the preceding and subsequent epochs. Suidas doubtless refers to this same contest in his words (s.v. Θέσπις) ἐδίδαξε δὲ ἐπὶ τῆς πρώτης καὶ ξ' ὀλυμπιάδος.

² s.v. *Thespis*.

³ v, 92 : φησὶ δ' Ἀριστόξενος ὁ μουσικὸς καὶ τραγῳδίας Ἡρακλείδην Ποντικὸν ποιεῖν καὶ Θέσπιδος ἐπιγράφειν.

⁴ *Rhet.* III, 1 : ὑπεκρίνοντο γὰρ αὐτοὶ τὰς τραγῳδίας οἱ ποιηταὶ τὸ πρῶτον.

of tragedy the poets themselves acted in their own dramas," but we know from Plutarch[1] that Thespis himself took the leading part in his own pieces. Tragedy must have become a definite form of art and literature before Pisistratus gave it so honourable a place in his new or expanded Athenian festival of Dionysus.

By universal consent Thespis made the grand step in the evolution of the Tragic art. In what did this consist? According to Diogenes Laertius[2] " in ancient times the chorus alone carried on the action, but Thespis invented a single actor." But this cannot mean, as is commonly held, that Thespis first separated in some degree the coryphaeus from the chorus and made him interrupt the dithyramb with epic recitations, for as we have seen above (p. 40) before his time the poet or coryphaeus used to mount a table and hold a dialogue with the chorus.

There seems no reason to doubt that Thespis in some way defined more exactly the position of the actor, especially by the introduction of a simple form of mask. We are told by Suidas[3] that at first he smeared his face with white lead, next he covered it with purslane in his exhibitions, and finally he introduced the use of masks made of linen only. But it is likely that another and still more important step was made by him, as is asserted in the tradition embodied by Horace[4]. Prof. Mahaffy[5] says that " we must cast aside the nonsense talked by Horace of his (Thespis) being a strolling player, going about in a cart to fairs and markets," and he holds that "an acquaintance with the mysteries and deeper theology of the day suggested to Thespis the representation of human sorrow for a moral purpose," and that " with Thespis may have arisen the great conception, which we see full-blown in Aeschylus—the intention of the drama to purify human sympathy by exercising it on great and apparently disproportioned afflictions of heroic

---

[1] *Solon* 29.   [2] III, 56.

[3] s.v. *Thespis*: καὶ πρῶτον μὲν χρίσας τὸ πρόσωπον ψιμμυθίῳ ἐτραγῴδησεν, εἶτα ἀνδράχνῃ ἐσκέπασεν ἐν τῷ ἐπιδείκνυσθαι, καὶ μετὰ ταῦτα εἰσήνεγκε καὶ τὴν τῶν προσωπείων χρῆσιν ἐν μόνῃ ὀθόνῃ κατασκευάσας ; Horace, *A. P.*, 277, makes him use lees (peruncti faecibus ora).

[4] *Ars Poet.*, 275–6.   [5] *Hist. of Greek Literature*, vol. I, pp. 234–5.

men, when the iron hand of a stern and unforgiving Providence chastises old transgressions, or represses the revolt of private judgement against established ordinance."

Others[1] also reject the Horatian tradition on the grounds that it arose from confusing the first beginnings of Tragedy with those of Comedy. In the latter beyond question "jests from a waggon" played a very important part, but there is no reason why a waggon should not likewise have taken a due share in the first efforts of the tragic actor, though for a purpose very different from that to which it was put by the scurrilous jesters who were the forerunners of Comedy proper. After all Horace is probably right. In early days the tragic choruses and dithyrambs were closely attached to the tombs of heroes and were only performed on festival occasions at these sacred spots. Thespis detached his chorus and dithyramb from some particular shrine, probably at Icaria his native place, and taking his company with him on waggons gave his performances on his extemporised stage when and where he could find an audience, not for religious purposes but for a pastime. Thus not merely by defining more accurately the *rôle* of the actor but also by lifting Tragedy from being a mere piece of religious ritual tied to a particular spot into a great form of literature, he was the true founder of the Tragic art.

This view offers a reasonable explanation of Solon's anger on first seeing Thespis act. A performance which he would have regarded as fit and proper when enacted in some shrine of the gods or at a hero's tomb, not unnaturally roused his indignation when the exhibition was merely "for sport," as Thespis himself said (and doubtless also for profit), and not at some hallowed spot, but in any profane place where an audience might conveniently be collected. It may of course be said that the offence of Thespis in Solon's eyes consisted in the impersonation of heroes or of gods. But it is very likely that long before this time sacred dramas with impersonations of the gods were regularly performed in temple precincts, as for instance the Mystery Plays at Eleusis, as part of the regular ritual of the deity.

[1] W. Christ, *Geschichte der Griechischen Literatur*, p. 175.

It can hardly be maintained that it was simply the introduction of an actor who held a dialogue with the chorus that
angered the great statesman and reformer, for as we have seen
above (p. 40) long before the time of Thespis some sort of
dialogue had been held between the chorus and a person
mounted on a table.

On the other hand, the representation of gods, not in or
near their shrines, and of dead heroes far away from the graves
in which their bones were at rest in the lap of their native land,
must indeed have been not merely a great "novelty," as we are
told it was, but a great shock, to the Greeks of the sixth
century B.C. If this explanation of the grand step made by
Thespis is correct, it can be exactly paralleled in the history of
the mediaeval Drama.

Mysteries and Miracles. The Mysteries and Miracles
were essentially part of a religious ritual performed in honour
of Christ or of some saint, as for instance the play of
St Catharine, which the Norman Geoffrey, afterwards abbot of
St Albans, caused to be represented at Dunstable some time
prior to A.D. 1110, the earliest play of any kind known by name
to have been acted in England. In process of time actors who
had given successful performances of such Mystery and Miracle
plays at some church in honour of some holy personage and for
the edification of the faithful, began to wander about as strolling
players ready to perform their piece wherever they could secure
an audience, be it sacred edifice or inn-yard. In so doing they
were transforming such plays from being merely a piece of
religious ritual attached to some particular shrine into a true
form of dramatic literature.

Nor is it only in these respects that the mediaeval
Christian drama may be compared with that of early Greece.
Not only was the process of development similar, and not only
did each rouse the same prejudices on the part of the more
religious and staid part of the community, but each sprang
from the same deep-rooted principle—the honouring and propitiation of the sacred dead, the hero and the saint—and as a
corollary even of the gods themselves. As the men of Sicyon
thought that they pleased Adrastus by rehearsing and repre-

senting his sorrows, so the Christian Church honoured its Divine Founder by continually keeping his Passion in remembrance, as he himself had ordained at the Last Supper.

The Roman Church still further carries out this same principle of honouring Christ by exhibiting the manger-cradle and holy child at Christmas and his sepulchre at Easter. To this day when every ten years the peasants of Ober-Ammergau perform their Passion Play, they believe that by this solemn representation of the sufferings of Christ, they are doing what is pleasing in his sight.

But if the leader of that company of peasant actors were to take it to some town or city and there perform the sacred drama in a theatre " for pastime " and for lucre, the feelings of their fellow-villagers and, I doubt not, of a far wider community, would not unnaturally be much the same as those roused in Solon's breast by the performance of Thespis.

But before discussing other forms of primitive drama, let us briefly review the successors of Thespis and the immediate forerunners of Aeschylus in the development of the Tragic art.

THE IMMEDIATE PRECURSORS OF AESCHYLUS.

Pratinas. First of these comes Pratinas, a native of Phlius in Argolis. His father's name is variously given as Pyrrhonides or Encomius. According to Suidas[1] he is said to have been the first to compose a Satyric drama, and the lexicographer ascribes to him fifty plays of which thirty-two were Satyric. In B.C. 499 when Aeschylus made his first appearance before the Athenian audience, Pratinas and Choerilus were his competitors, but nothing is known of the plays produced on that occasion. It was the collapse, during the performance of one of his pieces, of the temporary platforms ($i\kappa\rho\iota\alpha$) on which the spectators were standing that led to the erection of the first regular theatre at Athens[2].

His son Aristeas followed in his father's footsteps, and the name of one of his Satyric dramas—*Cyclops*—has come down

---

[1] s.v. *Pratinas*.   [2] **Suidas,** *loc. cit.*

to us. This is of special interest since, as we have seen above, the only extant Satyric drama bears the same title and doubtless was composed on the same theme. But in B.C. 467 when Aeschylus competed with *Laius, Oedipus, Seven against Thebes,* and the Satyric play *Sphinx,* Aristias was second with the *Perseus, Tantalus,* and the Satyric play *Palaestae,* composed by his father Pratinas[1]. Polyphradmon, son of Phrynichus, was third with the tetralogy of the *Lycurgeia.* The *Palaestae* is the only play of Pratinas of which the name has survived.

A fragment of a *hyporchema* probably belonging to one of his Satyric dramas is extant. In a lyrical fragment still preserved Pratinas[2] complains that the flute is now overpowering the voice:

" The Muse made Song the queen. Let the flute keep its place in the chorus.
It is but the servant of Song."

This was probably due to the great changes made by Lasus of Hermione, a contemporary of Pratinas, who, as we have seen above (p. 9), deeply influenced the music of the day, amongst his innovations being a greater use of the flute.

Choerilus. If Pratinas was the first to introduce the Satyric drama into Athens, his contemporary and rival Choerilus seems to have surpassed him in public estimation as a composer of this class of play. So great was his distinction in this branch of dramatic art that it gave rise to the proverb: " When Choerilus was king amongst the Satyrs[3]." Choerilus first began to exhibit in B.C. 523, and according to Suidas[4] he wrote no less than one hundred and sixty plays and was victorious thirteen times. From the same source we learn that he made some improvements in masks, but what these were is uncertain; perhaps they were Satyric. He, like Pratinas, was a competitor of Aeschylus when the latter made his first appearance in B.C. 499.

Phrynichus. Pratinas and Choerilus are chiefly remembered for the part they took in the introduction and development

---

[1] *Arg.* to Aesch. *Sept. c. Theb.*

[2] Athen. 617 B : τὰν ἀοιδὰν κατέστασε Πιερὶς βασίλειαν ὁ δ' αὐλὸς ὕστερον χορευέτω. καὶ γάρ ἐσθ' ὑπηρέτας.

[3] Ἡνίκα μὲν βασιλεὺς ἦν Χοιρίλος ἐν Σατύροισι.   [4] s.v. Χοιρίλος.

of the Satyric drama at Athens. But on the other hand their
contemporary Phrynichus, son of Polyphradmon, is memorable
for his share in the evolution of that true Tragedy which in the
hands of Aeschylus was moulded into the greatest form of
literature. Phrynichus made improvements on various sides of
the tragic art—metre, dances, structure of plot, and *mise en scène*.
Thus he was the first to use trochaic tetrameters in Tragedy,
and indeed he is called the inventor of that metre[1]—traditions
really not in conflict with the vague statement of Aristotle
already cited (p. 57), that the tetrameter was discarded along
with the short plot and that the iambic came into use along
with that of greater compass. He was the first to introduce
female characters and to employ female masks, and he invented
a great number of new dances. In an epigram composed by
himself[2] he boasts that he had devised " more figures in dancing
than there are waves in the sea on a stormy night."

All the early dramatists—Thespis, Pratinas, Choerilus and
Phrynichus—were called " dancers[3]," not only because of the pro-
minent part which the chorus and the dancing filled in their
plays, but also because they gave instruction in choric dancing.
Aeschylus himself is said to have personally trained his choruses
and to have invented many new dances and movements for them.
Partly from Suidas, partly from other sources, we know the
names of some half-score of the plays of Phrynichus : Αἰγύπτιοι,
Ἀκταίων, Ἄλκηστις, Ἀνταῖος ἢ Λίβυες, Δίκαιοι [ἢ Πέρσαι ἢ
Σύνθωκοι], Δαναΐδες, Μιλήτου ἅλωσις, Πλευρώνιαι, Τάνταλος,
Φοίνισσαι.

We know from Plutarch[4] that Themistocles acted as *choregus*
for Phrynichus in B.C. 475 in a contest in which the dramatist
was victorious, but unfortunately we are not certain respecting
the name of the successful drama or dramas. The conjecture
of Bentley that the *Phoenissae* was one of them is now generally

---

[1] Suidas, s.v. Φρύνιχος· εὑρετὴς τοῦ τετραμέτρου ἐγένετο, cf. Arist. *Poet.* 4.

[2] Plut. *Symp.* 732 F: σχήματα δ' ὀρχήσις τόσα μοι πόρεν, ὅσσ' ἐνὶ πόντῳ κύματα
ποιεῖται χείματι νὺξ ὀλοή.

[3] Athen. 22 A.

[4] *Them.* 5. Themistocles commemorated his victory on a *pinax*, Θεμιστοκλῆς
Φρεάρριος ἐχορήγει, Φρύνιχος ἐδίδασκεν, Ἀδείμαντος ἦρχεν.

held to be right. This play has a special importance as there seems little doubt that Aeschylus modelled his *Persae* upon it. But still more famous from its historical associations is the *Sack of Miletus*, which the poet exhibited in B.C. 494. In it he was again the forerunner of Aeschylus in the widening of the scope of Tragedy, but he was unfortunate in this experiment in using current political events for dramatic purposes. The play dealt with the capture of Miletus by the Persians in B.C. 495 (*Ol.* 71). But the horrors of the calamity suffered by their kinsfolk of Ionia were still too fresh in the minds of the Athenians. Herodotus[1] narrates how the whole theatre burst into tears, how his fellow-citizens fined the poet a thousand drachmae for having reminded them of their sorrows, and directed that no one for the future should dramatise this story.

We have few remains of Phrynichus, but from the references to him in the plays of Aristophanes[2], his compositions, especially his lyrics, were noted for their sweetness, and in the last quarter of the fifth century were still great favourites with the older generation.

From one of his fragments quoted by Pausanias[3] we learn "how the brand was given by the Fates to Althea and how Meleager was not to die till the brand was consumed by fire, and how Althea in her rage burned it." "This legend," says Pausanias, "was first dramatised by Phrynichus, son of Poly-phradmon, in his play of *The Pleuronian Women*":

> "For chilly doom
> He did not escape, for a swift flame consumed him
> While the brand was being destroyed by his grim mischief-working
> mother."

"Phrynichus, as we see, has not worked out the story in detail as an author would do with a creation of his own: he has merely touched it as a story already famous all over Greece."

Polyphradmon, son of Phrynichus, followed his father's art and with his *Lycurgeia* was third in the contest in B.C. 467, when Aeschylus won the first prize with his tetralogy, one play of which was the *Seven against Thebes*[4].

---

[1] VI, 21.   [2] *Aves* 750; *Vespae* 219.
[3] X, 31. 4.   [4] *Arg. ad* Aesch. *Sept. c. Theb.*

Let us now sum up the results of our survey of the rise of Tragedy in Greece.

There had been rude laments and dirges for the dead, certainly from Homeric days, and we know not how long before— unfeigned outpourings of the anguished heart for the loved one, later to be supplemented by the wail of the hireling. Such were those led by Achilles over Patrocles[1], and by white-armed Andromache over the body of her brave lord[2], when they had brought him to his famous house and " laid him on a carven bed and set beside him minstrels, leaders of the dirge, who wailed a mournful lay, while the women made moan with them." In the words of Achilles " Lamentation is the due of the dead." But the honouring of the dead did not end with the burning on the pyre or the consignment to the grave. Periodically solemn dances of a mimetic character, athletic contests and feats of arms, in honour of those long departed, had been the custom of the aboriginal population of Greece, long before the coming of either Achean or Dorian. This is amply proved by the celebrations in honour of Adrastus at Sicyon, of Iolaus at Thebes, and by the traces of similar cults of the dead in the Shaft-graves of Mycenae, which date from the Bronze Age.

At what precise date the gross rites of Dionysus were introduced into Athens we cannot say, though it was certainly early (pp. 51–2). On the other hand we can infer with high probability from the statements of Pindar and Herodotus respecting the first performance of the dithyramb at Corinth in the reign of Periander (B.C. 625—585), that it was within that period that the worship of the god was introduced, publicly at least, into Corinth. It may also have been about the same time that the cult of Dionysus Melanaegis of Eleutherae was set up in Hermione, the birthplace of Lasus.

Now as it was in the reign of Cleisthenes(*circa* B.C. 595—560) that the worship of Dionysus was introduced into Sicyon, it is not unlikely that when Cleisthenes was casting about for some way of ridding himself and Sicyon from the danger which he apprehended from the hero Adrastus (p. 27), the newly established cult of Dionysus at Corinth, with its famous dithy-

[1] *Il.* xxiii, 10.   [2] *Il.* xxiv, 720 *sqq.*

ramb and chorus, came under his notice. He accordingly may
have brought in not merely the hero Melanippus, but also the
powerful new god from Thrace to aid him against his ghostly
enemy. Whether this be so or not, the introduction of the
cult of Dionysus into Sicyon cannot be set earlier than B.C. 600,
and may have been some twenty years or more later.

Now as Thespis was an old man in B.C. 535, and as Solon
died in B.C. 558, Thespis must have been engaged in his profession at least before the latter date and probably many years
earlier, unless he had only taken to the dramatic calling rather
late in life. We may not be far wrong if we place his public
performances as early as B.C. 570. But as we are told that there
were at least fifteen writers of Tragedy before him, the first of
whom, according to Suidas, was Epigenes of Sicyon, the latter
must have been living and working at the very time when the
cult of Dionysus had not yet been set up in that city, and when
Adrastus was still the chief object of worship and was still
honoured with "tragic dances which referred to his sorrows."

Now the orthodox writers on the history of Greek Tragedy
infer from the scanty data respecting Epigenes that he had
already overstepped the narrow ring of Dionysiac themes and
had celebrated ancient heroes without any reference to Dionysus.
In other words, those who hold that Tragedy was originally
confined to Dionysus and his vicissitudes, admit that in Sicyon
at the very time when tragic dances in honour of Adrastus were
still or had lately been a chief feature of that town, and when
the cult of Dionysus had either not yet or but recently been
introduced, Epigenes was writing dramas which had no reference
to that god. But as he was writing dramas on subjects not
Dionysiac either before or very shortly after the cult of that
deity had been brought in by Cleisthenes, we must regard him
as not breaking away from a tradition which strictly confined
tragedies to Dionysiac themes, but rather as continuing the
ancient practice of celebrating heroes in such compositions.
Thus the unsubstantial fabric erected on the assumption that
Tragedy in its first stage dealt with nothing else but Dionysiac
subjects falls to the ground.

When we come to the rise of Attic Tragedy the evidence,

as far as it goes, points clearly in the same direction. The names of several of the plays of Thespis have been preserved, but these have been regarded as of doubtful authenticity, because, according to Aristoxenus, Heraclides Ponticus wrote plays to which he prefixed the name of Thespis. But as we are not told that these plays bore the same titles as those ascribed to Thespis by Suidas, it does not by any means follow that the latter are spurious. But even if the titles were the same, it is not unlikely that Heraclides would have chosen as titles for his spurious compositions names declared by tradition to be those of genuine works of the Father of Attic Tragedy.

The titles as they have reached us indicate that the ancients most certainly did not believe that Thespis confined himself to Dionysiac subjects. Neither the *Bachelors*, nor the *Priests*, nor *Phorbas* imply any such connection, though the name *Pentheus* clearly indicates that the play was on the same subject as the *Bacchae* of Euripides, and was therefore in some sense on a Dionysiac theme. Thus the Attic tradition seems to be against any such limitation of plays to Dionysiac subjects even in the infancy of Tragedy. We may therefore not unreasonably conclude that Thespis, like Epigenes, dramatised from the first the sorrows of heroes and heroines. This is confirmed by the fact that his younger contemporary, the lyric poet Simonides of Ceos, wrote a dithyramb called *Memnon*, whilst it is possible that Lasus also sang the sorrows of them of old time.

The foregoing arguments gain further support from the fact that Thespis does not appear to have written Satyric dramas, for, as we have seen above, Pratinas of Phlius first introduced them into Athens, whilst his contemporary Choerilus developed this style. But as it is admitted that the Satyric dramas specially dealt with the adventures of Dionysus, it follows that Dionysiac themes did not form any considerable element in the plays of Thespis.

When we pass to Phrynichus our arguments are again strengthened, for not one of the nine or ten titles of his plays which have come down to us betrays the slightest indication that the plot has any reference to Dionysus. On the contrary, we have good reason for believing in the case of most of them that they dealt purely with heroes, and not with the Thracian deity.

We may therefore conclude with high probability that there was never a period, either at Corinth, Sicyon or Athens, or anywhere else in Greece, when dithyrambs and tragedies were restricted to the celebration of the exploits and sufferings of Dionysus, but that on the contrary from the first inception of anything like formal dithyrambs and tragedies, these were employed like the ruder forms out of which they sprang, to honour the illustrious dead, whose tombs, as in the case of Adrastus and Iolaus, had been centres of worship for untold generations. This is quite in keeping with Aristotle's view that the tragedians were the lineal successors of the Epic poets, for the latter sang of the exploits and deaths of mighty men and the sorrows of heroines.

At Sicyon itself the rhapsodists were reciting the poems of Homer, when the "tragic chorus" celebrated year by year in mimetic fashion the sorrows of Adrastus. In the Greek tragedies, as we have seen, the epic element has long been recognised in the speeches of the messengers (p. 7). Thus Tragedy is really a combination of the lyrical outburst of spontaneous grief for the dead and the heroic lay in which the deeds and trials of hero or heroine were recited in narrative form. In the fully developed Tragedy the lyrics sung by the chorus represent the immemorial laments for the dead, whilst the messengers' recitals and the dialogues of the *dramatis personae* correspond to the narrations and speeches of the Epic.

The Origin of the terms Tragoedia and Tragic.

Whilst in the preceding pages we have reviewed the origin and development of Tragedy in Peloponnesus and Attica we have restricted ourselves to the *thing* and have not attempted to discover the true origin of the *name* or to build any argument upon it. As facts are always more important than mere terms, such an order of treatment seemed distinctly the most scientific. Now that we have completed our survey of the more material evidence, we are in a better position to attack the problems presented by the nomenclature of this branch of the Dramatic art and Literature.

Τραγῳδία. Let us first examine the word τραγῳδία. It is admitted by all that it is derived from τραγῳδός, and that the latter is derived from τράγος, *he-goat*, and ἀοιδός, *singer*. This may mean (1) one who sings about a *goat*, and (2) one who sings as a *goat*, according as the first part of the compound is objective or subjective. Thus τραγῳδία can mean either (1) a song about a *goat*, or (2) a song sung by a *goat*.

Τραγικός. In discussing the term τραγῳδία we must also take account of the term τραγικὸς χορός, applied by Herodotus to the choruses which at Sicyon performed some dramatic representation of the sorrows of Adrastus. The term τραγικός can mean either (1) something done in reference to a *goat*, or (2) something done by a *goat* or *goats*[1]. Thus τραγικὸς χορός may mean either (1) a chorus which celebrates a *goat* or *goats*, or (2) a chorus composed of *goats*. Thus both the possible meanings of the simple adjective correspond to those of the compound τραγῳδία.

Let us next consider the various views respecting the origin of the word τραγῳδία and consequently of τραγικός.

I. It has been held by writers, both in ancient and modern times, that the name arose from the circumstance that a goat was the prize in the early Tragic contests. This, as we have seen (p. 6), is said to have been the case in the first Tragic competition, that established by Pisistratus at Athens in B.C. 535. Such a view implies that the term only arose after B.C. 535, and consequently the same must be held respecting the adjective *tragic*. Herodotus however speaks of tragic choruses at Sicyon long before this period. To this it is replied that Herodotus is only applying the language of his own day to certain choruses of an earlier period, when as yet the terms *tragic* and *tragedy* were still unknown. But to this question we shall return. It will suffice for the present to point out that, even if this allegation were true, it does not alter in the least the history of the rise of Tragedy. For though the name

---

[1] Cf. ἱππικὸς ἀγών, a contest in which horses took part, and ἱππικὴ φάτνη, a manger for horses.

tragic may not have been employed, yet solemn dances of a mimetic character, such as those termed *tragic* in the time of Herodotus, were already in use at Sicyon to honour the hero Adrastus. But there are two strong objections to this explanation of the origin of the term. (*a*) Although Tragedy had been virtually developed long before the time of Pisistratus, not only in Athens but in Peloponnesus, it is assumed that, it had no name until after the foundation of the public competitions. But for this there is not the slightest evidence. (*b*) The analogy of the terms κιθαρῳδός, κωμῳδός, κωμῳδία point rather to a subjective meaning, though it has to be confessed that τρυγῳδός, the oldest term for a comic actor, may be explained in either way.

II. The next explanation is that of Bentley, who held that *tragoedia* meant the song of the *goats* or *goatmen*, that is, the satyrs, whom he and many others assumed to have been always in caprine shape. However it is now established that in Thracian representations they were never regarded as goats, for they have always the ears, tails, and even the feet of horses (Figs. 2—5). The reason for this is not far to seek. When Man desires to attribute inordinate sensuality to his fellow-men, he assigns to them the moral qualities of the horse, the bull, or the goat. But Aristotle knew that this was a libel on these animals and did not hesitate to say so. "Next after man," he wrote[1], "the horse is the most lustful of all animals." In later times Satyrs were certainly pourtrayed in caprine form, as for instance on the Pandora vase[2]. This exhibits a group of masked Satyrlike beings pourtrayed as half-men, half-goats, dancing round a flute-player; they have goat's horns on their heads and goat's hoofs instead of equine or human feet, their tails also being those of goats. But there is no evidence that this scene depicts a Satyric chorus. On a Naples vase[3] dated some fifty years later, Satyrlike beings are seen, but without goat's hoofs or horns, and with horse-like tails, the only part resembling a goat being a shaggy skin round the loins. This type with horsetails and goatskin loin cloths is likewise found

---

[1] *Hist. An.* VI, 2. 22.   [2] *Jour. Hell. Stud.* vol. XI, pl. XI.
[3] Haigh, *The Attic Theatre*, p. 328, fig. 29.

in the later representations[1] of Satyric choruses. If the Greeks conceived the Satyrs as goat-men and goat-footed, it is very strange that throughout the whole of Greek literature the epithet "goat-footed" is never found applied to them, an omission all the more significant since by the Roman writers they are regularly termed *capripedes*[2]. The Satyrs therefore cannot be themselves regarded as the origin of the term, more especially as their name gives its title to the Satyric drama, which, as we have seen, stood clearly apart from Tragedy. It seems unlikely that both the terms *tragoedia* and *Satyric Drama* would have been adopted from the Satyrs, more especially as it is clear that the very essence of Tragedy—the rude dithyramb and the mimetic dance—was already in use long before the introduction of the cult of Dionysus and his Satyrs.

III.   In May 1909, Dr L. R. Farnell read a paper before the Hellenic Society entitled "The Megala Dionysia and the Origin of Tragedy[3]." In this he put forward a modification of Bentley's view, on which he based a criticism directed against the main theory of the present work. His paper has as yet only appeared in a summary, which I quote in full:

"The origin of tragedy partly turned on the question about the date of the introduction of the cult of Dionysos 'Ελευ-θερεύς from Eleutherai. Vollgraff's view was that this was only introduced shortly before the peace of Nikias; if so the legend and cult of Eleutherai would not necessarily throw light on the origin of tragedy. But there were strong reasons against Vollgraff's view, and for supposing that the cult and cult-legends of Eleutherai reached Athens as early as the middle of the sixth century B.C. and that a new 'cathartic' festival in spring was instituted to provide for the god of this new cult. Scholars had long felt the difficulty in the Aristotelian dogma that 'Tragedy' arose somehow from the Dithyramb and was primarily 'Satyric': a new theory had been put forward that Tragedy arose not from Dionysiac ritual but from a mimetic service performed at the graves of heroes.

---

[1] Baumeister, *Denkmäler*, fig. 424.

[2] Lucr. IV, 582; Hor. *C.* II, 19. 4.

[3] *Jour. Hell. Stud.* vol. XXIX (1909), p. xlvii.

But whatever advantages attached to this theory, it did not account, any more than the older theory accounted for, the name τραγῳδία. No explanation of this word of any probability had ever been put forth other than the obvious one, that it meant 'goat-song'; that is, according to the most likely analogies, the song of men dressed in goat-skins. The mistake hitherto made was to suppose that men so dressed were satyrs. The original performers in the τραγῳδία were worshippers of Dionysos Μελάναιγις, a god of the black goat-skin; and their mimetic dance was solemn, sad, always tragic, probably originally a winter rite. The true meaning of the primitive service was indicated partly by the legend concerning Dionysos Μελάναιγις, and the duel between Melanthos and Xanthos, in which Blackman killed Fair-man, partly by the story of the Minyan ψολόεις of Orchomenos, who had to do with a ritual in which the young god was killed, partly by the discovery by Mr R. M. Dawkins of a Dionysiac Mummers' play in modern Thrace, in which goat-men appeared and a goat-man was slain and lamented. They must look for the origin of Attic tragedy in an ancient European Mummery, which was a winter-drama of the seasons, in which the Black personage Dionysos Μελάναιγις or Μέλανθος, or οἱ ψολόεις killed Xanthos the Fair One. The actors wore the black goat-skin of their god. Such a peasant mummery-play spreading through the North-Greek villages would often attract the local dramatic legend of some priest like Ikaros, who was slain in the service of the god: this would bring in the 'heroic' element, the death of the Dionysiac 'hero': the heroic element triumphed, all heroes were admitted, and the black goat-skin was discarded. Finally the religious intention of the festival explained the Aristotelian theory of 'Katharsis.'"

Let us now examine the various points in this statement *seriatim*.

(1) The first to be noticed is that Dr Farnell admits that the Dionysiac Mummers' play, spreading to the North-Greek villages, found there local dramatic legends, and that "this would bring in the heroic element." In other words, after denying that Tragedy arose in the worship of heroes, he admits

for it the dual origin, which I have put forward—a native Greek
and a Thracian—since he holds that a "local dramatic legend"
was often already in full operation, such as was the case at
Sicyon, where there had already been mimetic choruses long
before the worship of Dionysus Melanaegis (according to
Dr Farnell) had been introduced into Athens and long before
any cult of Dionysus had been brought into Sicyon.

(2)   Dr Farnell speaks as if Dionysus had come into Greece
as *Melanaegis*, and was universally worshipped there under that
title.   But what are the facts ?   It was only at Eleutherae,
Athens, and Hermione in Argolis that he was worshipped under
this cult-name.   There is not a tittle of evidence to show that
Dionysus was celebrated at Corinth under that name in the
famous dithyramb of Arion, or that the god was brought into
Sicyon in that form : indeed the two ancient statements respecting the origin of the name *Melanaegis* distinctly indicate
that it was a very special phase of the god and by no means
the ordinary form under which he was venerated.

The account given by Suidas[1] is as follows: "They set up
the worship of Dionysus Melanaegis for the following reason:
the daughters of Eleuther beheld an apparition of Dionysus
clad in a black goatskin, and found fault with it.   Thereat the
god was enraged and drove them mad.   After that Eleuther
was instructed by an oracle to cure their madness by honouring
Dionysus of the Black Goatskin."   The other account is given
by the Scholiast on Aristophanes[2].   "War broke out between
the Athenians and the Boeotians for the possession of Celaenae,
a place on their borders.   Xanthus, the Boeotian, challenged
the Athenian king Thymoetes.   When the latter declined the
challenge, Melanthus a Messenian (of the race of Periclymenus,
the son of Neleus), then living at Athens, took up the challenge
with an eye to obtaining the kingdom.   When they met in
single combat Melanthus saw someone behind Xanthus clad
in the skin of a he-goat ($\tau\rho\alpha\gamma\hat{\eta}$), that is, a black goatskin
($\alpha\mathrm{i}\gamma\acute{\iota}\varsigma$), and he cried out that it was not fair for him to bring
a second.   The other looked behind, and Melanthus at once
struck him and slew him.   In consequence of this the festival

---

[1] s.v. μέλαν.   [2] *Ach.* 146.

of the Apaturia and of Dionysus Melanaegis was established."
It is quite plain from these two passages that the form under
which Dionysus was supposed to have appeared at Eleutherae,
whether it was to the daughters of Eleuther, the eponymous
hero of that village, or to Melanthus, the Messenian, was in a
guise hitherto unknown to Greece. Otherwise there would
have been no reason for setting up a brand new cult of him
under this particular title. Exact parallels occur in modern
times. At some particular place, be it Lourdes or Knock or
Loretto, someone sees a vision of the Madonna, and in consequence of this a new cult of a particular phase of the Virgin is
set up. But it does not follow that this particular phase
becomes universal. Just as the cult of a special aspect of
Dionysus was brought into Athens and Hermione, so too that
of Our Lady of Loretto is set up in various places.

Again though Dr Farnell assumes that the cult of Dionysus
Melanaegis only got into Athens about the middle of the sixth
century B.C., shortly before the Great Dionysia with their tragic
contests were established by Pisistratus in B.C. 535, yet the
ancients thought that it had been introduced *circa* B.C. 1100 in
the regal period, and associated it with the very ancient festival
of the Apaturia. But the latter was already of great importance
when the Ionians[1] settled in Asia after the Doric invasion
(B.C. 1104). Now if Attic Tragedy and the name *Tragoedia*
arose at Athens from the worship of Dionysus Melanaegis,
we ought to find Tragedies, which are supposed by Dr Farnell
to be an essential element of that cult, forming an integral part
of the Apaturia. Yet it was only at the Lenaea and the
Great Dionysia that such plays were acted, whilst no dramatic
performance of any kind was included in the ceremonies of
the Apaturia. Nor is there any evidence that the acting
of tragedies formed a part of the ritual at Eleutherae or
Hermione, although we know that in the latter place his
festival was annually celebrated with musical contests and a
regatta and swimming races[2]. Nor was Dionysus the only or
the chief deity venerated at the Apaturia, that great festival of
the *Phratriae*. On the first day, called *Dorpeia*, every citizen

[1] Herod. i, 47.   [2] Paus. ii, 35. 1.

went in the evening to the *phratrium,* or to the house of some wealthy member of his own *phratria,* and there feasted. The second day was termed *Anarrhusis,* from the sacrifice offered on that day to Zeus *Phratrius,* and to Athena and *sometimes* to Dionysus Melanaegis. But according to Harpocration the Athenians on that occasion dressed in their finest apparel, kindled torches on the altar of Hephaestus, and sacrificed to, and sang in honour of, that deity. On the third day, called *Koureotis,* the children born that year in the families of the *phratria,* or such as had not yet been entered on the roll of the *phratria,* were presented by their fathers or guardians to the *phratores.* For each child a *probaton*[1] was sacrificed. It is therefore quite clear that Dionysus Melanaegis formed but a mere adjunct of a very ancient festival, that his worship had been brought from Eleutherae to Athens long before the sixth century B.C., that there was at no period any dramatic performance, tragic or otherwise, at the festival of the Apaturia, that the sacrifices offered on the third day were not confined to a he-goat, as it is termed a *probaton,* a word which in Attic Greek is almost always confined to a sheep and is not used of goats.

To Dr Farnell's fanciful explanation of the names Xanthus and Melanthus, and to his comparison with the *Psoloeis,* we shall return later.

(3) Dr Farnell, in confining his thesis to the origin of *Attic* Tragedy, shuts his eyes to the historical facts which preclude us from treating the origin of Attic Tragedy and the name *tragoedia* apart from the rise of that art in other parts of Greece, and he ignores the statements of the ancient authorities that Thespis was already acting dramas, known to them as tragedies, long before the death of Solon in B.C. 558 and the institution of the Great Dionysia in B.C. 535. Thespis was not the first composer of such tragedies, for already Epigenes of Sicyon had written tragedies, and there is reason for believing that some of these at least had no reference to Dionysus (p. 68). Furthermore, there are said to have been many other dramatic writers in the interval between Epigenes and Thespis.

(4) Dr Farnell told us that we "must look for the origin

[1] Schol. Ar. *Ran.* 810.

of Attic tragedy in an ancient European Mummery, which was
a winter-drama of the seasons, in which the Black personage
Dionysos Μελάναιγις or Μέλανθος, or οἱ ψολόεις killed
Xanthos the Fair One. The actors wore the black goat-skin of
their god." Dr Farnell does not in his summary expressly term
Dionysus a goat-god, though it is distinctly implied in his words
just cited. He bases his view principally on the modern play
seen in Thrace by Mr Dawkins "in which goat-men appeared
and a goat-man was slain and lamented." Thus there can be
little doubt that he means that Dionysus was a goat-god.
What is the proof of this? If he were really worshipped under
an animal form when he was brought into Greece, evidence of
this ought easily to be found in the shapes which he takes in
literature and art, and in the victims sacrificed to him. A brief
investigation will demonstrate that there is little evidence for
his connection with the goat, but an overwhelming mass of
proof for his intimate relation with the bull[1].

The Bull. Dionysus is specially conceived of as in taurine
form. Thus he is called "Cow-born," "Bull-shaped," "Bull-faced,"
"Bull-browed," " Bull-horned," " Horn-bearing," " Two-horned,"
and " Horned." The last three epithets of course might apply
equally well to him, if there were other evidence for his representation in goat-form. Again, he was believed to manifest himself
at least occasionally as a bull; his images, as at Cyzicus, were
often made in the form of a bull, or with bull's horns, and he was
similarly represented with horns in paintings. In one statuette
he is shown clad in a bull's hide, the head, horns and hoofs
hanging down behind. The women of Elis, as we are told
by Plutarch[2], hailed him with this invocation: " Come hither,
Dionysus, to thy holy temple by the sea; come with the Graces
to thy temple, rushing with thy bull's foot, O goodly bull, O
goodly bull!" According to the myth he was in the shape of a
bull when he was torn to pieces by the Titans, and when the
Cretans acted his sufferings and death, they rent a live bull in
pieces with their teeth. "Indeed," writes Prof. Frazer, "the

---

[1] Prof. J. G. Frazer, *Golden Bough*, vol. II, p. 164 (2nd ed.) has collected all
the evidence for the bull, goat and fawn.

[2] *Quaest. Graec.* 36; *Isis and Osiris*, 35.

rending and devouring of live bulls and calves appears to have been a regular feature of the Dionysiac rites." This last practice needs no better illustration than the famous passage in the *Bacchae* of Euripides[1]. Again he is represented as a child with clusters of grapes round his brow, and with a calf's head with sprouting horns attached to the back of his head. On a red-figured vase the god is pourtrayed as a calf-headed child seated in a woman's lap.

When treating of the Dithyramb (p. 6) we have had occasion to notice the practice of the Cynaethians who, at their feast in honour of the god, went forth and seized from a herd the bull which the god himself directed them to take and to bear away to sacrifice. What is still more important for our present inquiry is that on the first day of the Great Dionysia at Athens, the Ephebi provided as the victim for the god, not a goat but a bull. Yet Dr Farnell holds that the Great Dionysia and its tragic contests were especially associated with the cult of Dionysus Melanaegis, the goat-god.

We have already seen that to the first fully matured Dionysiac dithyramb, that of Arion at Corinth, the name *ox-driving* was given by Pindar, which may well mean, as explained by the scholiast, that the victim was a bull, as was the case with the Cynaethians and the Athenians.

Thus then in classical times, Dionysus was regularly worshipped as tauriform, and as appearing in this guise to his votaries, whilst the victims torn to pieces or offered with less frantic rites, as at Athens, were normally bulls or calves and not goats.

The Goat. Now let us turn to the evidence for the connection of the goat with Dionysus. That god is never termed *tragos*, though, according to a legend preserved by Apollodorus[2], he is said to have been changed into a kid (*eriphos*) to save him from the wrath of Hera; again, according to Ovid[3], when the gods were led to Egypt to escape Typhon, Dionysus was turned into a goat; finally Arnobius[4] says that the worshippers of the god tore goats asunder.

---

[1] 735 *sqq.*
[2] III, 4. 3.
[3] *Met.* v, 329.
[4] *Adv. nationes*, v, 19.

But it must be pointed out that these allusions to his having a goat form are all from late writers. At Eleutherae and at Hermione he was worshipped as Melanaegis, "the Wearer of the black goat-skin," but with this point we shall deal fully later on. In the market-place at Phlius, the birthplace of Pratinas the satyric playwright, stood a bronze statue of a she-goat gilded almost all over. "The image," says Dr Frazer, "probably represented the vine-god himself." But apart from the difficulty occasioned by the sex of the statue, the explanation given by Pausanias[1] is probably the more correct: "It was honoured by the Phliasians for the following reason. The constellation named the Goat always blights the vines at its rising and to avert its baleful influence they worship the bronze goat in the market-place and adorn it with gold." This is plainly a simple case of sympathetic magic. This view is corroborated by the occurrence in Greece of similar dedications of goats to gods other than Dionysus. Thus "the people of Cleonae[2], like the Athenians, had suffered from the pestilence, and in obedience to an oracle from Delphi sacrificed a he-goat to the rising sun. So finding that the plague was stayed, they sent a bronze he-goat to Apollo." Pausanias[3] also relates how the people of Elyrus in Crete sent a bronze goat to Delphi: "The goat is suckling the infants Phylacides and Philander, who according to the Elyrians were the children of Apollo by a nymph Acacallis, whom Apollo visited in the city of Tarrha." Other divinities are likewise closely associated with the he-goat. Thus Aphrodite Pandemus at Olympia was represented in a statue seated upon a bronze he-goat[4] and the same goddess was worshipped as *Epitragia* ("Seated on a He-goat") in one shrine at Athens.

There is one clear case of the sacrifice of a he-goat to Dionysus, but on investigation this turns out not to have been the original form of offering, but a substitution for a human victim. At Potniae in Boeotia there was a temple of Dionysus *Tragobolos* ("Goat-shooter"). "Once when sacrificing to the god, flushed with wine, they grew so outrageous that they killed the priest of Dionysus. Pestilence fell upon them and from

[1] ɪɪ, 13. 6.   [2] Paus. x, 11. 5.
[3] x, 16. 5.   [4] Paus. ᴠɪ, 25. 1.

Delphi word came to sacrifice a youth to Dionysus. But they say that not many years afterwards the god substituted a goat as a victim instead of the boy[1]."

Thus then the he-goat at Potniae was not his original victim. But it is easy to show that he had no monopoly of goat sacrifices. Such victims were certainly offered to other deities and heroes, not as substitutes for human victims, but as the offerings of a primitive time. The Lacedaemonians, according to Pausanias[2], surnamed Hera "Goat-eating" (*Aigophagos*) and sacrificed goats to the goddess. "They say that Heracles founded the sanctuary and was the first to sacrifice goats. The reason why he sacrificed goats was because he had no other victims to offer."

The worship of the hero-god Aesculapius, had been introduced from his great sanctuary at Epidaurus into the Cyrenaica and set up at Balagrae. There he was worshipped under the title of Physician. From this Cyrenian sanctuary was founded the one at Lebene in Crete. "The Cyrenians[3] differ from the Epidaurians in this, that whereas the Cyrenians sacrifice goats, it is against the Epidaurian custom to do so." Conversely, at Tithorea in Phocis, there was a shrine of Aesculapius[4] where they sacrificed to him all animals except goats. There was also a legend that Aesculapius, like the Cretan Zeus, had been suckled by a goat in the land of Epidauria[5].

The legend that Heracles offered goats to Hera, because he had nothing better, explains why we do not more frequently hear of such victims being offered to heroes or gods. Although goats were almost certainly constantly sacrificed, yet we naturally do not hear of them in connection with the more important festivals of gods and heroes, for more costly victims were offered on those occasions.

The goat victim offered to Dionysus at Potniae was a substitute for a youth, just as the she-goat sacrificed in later times to Artemis at Munychia in Attica was instead of a bear, which in its turn had almost certainly replaced a maiden, for the priest when sacrificing the she-goat uttered the significant

---

[1] Paus. IX. 8. 1.   [2] III. 15. 9.   [3] *ib.* II. 26. 9.
[4] *ib.* X. 32. 12.   [5] *ib.* II. 26. 4.

formula " This is my daughter." Therefore it cannot in face of these facts be maintained that when the cult of Dionysus came into Greece from Thrace the proper victim for the god was a goat. We have already seen that bulls and calves were the normal offerings, but there are a series of grim facts which point distinctly to human victims as in the case at Potniae.

Though one phase of Dionysus had been introduced into Athens under the particular local title borne by him at Eleutherae, and had been attached in its new home to the festival of the Apaturia, the normal offering to the god was not a goat either at that festival or at the Great Dionysia. What was the true nature of the offerings made to the god in his primal and more universal cult ? It is in times of stress and anxiety that the true primitive character of a ritual comes boldly to the light. In B.C. 476 Themistocles, the greatest of Athenian statesmen, furnished the expenses of the chorus which performed the tragedy of Phrynichus at the great festival of Dionysus. Four years earlier on that awful night before Salamis, when men and women prayed as they had never prayed before to the gods for deliverance from slavery and death, Themistocles sacrificed to Dionysus not three he-goats, or three bulls, but three Persian youths. In doing this he was certainly reverting to what tradition taught was by far the most acceptable offering to that god. This beyond question was the practice in Thrace itself, the true home of the god. For the rending in pieces not merely of animals, but of human beings, in the worship of Dionysus in that region is manifest in the legend of the death of Orpheus. The frantic Thracian women as they were celebrating the Bacchic orgies rent him limb from limb and his head was borne

"Down the swift Hebrus to the Lesbian shore."

The title " Cannibal " ('Ωμηστής) under which Themistocles propitiated him on the eve of Salamis and the like one ('Ωμάδιος) which he bore in Chios and in Tenedos, where human victims were his regular tribute, indicate clearly that the wearing of a goat-skin of a particular colour was merely an accident and did not appertain to the essence of the god.

Goat-skin Dresses. But the view just stated is strongly emphasised by the fact that Dionysus had no monopoly of the epithet *Melanaegis*, any more than he had of goat-skins in general. For example the Erinys is described as Melanaegis by Aeschylus[1]. Yet no one will contend that because the Erinyes play so prominent a part in the *Eumenides*, that play is a " winter-drama of the seasons."

But Dionysus has just as little monopoly of goat-skin dresses in general as he has of those of a black colour. For example Zeus himself is regularly termed " Wearer of the goat-skin " (αἰγίοχος) in Homer and is constantly represented with that attribute in works of art. Again, Athena wears as one of her special characteristics her goat-skin (*aegis*). Indeed, if the argument on which Dr Farnell has based his theory that Dionysus was a Thracian or European goat-god were sound, we should have little difficulty from the facts just presented in turning the Olympian gods into a herd of goats; for the evidence in favour of Zeus, Apollo, Hera, Athena, Aphrodite and Aesculapius being goats, is in some cases far stronger than, in others just as strong as, that which can be urged for Dionysus.

To the origin of such goat-skin garments we shall soon return. In addition to the epithet Melanaegis Dr Farnell finds his chief support for Dionysus the goat-god in the story of the combat between Xanthus the Boeotian and Melanthus the Messenian, identifying the god with Melanthus (Black man) and with the Minyan ψολόεις of Orchomenus. We have shown the invalidity of his argument that Melanaegis was the primitive form under which Dionysus came into Greece. The evidence from the story of Melanthus and Xanthus is just as insubstantial as the phantom seen by the former. It is easy to turn any story or name, ancient or modern, into a nature myth. Thus Prof. Max Müller himself was once well explained on this principle[2]. On the other hand there is every reason to believe in the substantial accuracy of the non-miraculous part of

[1] *Theb.* 699.

[2] *Kottabos*, vol. I, pp. 145–54, The Oxford Solar Myth. A contribution to Comparative Mythology. (Dedicated, without permission, to the Rev. G. W. Cox, M.A.) (By the late Dr R. F. Littledale.)

the story of Xanthus and Melanthus. There were constant border wars between Boeotia and Athens in historical times, and it is more than probable that their relations were much the same in the earlier period, whilst the citing of the pedigree of Melanthus points to his being a real historical personage. Of course it is the contrast in colour indicated in the names of the combatants that has led Dr Farnell to take up his position. Yet there is no need to resort to mythologising, since history offers a simple explanation of these names. The ruling element in Boeotia, from at least B.C. 1000, was a people who had passed down from the Upper Balkan, and in classical times the Thebans were distinguished by their fair hair and great stature, their women for these two qualities being regarded as the handsomest in Greece. The Boeotians thus stood in contrast to the dark complexioned aboriginal race of Greece to which the Neleidae of Pylus, the family of Melanthus, belonged.

The names Xanthus and Xanthias ("Fair Hair") were as well known in Greece as Pyrrhus ("Red-head"), whilst no less familiar were such names as Melanthus, or Melanthius (the unfaithful goat-herd of Odysseus). We may therefore safely reject the nature-myth explanation of the combat and regard it as embodying an actual border war. The miraculous appearance of the "Wearer of the black goat-skin" does not in the least invalidate the substantial truth of the story. If such supernatural adjuncts are sufficient grounds for rejecting the truth of historical events, then the battle of Antioch did not take place in A.D. 1098 and Aubrey de Vere, the great "earl of Genney," never lived, because "the night coming on in the chase of this battayle, and waxing dark, the Christians being four miles from Antioch, God willing the safety of the Christians, showed a white star or mullet of five points, on the Christian host, which to every man's sight did alight and arrest upon the standard of Aubrey de Vere, there shining excessively[1]." Eight centuries have mouldered into shadow since de Vere and his night-foundered comrades believed that they saw this divine light. But who will venture to mythologise this story and see in the contrast between the bright glistering star and the murky night a

[1] Leland, *Itin.*, vol. VI, pp. 37–8 (ed. II, 1744).

struggle between the powers of light and darkness ? The five-point star became the badge of the great house of de Vere, of which in 1625 in reference to its famous earldom, the Chief Justice of England said, " No king in Christendom hath such a subject as Oxford." And well might he say so, for the " fighting Veres " had taken a foremost part in the making of England for more than 500 years.

Finally, Dr Farnell identifies Dionysus Melanaegis with the ψολόεις of Orchomenus in Boeotia. Speaking of the persons named Psoloeis and Aeoleiae in Boeotia, Plutarch[1] writes : "The story is that Leucippe, Arsinoe, and Alcathoe, the daughters of Minyas, went mad and longed for human flesh ; they cast lots to decide whose child should be taken, and the lot decided that Leucippe must give up her son Hippasus to be torn in pieces. The husbands of these women got the name Psoloeis because they wore filthy garments in consequence of their grief and mourning. Their wives were termed Aeoleiae, that is 'Baleful,' and to this day the Orchomenians apply the name to the women of that family. Each year at the festival of the Agrionia these women have to flee away and they are pursued by the priest of Dionysus, armed with a sword. It is lawful for him to slay the woman he catches, and in our own day Zoilus the priest slew one. But this brought about no good, for the priest sickened from some trifling sore and found a lingering death from gangrene, whilst the Orchomenians themselves, in consequence of public disasters, took away the priesthood from his family and now elect the best man in the whole community."

Let us recall for a moment Dr Farnell's own words : " The true meaning of the primitive service was indicated partly by the legend concerning Dionysos Μελάναιγις, and the duel between Melanthos and Xanthos, in which Black-man killed Fair-man, partly by the story of the Minyan ψολόεις of Orcho-menos, who had to do with a ritual in which the young god was killed, partly by the discovery by Mr R. M. Dawkins of a Dionysiac Mummers' play in modern Thrace, in which goat-

---

[1] Quaest. Graec. 299 E, F. The MSS. read τοὺς μὲν ἄνδρας αὐτῶν δυσειματούν-των...ψολόεις, τὰς Αἰολείας Οἰωνολόας. I have followed Reiske's reading δυσειμα-τοῦντας...αὐτὰς δὲ Αἰολείας οἷον Ὀλοάς.

men appeared and a goat-man was slain and lamented." But it
will be noticed that the name Psoloeis ("Sooty") was not given
either to the child Hippasus, who was slain by his mother
Leucippe and her sisters, nor yet to the women of that family.
Plutarch only states that the name Aeoleiae was still applied to
the women of the house of Minyas, but makes no such assertion
about the application of the term Psoloeis to the males of that
race.

Now Dr Farnell's argument based on Melanaegis and
Melanthus depends upon the assumption that in each case we have
a personage "Black-man" killing "Fair-man." But the Psoloeis,
the "Sooty" ones, did not kill either the boy Hippasus, nor did
they kill the Aeoleiae in historical times, nor were they themselves killed. Accordingly they cannot be compared with either
Melanaegis or Melanthus or the goat-men who kill a goat-man
in the Thracian Mummery. Nor is there the slightest trace of
any connection between the Psoloeis and the goat. Furthermore Dr Farnell ignores the sex of the victims at the Agrionia
in later times. The women of the house of Minyas cannot
be paralleled offhand with a boy representing the young god.

The story undoubtedly points to human sacrifices as part of
the rites of Dionysus at Orchomenus, the boy corresponding
probably to the youth once sacrificed to Dionysus Tragobolus at
Potniae, another Boeotian town. But the Aeoleiae represent a
different type of sacrifice, possibly the provision of a wife for the
god.

(5) Dr Farnell holds that "the actors wore the black goat-
skin of their god," and that "their mimetic dance was solemn,
sad, always tragic, probably originally a winter rite." But there
is no more evidence for his description of the early Dionysiac
dance than there is for his European goat-god. Half a century
before the date at which Dr Farnell supposes that the worship
of Dionysus Melanaegis had been introduced into Athens, Arion,
who had given its full shape to the dithyramb performed by
his chorus at Corinth in honour of Dionysus, had introduced in his
songs "Satyrs speaking in metre" (p. 5). But we have not the
slightest reason for supposing that their utterances and dances
were uniformly sad and grave any more than are those of the

actors in the modern Thracian Mummery. Though the latter
contains the slaying of a man, it is far from being all grave,
as it has a very large element of indecent buffoonery. But the
ancients themselves did not consider the Satyric drama at all
grave or sad, but gave it the name of "Sportive Tragedy" (p. 52),
because it was regarded by them as partly tragic, partly ludicrous,
like the modern mummeries in Thrace and Northern Greece.

Dr Farnell holds that the Satyrs were "goat-men" and that
they wore the goat-skin in honour of their god. That the
Satyrs wore goat-skins there can be no doubt, for we have the
evidence of Euripides in the *Cyclops*[1] itself, his own Satyric
drama. This passage will show whether Dr Farnell is right in
his assumption that the goat-skins are the sacred vestments
worn in a solemn sad ritual of a "god of the black goat-skin."
The chorus of Satyrs sings: "O dear one, O dear Bacchic god,
whither roaming alone art thou tossing thy fair locks? But I,
thy servant, am the serf of the one-eyed Cyclops wandering as a
slave with this miserable garment of a he-goat's skin, bereft of
thy loving care." But far from these lines indicating that the
goat-skin was a peculiarly sacred vestment and an important
part of the ritual, they clearly prove that it was simply regarded
as the meanest form of apparel that could be worn by a slave.
In fact it is nothing more than the goat-skin or sheep-skin
cloak (*baite, sisura*), worn by country people and shepherds in
Greece, not only in classical times but down to the present day.
This gives us the true explanation of a line from a Satyric play
of Aeschylus[2], in which one of the chorus is addressed as a
he-goat. The speaker simply makes a jesting allusion to the
skin of that animal which the other wears as his dress, like the
Satyrs in the *Cyclops*. This too gives both a true and simple
explanation of the goat-skins seen on the loins of Satyrs in

[1] 74—81:   ὦ φίλος, ὦ φίλε Βακχεῖε, ποῖ οἰοπολῶν
                 ξανθὰν χαίταν σείεις;
                 ἐγὼ δ' ὁ σὸς πρόπολος
                 θητεύω Κύκλωπι
                 τῷ μονοδέρκτᾳ, δοῦλος ἀλαίνων
                 σὺν τᾷδε τράγου χλαίνᾳ μελέᾳ
                 σᾶς χωρὶς φιλίας.

[2] Fr. 207 (Nauck): τράγος γένειον ἆρα πενθήσεις σύ γε.

later representations who are furnished not with goats', but with horses' tails (p. 72).

Thus the wearing of the goat-skin by the chorus of Satyrs in what is admittedly the Dionysiac element in dramatic performances was in no wise a piece of ritual and still less was it worn by his votaries in special honour of a goat-god, of whose existence there is no proof.

Dr Farnell's hypothesis depends entirely on the wearing of goat-skins by the Satyrs, and as he makes not only the names *tragoedia* and *tragic* arise from the latter, but also Attic Tragedy itself, he thus postulates that they played the most prominent part in the beginnings of Tragedy in Attica. If that is so we ought (1) to find evidence for them in Attica before they were in Peloponnesus, and (2) to find them associated closely with Thespis. But the facts point all the other way. Arion, the composer of the great dithyramb in honour of Dionysus, was employing Satyrs by B.C. 600, whilst to Pratinas of Phlius are ascribed the first composition of regular Satyric dramas and their introduction into Athens at a comparatively late date in the sixth century B.C., when he probably also introduced the Satyric mask (Fig. 10). It must therefore be admitted that the Satyrs played an important part in the first beginnings of Tragedy in Peloponnesus[1] before Thespis had appeared and long before Pratinas of Phlius. As the Satyric "goat-men," from whom Dr Farnell derives *tragoedia* and *tragic*, had taken so prominent a place in the development of Tragedy in Peloponnesus before there is any evidence for them in Attica, it follows that if *tragoedia* and *tragic* are derived from them, these terms were not invented for the first time in Attica, but rather in Peloponnesus and thence introduced into Attica. Moreover no ancient writer even hints that Thespis wrote Satyric dramas, and there is no evidence that he composed plays other than those on heroic subjects in his early period, though he may

---

[1] This is quite in keeping with the earliest mention of the Satyrs, that in a fragment of Hesiod preserved by Strabo, p. 405, 13 (Didot), where they seem connected with Argolis :

ἐξ ὧν οὔρειαι νύμφαι θεαὶ [ἐξ]εγένοντο,
καὶ γένος οὐτιδανῶν Σατύρων καὶ ἀμηχανοεργῶν
Κουρῆτές τε θεοὶ φιλοπαίγμονες, ὀρχηστῆρες.

have combined Dionysiac and heroic themes in his *Pentheus*, if that was really a genuine work of his. This view gains considerable confirmation from his method of disguising his face. At first he coated it with white lead, then he covered it with purslane, and finally he used a plain linen mask (p. 60). Now as the next step in the development of masks was that made by Choerilus, the great writer of Satyric dramas, it is probable that the improvements made by Choerilus were for Satyric masks. But as Thespis at first used white lead, then purslane, and finally a mask of unpainted linen, his "make-up" was very ill adapted for representing Dionysus, Silenus or Satyrs. On the other hand the pale white colour was well suited for the representation of heroes, whose ghosts might be supposed to appear, like that of Darius in the *Persae*. It is

FIG. 10.　Masks of Dionysus, Satyr and Silenus.
(From a terra cotta in British Museum.)

easy to prove from Aristophanes[1] that to the ordinary Athenian the proper colour to use in the representation of the face of one who had come back from beyond the tomb was white lead.

The young man asks: "Is this a baboon covered with white lead, or an old woman that has risen up from the dead?" It is quite clear that the fit colour for a *revenant's* face was white, and this Thespis could effect by his use of white lead and by his unpainted linen masks. On the other hand to have represented Dionysus with the pallor of death would have shocked his audience.

IV. Some years ago the present writer explained the *aegis* and *gorgoneion* of Athena as nothing more recondite than the

---

[1] *Eccl.* 1072:　πότερον πίθηκος ἀνάπλεως ψιμυθίου,
　　　　　　　　ἢ γραῦς ἀνεστηκυῖα παρὰ τῶν πλειόνων;

primitive goat-skin covering used in ancient Athens as the ordinary dress. A slit was made in the back of the skin through which the wearer's head was put, and the grinning skin of the animal's face hung down on the breast of the wearer. Herodotus[1] compared the goat-skin dresses (*aegides*) of the Libyan women in his own day to the *aegis* of Athena, the only difference being that whilst the former had leathern fringes, that of the goddess had one of snakes. But these snakes and the Gorgon's head were but later additions, for in the *Iliad*[2] she wears an *aegis* with an ordinary fringe, and " a grim head of a beast upon it." The addition of the fringe of snakes and the development of the skin of the goat's head into the *gorgoneion* came much later. And though in the course of time the Athenian women wove and embroidered beautiful robes for themselves and for their goddess, the primaeval goat-skin still remained as part of the dress of Athena.

In like fashion the *aegis* of Zeus has nothing cryptic about it. It was the skin of the goat Amalthea, which according to the myth had suckled the child Zeus. Very ungratefully, when he grew up he slew his foster-mother and made her skin into his covering, the ancient goat-skin garment of Crete. Such *aegides* were still worn by the Lycians serving in the host of Xerxes, who according to Herodotus were emigrants from Crete. The *baite* of the Greek shepherds was only the continuation of the skin garments of the aborigines of Greece. Jason[3] is represented as wearing a panther-skin when he came down from Pelion to claim his heritage from Pelias, but he was not a panther-god, for we are told that the skin was to protect him from the pelting rains. In the time of Pausanias (A.D. 180) the Arcadians still wore the skins of wolves and bears, and the poor people in Phocis and Euboea regularly used pig-skins.

We are now in a position to explain the "Song of the Goats" and the "Dance of the Goats." In view of the evidence cited above, it will be admitted that goat-skins had been worn in Greece as the commonest and cheapest form of dress, centuries before the introduction of Dionysus Eleuthereus into Athens, whether that was about B.C. 550, as Dr Farnell holds,

---

[1] IV, 189.　　　[2] V, 738 *sqq*. etc.　　　[3] Pind. *Pyth.* IV, 81.

or far earlier, as is shown by its attachment to the Apaturia and by the statement that it took place in the regal period of Athens, long before Cleisthenes had brought the cult of Bacchus into Sicyon.

Let us now return to the terms *tragoedia* and *tragic*. In all kinds of ritual and mummery ancient costumes are rigorously retained. No better examples are needed for Greece than the *aegis* of Athena just mentioned or for modern times than ecclesiastical vestments, robes of state, academic costumes and legal gowns and wigs. Just as the Bacchants wore fox-skins and fawn-skins, the typical Thracian dress, which survived till recently in the modern Thracian play, and as the Satyrs wore the common goat-skin garb, now used solely in the dress of the mummers in Thrace and North Greece, doubtless because of its cheapness, so the men who danced solemnly round the tomb of Adrastus, with no element of the grossness of the Satyric chorus, wore the dress of ancient days in this ritual performance. Accordingly, when Herodotus calls such a chorus a *goat* chorus, he is not applying in an anachronistic fashion the nomenclature of his own day to earlier times. At Sicyon, by that date, woven woollen garments were in common use, but for sacred purposes the immemorial garb of the goat-skin had to be donned.

V. Another explanation is also possible, though not so probable. As the dithyramb sung by the cyclic chorus in honour of Dionysus was called "ox-driving," probably because it accompanied the sacrificial bull, so the chorus which danced at the tomb of Adrastus may have led along a goat to be offered. There is just as much evidence for goats being offered to heroes as to Dionysus. The people of Balagrae continued so to sacrifice to Aesculapius, a hero who only became a god at a comparatively late date. We saw that the sacrifice of goats to Hera was considered exceptional, and Pausanias explains it by the poverty of the founder of the sacrifice. We hear almost nothing of the offerings made at the tombs of ordinary heroes and heroines, and we must therefore not argue from such silence that goats were not regularly sacrificed to them. Of course in more important shrines and in wealthy communities, costlier victims would be offered. It may therefore be that the term *tragikos* was applied both to the goat-skin dresses of the chorus and to the victim led to the tomb.

From the foregoing survey of the facts we may conclude (1) Dionysus was not a goat-god when he entered Greece, but, if an animal god, rather a bull-god; (2) that the name Melanaegis was given to him at Eleutherae because of a local incident, and did not refer to the essence of the god, but only to an accidental attribute; (3) that when the worship of Dionysus Melanaegis was brought into Athens, it was an obscene cult; (4) that it was brought into Athens in the regal period; (5) that it was then attached to the ancient Ionic festival of the Apaturia, of which tragic performances at no time were part, in which Dionysus held a very inferior position, and in which the normal sacrifice was a sheep and not a goat; (6) that the cult of Dionysus Melanaegis is thus in no wise connected with the origin of Tragedy; (7) that the Satyrs wore goat-skins not in honour of that god, but because it was the ordinary dress in primitive days, and so continued amongst shepherds and other peasants into historical times; (8) that in Peloponnesus, as well as elsewhere in Greece, and in Thrace and Crete, goat-skins were the ordinary dress of the aborigines; (9) that for this reason the chorus which celebrated the ancient heroes, such as Adrastus, wore the primaeval dress of goat-skin and was therefore fitly termed a *goat chorus*; (10) that Herodotus is therefore not guilty of an anachronism when he applies the term *tragic* to the chorus which performed a mimetic dance at the grave of Adrastus in Sicyon as early as B.C. 600; (11) that, since it was from this rude chorus that Tragedy proper developed, that art was rightly described as the *goat-song*; (12) that as such tragedies were being performed in Peloponnesus and in Athens before the establishment of the Great Dionysia in B.C. 535, the term *tragedy* which was always kept distinct from the term *Satyric drama* was in full use in Peloponnesus and Athens before the institution of the tragic contests in B.C. 535; (13) that Satyrs had been employed in Peloponnesus since the time of Arion, and that Pratinas of Phlius was the first to compose regular Satyric dramas and to introduce them into Athens in the last quarter of the sixth century B.C.; (14) that, even if Dr Farnell were right in deriving the terms *tragoedia* and *tragic* from the Satyrs dressed in goat-skins, since there is evidence for the use of Satyrs in Peloponnesus from B.C. 600, and as Thespis did not write Satyric dramas, the terms *tragoedia* and *tragic* as well as the actual art itself arose rather in Peloponnesus than in Attica; (15) that Tragedy arose from the worship of the dead, and not from that of Dionysus; (16) that as Dionysus himself had almost certainly once been only a Thracian hero, even if it were true that Tragedy had risen from his cult, its real ultimate origin would still be in the worship of the dead[1]; and (17) that dramatic representations in honour of gods, such as those at Eleusis, were simply an extension of the method of propitiating dead ancestors to secure the favour of the great divinities.

[1] As the oracles of Amphiaraus and Trophonius at Oropus and Lebadea respectively were certainly shrines of heroes (Paus. i, 34. 5; ix, 39. 5—14), it is probable that the oracle of Dionysus amongst the Bessi, his most ancient cult-centre, had a like origin.

CHAPTER III

PRIMITIVE DRAMAS AMONGST ASIATIC PEOPLES

All the world's a stage,
And all the men and women merely players.
SHAKESPEARE, *As You Like It*, II, 7.

WE have seen in an earlier section that the Christian *Mysteries* and *Miracle* plays of the Middle Ages sprang from the same psychological standpoint as that from which Greek Tragedy appeared to have arisen. If we pass to Asia, we shall meet amongst various peoples widely different in race dramatic performances, which without doubt must be regarded as indigenous and most certainly as completely independent of all influence from the Greek or other European drama. If it should turn out that all these native mimetic performances have originated in the same principle as that which has given birth to the ancient Greek and mediaeval Christian dramas, we shall have greatly corroborated our argument that Greek Tragedy did not arise merely in the cult of a particular deity, but rather from beliefs respecting the dead as widespread as the human race itself.

Let us first turn to Hindustan and to the Sanscrit literature of its Aryan conquerors.

The Ramayana. The oldest Hindu drama the *Ramayana* celebrates the life, exploits and sufferings of Rama, son of Dasaratha, who reigned in Ayodhya (Oude), and it includes the loves of Rama and his wife Sita, the rape of the latter by Ravana, the demon-king of Ceylon, the overthrow of Ravana by Rama, the subsequent sorrows of the hero and his wife, the death of Sita, and her husband's translation into heaven.

Since Rama was regarded as an incarnation of Vishnu, and since a verse in the introduction of the work declares that "he who reads and repeats this holy life-giving *Ramayana* is liberated from all his sins and exalted with all his posterity to the highest heaven," it is the keeping in remembrance of the hero-god, his exploits and his sufferings, that is the essential element in this great drama.

The Sacred Plays of Tibet and Mongolia. No less evident is the same root-doctrine in the religious Mystery plays performed by the Lamas of Tibet and Mongolia. They represent scenes in the life of Buddha, of incarnations of Buddha, or of Buddhist saints, who were sorely beset and tormented by devils, but in the end prevailed over evil. It would appear however that beyond doubt Buddhism has simply incorporated mimetic dances of the Shamanistic ancestor-worship, which it has nominally supplanted.

The ritualistic form of Buddhism, found in Tibet, Mongolia, and China, commonly termed Lamaism, has incorporated a very large element of the primitive rites of many Shamanistic tribes. The Buddhist missionaries in order to make conversion more easy, adopted the gods and rites of their proselytes under new names or with slight modifications, just as was done by the early Christians who evangelised various parts of Europe.

One of these Tibetan Mysteries called *The Dance of the Red Tiger-Devil* is said by Colonel Waddell[1] to have originated in a Shamanistic exorcism of evil spirits, with perhaps a human sacrifice in earlier times, a feature which can be easily paralleled from Greek legend, and even from Greek history itself, and which plays an important part in more than one Greek tragedy. In its modern form the motive is the assassination of a great enemy of Lamaism by a Lama disguised as a Shamanist dancer, thus holding up for reverence the triumph of the holy man over the sinner.

The Lamas reserve to themselves the exclusive right of acting in the Mystery Play[2] with its manifestation of the gods and demons by awe-inspiring masks and the like, whilst they

---

[1] *The Buddhism of Tibet*, pp. 516 *sqq.*

[2] Waddell, *op. cit.*, p. 540.

relegate to lay actors the sacred dramas illustrating the former births of Buddha and other saints, the *Jatakas*. The most popular of all the dramas played by the lay actors and actresses are the Visvantara (Vesantara) Jātaka, or the great Birth of Buddha, and the indigenous drama of Nan-sa, or the Brilliant Light. But they also at times play among other things the Sudhana Jātaka, the Marriage of king Sron Tsan Gampo, the Indian king (?) Amoghasiddha, and the fiendess Do-ba-zan-mo.

An admirable description of the great drama performed by the Lamas of Ladak is given by Mr E. F. Knight[1]. It was on the 16th of June that Knight saw the grand mystery. "We were awoken at an early hour to a realisation of where we were by the sounding of the priestly shawms in the different quarters of the great monastery. After breakfast we repaired with the Naib Wazir, the Treasurer, and other notables to the gallery overlooking the quadrangle, where seats had been prepared for us. The jovial Treasurer, finding that I appreciated the national beverage, produced at intervals flowing bowls of chung to cheer us as we gazed at the successive whirling troops of devils and monsters that passed before us.

"It is difficult to give an account of the ever-changing and very interesting mummery which was carried on for the whole of this long summer's day—a bewildering phantasmagoria of strange sights, a din of unearthly music, that almost caused the reason to waver, and make one believe that one was indeed in the magic realm represented by the actors, a dreadful world affording but dismal prospects, being even as these Buddhists regard this present existence of ours, and of which, if it were thus, one would indeed be well quit. For the principal motive of this mystery play appeared to be the lesson that the helpless, naked soul of a man has its being in the midst of a vast and obscure space full of malignant demons—the earth, the air, the water, crowded with them—perpetually seeking to destroy him, harassing him with tortures and terrors; and that against this infinite oppression of the powers of evil he can of himself do nothing, but that occasionally the exorcisms or prayers of some

[1] *Where Three Empires Meet*, pp. 206 *sqq.* ; Waddell, *The Buddhism of Tibet*, p. 522.

good Lama or incarnation may come to his assistance and shield him, and even then only after fierce and doubtful contests between the saint and the devils. And only for a time, too, can this relief from persecution endure, for all the exorcisms of all the saints are of little avail to keep back these advancing hordes. The shrieking demons must soon close in upon the soul again. Such is the gloomy prospect of human existence as depicted by the Tibetan Lamas. The extraordinary resemblance between much of the pageantry and forms of Tibetan Buddhism and those of the Church of Rome has been observed by all travellers in these regions. The Lamas who represented the saints in this mummery, had the appearance of early Christian bishops; they wore mitres and copes and carried pastoral crooks; they swung censers of incense as they walked in procession slowly chanting. Little bells were rung at intervals during the ceremony; some of the chanting was quite Gregorian. There was the partaking of a sort of sacrament; there was a dipping of fingers in bowls of holy water; the shaven monks, who were looking on, clad almost exactly like some of the friars in Italy, told their beads on their rosaries, occasionally bowed their heads and laid their hands across their breasts; and there was much else besides that was startlingly similar to things that one has seen and heard in Europe. I will only attempt a description of some of the principal features of this two days complicated ceremony, to rehearse for which is one of the chief occupations throughout the year. Some of the sacred dances have intricate figures and gesticulations, and must need a great deal of preparation. The musical instruments employed by the Lama orchestra on this occasion included shawms and other huge brazen wind instruments, surnais, cymbals, gongs, tambourines, and rattles made of human bones. The many-coloured and grotesquely-designed robes worn by the mummers were of beautiful China silk, while the masks exhibited great powers of horrible invention on the part of their makers.

"The gongs and shawms sounded and the mummery commenced. First came some priests with mitres on their heads, clad in rich robes, who swung censers, filling the courtyard with the odour of incense. After a stately dance to slow music these went out; and then entered, with wild antics, figures in yellow robes and peaked hoods, looking something like victims destined for an *auto da fé*; flames and effigies of human skulls were on their breasts and other portions of their raiment. As their hoods fell back, hideous features, as of leering satyrs, were disclosed. Then the music became fast and furious, and troop after troop of different masks rushed on, some beating wooden tambourines, others swelling the din with rattles and bells. All of these masks were horrible, and the malice of infernal beings was well expressed on some of them. As they danced to the wild music with strange steps and gestures, they howled in savage chorus. These, I believe, were intended to represent some of the ugly forms that meet the dead man's soul in space, while it is winging its way from one sphere to the next.

"The loud music suddenly ceased, and all the demons scampered off, shrieking, as if in fear, for a holy thing was approaching. To solemn chanting, low music, and swinging of censers, a stately procession came through the porch of the temple, and slowly descended the steps. Under a canopy borne by attendants walked a tall form in beautiful silk robes, wearing a large mask representing a benign and peaceful face. As he advanced men and boys, dressed as abbots and acolytes of the Church of Rome, prostrated themselves before him, and adored him with intoning and pleasing chanting. He was followed by six other masks who were treated with similar respect. These seven deified beings drew themselves in a line on one side of the quadrangle, and received the adoration of several processions of masked figures, some of abbots, and others beast-headed, or having the faces of devils. 'These seven masks,' said the Treasurer to us, 'are representations of the Dalai Lama of Lassa and his previous incarnations. They are being worshipped, as you see, by Lamas, kings, spirits and others.' But a few minutes later the steward of the gompa came up to us and explained that these were intended for the incarnations of Buddha, and not of the Dalai Lama; whereupon he and that other erudite theologian, the Treasurer, discussed the point at some length in their native tongue."

Amongst the Buriats, an important tribe of Mongolia, the

Mystery play or *Tsam*, as they term it, is of a much simpler character and is again the triumph of good over evil spirits. The Buriats, who number over two hundred thousand souls, live on the south-eastern side of Lake Baikal chiefly around Selenginsk. Only a few thousand still remain pagans. The chief *Datsan* (Lamaserai or monastery) of the Buriats is at Gelung Nor (Lake of Priests), a lake of about fourteen miles long separated from the south-eastern end of Lake Baikal by the Khamar Daban range. Here is a great temple in the Chinese style[1].

"Down in a space railed off in the front of the temple is to be seen a vast crowd. Thousands of Buriats have come from great distances to witness the scene. As the audience waits expectantly the noise of many musical instruments is heard.... Suddenly several wild figures, in the strangest of masks, rush upon the scene. Some wear death's-head masks, or a combination of Father Christmas and Neptune, another a stag's head and antlers, and yet others the heads of beasts horned and not horned that would puzzle even the President of the Zoological Society. Grinning demons mingle in the crowd of hideous figures, one wearing a great open-mouthed devil

Fig. 11.
Archaic Greek Scarab.

mask, with little flags fluttering, and several other actors, who are maskless, having on their heads great hats with gilded filagree work. The spectator, dazzled by the brilliancy of the scene and dazed by the din of the musical instruments, at length makes out persons without masks and armed with daggers, who appear to typify the good spirits who have vanquished the death's-heads and the miscellaneous demons and monsters of evil."

The strange masks worn by some of the performers—stag's head and antlers, and others in the shapes of the heads of beasts, horned and not horned—recall the animal masks worn by personages seen on various objects, such as engraved gems

[1] C. H. Hawes, *In the Uttermost East*, pp. 446 *sqq.*; Waddell, *op. cit.*, p. 43.

(Fig. 11) and frescoes, belonging to the Bronze Age of Greece, and also the beast costumes worn in the Bear dance at Brauron and similar mimetic ceremonies of Greece. As the more primitive forms of masks survive in the Buddhist dramas, so the strange and fearsome forms—the "Horse-Cocks" and "Goat-Stags" introduced by Aeschylus in some of his tragedies—may well be survivals from the elder days of Greece.

We have seen above good reason for believing that the Buddhist dramas enacted by the Lamas in Tibet and Mongolia are little else than adaptations of primitive or mimetic dances, once performed as part of their religious rites in the days before Buddhism by the pagan shamans, of whom the Lamas are the living representatives. If in the primitive drama of another non-Aryan Asiatic race it should turn out that the leader of a company of actors is always a shaman, the view given above respecting the origin of the Lamas and their sacred plays will be substantially confirmed. In south-eastern Asia the Malays will at once furnish the evidence required.

The Malay Drama. In the primitive drama of the Malay Peninsula, in spite of the influence of Hinduism and Muhammadanism, there are not wanting traces of its close connection with the spirits of the dead.

"The most important of the ceremonies," says Mr W. W. Skeat[1], "which relate to the Malay theatre is that of inaugurating or 'opening' (as it is called) a site for the performance." Citing Mr Hugh Clifford, he says that the space railed in is called a *Panggong*.

"Before the play begins, a ceremony called *Bûka Panggong*, which has for its object the invocation and propitiation of certain spirits, is gone through....

"The ceremony, which is a curious one, is performed in the following manner: The company having entered the shed and taken their seats, a brazier is placed in front of the *Pâwang* or Medicine-Man, who is also the head of the theatrical troop. In this brazier precious woods and spices are burned, and, while the incense ascends, the *Pâwang* intones the following incanta-

[1] *Malay Magic*, 504 *sqq.*

tion, the other members of the troop repeating each sentence in chorus as he concludes it.

" ' Peace be unto Thee, whose mother is from the earth, and whose father has ascended to the Heavens! Smite not the male and female actors, and the old and young buffoons with Thy cruelty, nor yet with the curse of poverty! Oh, do not threaten with punishment the members of this company, for I come not hither to vie with thee in wisdom or skill or talent: not such is my desire in coming hither. If I come unto this place, I do so placing my faith in all the people, my masters who own this village. Therefore suffer not any one to oppress, or envy, or do a mischief unto all the body of male and female actors, together with the young and old buffoons, and the minstrels and bridegroom, together with Sri Gĕmûroh, Sri Bĕrdĕngong. Oh, suffer them not to be hurt or destroyed, injured, or maimed; let not the male or female actors be contused or battered, and let them not be injured or maimed; let them not be afflicted with headache, nor with undue physical heat, nor yet with throbbing pains or with shooting aches. Oh, let them not be injured by collisions like unto ships, the bows of which are telescoped, nor afflicted with excessive voiding. Suffer them not to vomit freely, nor to be overcome by heavy weariness or fatigue or weakness. I ask that Thou wilt suffer them to be as they have been accustomed to be in former times, and to feel cool and fresh like unto the snake, the chinta-mâni (a short snake of a yellow colour, the presence of which is lucky).

" Peace be unto Thee, Oh Black Awang (a very common man's name), who art King of the Earth! Be not startled nor deranged, and be not offended, for Thou are wont to wander in the veins of the ground, and to take Thy rest in the portals of the Earth. I come not hither to vie with Thee in wisdom, for I only place my trust in Thee, and would surrender myself wholly into Thy hands; and I beg thee to retire but three paces from the four corners of our shed, and that Thou shalt refrain from wandering hither and thither, for under Thy care I place the male and female actors, and all the buffoons, both young and old, together with all the musicians and the bridegrooms. I place them under Thy care, and do not oppress or envy them, neither suffer evil to befall them, do not strike against them as Thou passest by...'." A similar ceremony was witnessed by Skeat. A tray with the usual brazier of incense and small bowls of rice variously prepared was then brought in.

All this looks as if the worship of the spirits of the dead may have once been the chief motive in such performances, a view strongly supported by the fact that the leader of such companies of actors is always a medicine man. This circumstance also confirms the belief that the Tibetan Buddhistic dramas of to-day and the Lamas who perform them, are but the modern representatives of old pagan mimetic dances and of the shamans who enacted them for religious or magical purposes. If we could but find some primitive people of Asia whose religious beliefs and practices are still almost untouched by influences from without, whether Buddhist, Hinduist, or Muhammadan, and that this folk have dramatic performances of a most primitive kind, if it should furthermore turn out that such plays, if they can be termed such, are performed by the shaman for purely religious objects, and not for amusement as is the case with the Malay dramas, we might obtain very important evidence respecting the origin, not merely of the Buddhistic and Malay drama, but even of that of Greece itself.

The Drama of the Veddas of Ceylon. In one of the most primitive races of mankind which still survive—the Veddas of Ceylon—we can fortunately find the evidence of which we are in search. The recent investigations of my friends, Dr and Mrs Seligmann, have secured, before it was too late, much more accurate and precise information respecting these most interesting and important people than was hitherto available. Their complete results will shortly be published in a separate volume, but meantime they have generously placed at my disposal some fruits of their most valuable observations as well as the photograph reproduced (Fig. 12).

The Veddas, who still remain in a wild state, are but very few in number. These live practically by hunting, and scarcely till the ground at all except for growing yams. It is therefore obvious that a plentiful supply of game and success in capturing it and also good crops of yams are the chief objects of the hopes

and prayers of this simple folk. Naturally their religious
ceremonies bear directly upon the all-important question of
a supply of food. In order to secure these ends they have ceremonies in which they invoke the aid of the spirits of departed
members of their race, renowned in their day and generation for
their skill and success in the chase and in the growing of yams.
Such an honoured spirit is termed a *Yaka*, and the most
prominent amongst these *Yaku* is Kande Yaka, who was a
mighty hunter. Accordingly when it is desired to slay a deer,
they seek the aid of Kande Yaka, and this is done by a most

Fig. 12. A Vedda drama : 'How Kande Yaka killed the Deer.'

primitive dramatic performance—How Kande Yaka killed the
deer. I here give in Dr Seligmann's own words the account of
this remarkable ceremony.

The Kirikoraha at Bendiagalge. " The Kirikoraha was
danced at Bendiagalge after a fine buck had been killed, before
taking part in which all the men went to the stream and
bathed. A tripod, called *muk-kaliya*, was made by binding
three sticks together on which an open earthen pot (*kirikoraha*)
was placed and the *aude* was laid upon it.

" Some rice with cocoa-nut and chillies had previously been

cooked at the cave, together with certain portions of the deer—the flesh from the head, sternum and front of the ribs—and all were brought down to the dancing plot in the *talawa* (plain). This food formed the *aduk*, and the *adukudenawa*, or ' offering of the food,' was performed before the dance began. The shaman, Randu Waniya, squatted in front of the food, and with hands together, repeated a charm or *vadinau* to Kande and Belinde Yaku. This lasted nearly ten minutes and was full of repetitions. It was performed in gratitude for all deer and sambur, but not for birds, and in it the Yaku were invited to take food, which was left for them for a short while and was afterwards eaten by the Veddas themselves.

" The shaman took a cocoa-nut and the *aude* and held them to his head and salaamed, while Poromala smeared some beeswax on a stick and afterwards censed the *aude*: at the same time the invocation to Kande was repeated. The stick was so held that the smoke might touch the *aude* and in this way Kande Yaka would smell it and be pleased.

" This appeared to be one of many incidents pointing to the fact that when *Yaku* are invoked, they first come to their special properties (Kande always to an *aude*, other *Yaku* to leaves, swords, and various articles), and from these enter the person of the shaman. All sang the invocation and the shaman danced round the tripod, holding the *aude* and cocoa-nut together in both hands and waving them rhythmically, as he performed the orthodox Vedda step, *i.e.* one pace with each foot, each followed by a couple of pats on the ground with the ball of the foot, every two steps being followed by a half turn of the body to the accompaniment of sounds produced by those who were not dancing beating their sides. After a short time the shaman showed signs of becoming possessed. He began to shiver and to shake his head, and with the *aude* in his right hand he struck the cocoa-nut in his left and broke it in halves, letting the milk fall into the *kirikoraha*, and at this time he became possessed by Belinde Yaka. The way in which the nut split was prophetic: if a clear break was made, the animal to be promised later would be a female, if however the edges were jagged, a male would be shot. Then with half the nut in each hand, the shaman came to each of us in turn and placing his arms on our shoulders, in the hoarse gasping voice of the Yaka, promised us good hunting and protection from wild animals.

" All sang the incantation again and Randu Waniya continued to dance, holding the handle of the *aude* in his right hand and the point of the blade in his left, turning it with rotatory movement as he danced, now swaying his body and lifting his feet higher from the ground. He went to the *kirikoraha*, and inspected the milk, letting it run through his fingers and dropping some on the *aude* to see if it was rich enough : apparently he was satisfied with its quality. Soon he fell back and was supported by Sitawaniya. After a short time he revived with much quivering and gasping, and, taking a handful of the cocoa-nut milk, he shouted and approached the *arachi* (this man was known to the Bendiagalge community and was much respected, both because he boasted Vedda blood and because he was renowned as a *Vederale* charmer and medicine-man) who accompanied us, and scattered the juice over him, while with the right hand on his shoulder he expressed his pleasure in seeing him and promised him game to shoot. Then after prophesying good hunting to each of us in turn and to several of the Veddas, the Yaka of Belinde left him.

" Randu Waniya again danced eastward round the Kirikoraha, holding the *aude* in both hands, but soon he began to crouch and pointed to the ground, and then pretended to thrust the *aude* at imaginary slots. Here his excited manner showed that he had become possessed by Kande Yaka, and he imitated him as he followed the trail of a sambur. Sitawaniya took the *aude* and gave him a bow and arrow and the tracking continued amidst intense excitement, Sitawaniya following closely, ready to support the shaman if he should fall, and others pointing out the slots to him, till at last, a basket having been placed on the ground, he pulled his bow and shot it (Fig. 12). As the arrow sped from the string he fell back seemingly exhausted. The Yaka did not here finally depart from the shaman, but merely went to the quarry to ascertain if his shot had been fatal. The shaman soon came to himself, apparently satisfied, and bent his head over the *kirikoraha*, and then in the usual agitated manner of the Yaku, came to each of us in turn and placed the *aude* on our heads, thereby granting us jungle favour, and afterwards proceeded to various of the Veddas, prophesying good luck in hunting to each of them. Then taking the half shells in either hand and waving them about, he danced round the *kirikoraha*, and bent his head over the pot, so that the Yaka might drink, and afterwards fell into Sitawaniya's arms. Again he revived and, putting his arms on our interpreter, promised him victory in all undertakings. Then turning to the *kirikoraha*, having given the *aude* to one of the onlookers, who were all willing assistants, he filled the palms of his hands with milk and bounded forward, and with every step raised his hands and scattered the milk, and in this way the Yaka within him showed his pleasure.

" Next he took the *kirikoraha* from the tripod and with both hands spun it on the ground, and immediately it left his hands, he fell back. The spinning was prophetic, for in that direction towards which the bowl dipped, there game would be found. This time it dipped to the north. When the shaman came to himself, after a few seconds, Kande Yaka had left him and he was possessed by Belinde Yaka again. With shouts, gasping, and trembling he came to most of the onlookers and promised good hunting in the usual manner, and he took the *kirikoraha* and spun; and when it left his hands the spirit departed from the shaman and he fell back. The dance was now over and all were eager to partake of the cocoa-nut milk—Yaka food—and so valuable that none must be wasted. All the men took a little and also fed the children with it, but the women were not allowed to eat it. However, as the mere contact with the milk had intrinsic virtue, the shaman rubbed some on their heads. In other less sophisticated communities women were not looked upon as unclean, and it seemed that the idea might be borrowed from the Singhalese, among whom it is very strongly held[1]."

[1] It may be that this belief in the efficacy of some mimetic representation of a successful hunt may be found even among the lower animals. The following fact

No one on reading the account of this interesting ceremony, probably the most primitive of dramatic performances, will fail to recognise in it the same principle of propitiating the spirits of dead heroes by representations of their exploits, and even of their sorrows, which we have found in the case of Adrastus and in the mediaeval religious dramas. But there are even other points of contact between the simple Vedda ritual and some of the most stately of Greek ceremonies. As the simple aborigines of Ceylon invite their Yaku to partake of food, so the Greeks of the golden age of Hellas held entertainments for their gods and heroes. These Theoxenia—" Banquets of the gods "—were held in various parts of Greece. There were such festivals in honour of Apollo at Pellene and also at Delphi, where one of the months was called *Theoxenios*, whilst at Agrigentum a like feast was held to which Castor and Pollux were supposed to come: " For to them (the Dioscuri) he (Heracles) gave charge when he ascended into Olympus to order the spectacle of the Games, both the struggle of man with man and the driving of the nimble car. Anywise my soul is stirred to declare that to the Emmenidae and to Theron has glory come by the gift of the Tyndaridae of goodly steeds, for that beyond all mortals they do honour to them with tables of hospitality, keeping with pious spirit the rite of the blessed gods[1]."

may point in this direction. A tabby cat, of perhaps more than average intelligence, was seated on my knees one winter evening beside the fireplace. A mouse came out from under the further end of the fender, whereupon she sprang from my knee and caught it. Next evening she repeated the same performance, getting up and sitting on my knee, and then suddenly springing across the hearthrug to the spot where she had secured her prey on the previous night. Almost every evening that winter she repeated the experiment, never springing at the imaginary mouse from any other place than from my knee. The following winter she recommenced the mimetic performance of her successful hunt, and the next winter she again did the same. It was only last winter that she finally abandoned her attempts to elicit a mouse by repeating the action which had once proved eminently successful. I may add that in the interval the fire-place had been completely altered. Among primitive peoples, such as the Malays, in order to secure his game more easily, the hunter addresses it in beguiling words (Skeat, *Malay Magic*, p. 171). The same cat when searching for mice or when listening to them when beyond her reach, does not growl, but addresses them in the dulcet tones of endearment which she uses to her kittens.

[1] Pindar, *Ol.* III, 35 *sqq.*

So too at the great festival of the Eleutheria at Plataea, held in honour of those who had laid down their lives to deliver Hellas from the Mede, the chief magistrate each year headed a procession to the graves, and after laving the tombstones with water from the fount and anointing them with unguent, slew a black bull and after a preliminary prayer to Zeus and Hermes, invited the heroic dead to partake of the banquet and the blood[1].

To sum up then our results so far, we may arrive with some probability at the following conclusions:—that the Dorians did not invent Tragedy; that representations of the sufferings of heroes were familiar features in Greece before the incoming of the worship of Dionysus; that such solemn songs and dances were part of the propitiatory rites performed at the tombs of heroes in order that they might protect their people, and that the earth, through their kindly interposition, might bring forth her fruits; that on top of this primaeval ancestor-worship came in a Thracian cult of a wild orgiastic kind, a ritual likewise regarded as beneficial for promoting vegetation and the increase of food; that this new religion was gradually in many places engrafted on old local cults of heroes, and that the tombs of the latter now became the altars of Dionysus; that the only true Dionysiac element was the dithyramb that dealt with the sorrows and adventures of Dionysus and his Satyrs, and that from this grew the Satyric drama, whose close union with, and at the same time rigid distinction from, Tragedy as well as from Comedy is thus at last explained; further, that the grand step made by Thespis was to elevate the Tragic dance from being a mere piece of ritual inseparably connected with a particular shrine into true dramatic literature; finally, it would appear that the principle from which Tragedy sprang was not confined to Greece or to Mediterranean lands, but is world-wide and one of the many touches that make the whole world kin.

[1] Plut. *Aristides*, 21.

CHAPTER IV

SURVIVALS OF THE PRIMITIVE TYPE IN EXTANT GREEK TRAGEDIES

In that new world which is the old.
TENNYSON.

In the previous pages we have carefully tested the grounds for the doctrine traditional with scholars respecting the origin of the Tragic art, and we have been forced to reject the old view. Then a further search with new methods into the available data bearing on Greek mimetic performances and extending far beyond the limits of Greece and the Mediterranean led us to the conclusion that Tragedy originated in the worship of the Dead.

Let us now turn to the extant works of the great Greek dramatists, and let us examine the main ideas which pervade them, and see how far these are distinct survivals of the religious and social doctrines held by the Greeks in the ages before the full development of Tragedy in the beginning of the fifth century B.C., when in the hands of Aeschylus

> "The thing became a trumpet whence he blew
> Soul-animating strains,"

of which but too few have reached our ears. If it should turn out, that not only the tombs of kings and heroes, but also the offerings made at them, including even human sacrifices, the ghosts of the mighty dead, and the use of such tombs as sanctuaries take leading parts in a great number of the plays that still survive, we need have little doubt that our views respecting the origin of Tragedy rest on sure foundations.

Tombs in Greek Tragedies.   If the tomb of the hero or
heroine was really, as we hold, the centre round which grew up
the primitive Tragedy, we ought to find distinct evidence for
this in the plays of Aeschylus, the oldest of the three great
Tragic poets. Thespis, according to tradition, had made his
grand step long before his victory in the first Tragic contest
in B.C. 535. Ten years later Aeschylus, the son of Euphorion,
was born at Eleusis. He competed with his first play against
Pratinas, but not successfully, in B.C. 499, when he was but
twenty-five. Henceforward he was in constant rivalry with
Pratinas, Choerilus, Phrynichus, and in later times with his
younger contemporary Sophocles. He was thirty-five years
old when he and his two valiant brothers fought at the battle of
Marathon[1], where Cynegirus, the elder, fell in the final attack
on the Persian ships. He was forty-five at the battle of
Salamis, the chief glory of which probably belongs to his
other brother Ameinias.

Tradition[2] states that the poet was present on the ship
of his youngest brother Ameinias, who was the real hero
of that great victory. This man, when the Athenians, panic-
stricken at the sight of the Persian Armada, began to back-
water, alone of all urged his ship forward, charging a navy,
"whilst all the world wondered." On seeing him ram a
ship of the enemy, the Greeks took heart and joined battle
all along the line[3]. Not only then was the dramatist an
eye-witness of the mighty deeds which he has enshrined for
ever in his *Persae*, but it is almost certain that he himself
was one of that undaunted crew which saved Hellas and

---

[1] Suidas s.v. Αἰσχύλος, who also states that he fought at Plataea.

[2] *Schol. Med. Pers.* 431: Ἴων ἐν ταῖς Ἐπιδημίαις παρεῖναι Αἰσχύλον ἐν τοῖς
Σαλαμινιακοῖς φησί. The Medicean *Life of Aeschylus* says that the poet μετέσχε
τῆς ἐν Σαλαμῖνι ναυμαχίας σὺν τῷ νεωτάτῳ τῶν ἀδελφῶν Ἀμεινίᾳ. Ion was a contemporary of Aeschylus.

[3] Herod. VIII, 84: ἀναγομένοισι δέ σφι αὐτίκα ἐπεκέατο οἱ βάρβαροι. οἱ μὲν δὴ
ἄλλοι Ἕλληνες ἐπὶ πρύμνην ἀνεκρούοντο καὶ ὤκελλον τὰς νέας, Ἀμεινίης δὲ Παλληνεὺς
ἀνὴρ Ἀθηναῖος ἐξαναχθεὶς νηὶ ἐμβάλλει κτλ. To this incident Aeschylus himself
alludes (*Persae* 411):

> ἦρξε δ' ἐμβολῆς Ἑλληνικὴ
> ναῦς, κἀποθραύει πάντα Φοινίσσης νεὼς
> κόρυμβ'.

It is probable that Aristophanes refers to this same Ameinias and his exploit the western world. Critics of course have denied that this Ameinias was the brother of Aeschylus, chiefly on the ground that he belonged to the deme of Pallene, whilst Aeschylus belonged to Eleusis. But, as often happens in such cases, they have ignored a simple and probable solution of this difficulty. Adoption was a very common practice at Athens, and by Attic law, if a boy were adopted he passed from his own family and deme into those of his adoptive father. The fact that Ameinias was the youngest of the three brothers harmonises admirably with the view that he had been adopted into another family. No father would have given an elder son to another family, but rather his youngest.

The other objection is that Herodotus would certainly have mentioned that Ameinias was a brother of Aeschylus, had such been the case. But he does not tell us that Cynegirus was a brother of the poet, simply stating that he was the son of Euphorion[1]. Any biographical notes upon the relations of Ameinias would have been utterly out of place and have marred the grandeur of the account of the opening and decisive incident of the great struggle.

But even if Aeschylus was not on the ship of Ameinias of Pallene, either as a combatant or as a spectator, he must have looked upon that grand scene of which he has left an immortal picture in the *Persae*. The famous lines in which he describes the dead Persians flung helpless and inert by the pitiless waves against the unyielding shore of "dove-nursing" Salamis are as little likely to have been drawn from fancy as is that magnificent passage in which another soldier-dramatist, Cyril Tourneur, has pictured the dead soldier lying in the surf:

in *Eq.* 569-70, where I ventured to amend many years ago Ἀμυνίας to Ἀμεινίας (*Camb. Phil. Trans.*, vol. I, p. 210). The poet is speaking of the brave men who fought at Marathon in contrast to the poltroons of his own day:

οὐ γὰρ οὐδεὶς πώποτ' αὐτῶν τοὺς ἐναντίους ἰδὼν

ἠρίθμησεν, ἀλλ' ὁ θυμὸς εὐθὺς ἦν ἀμυνίας.

The name of *Amunias* occurs several times in the *Nubes* and the *Vespae* either as that of an usurer or of an infamous archon. Aristophanes therefore was not likely to use a name with such evil associations in such a passage, but rather that of one of the worthies who had fought at Marathon or Salamis.

Cf. R. A. Neil's ed. of the *Equites*, ad loc.

[1] Herod. VI, 114.

> " He lay in his armour as if that had been
> His coffin ; and the weeping sea (like one
> Whose milder temper doth lament the death
> Of him whom in his rage he slew) runs up
> The shore, embraces him, kisses his cheek ;
> Goes back again and forces up the sand
> To bury him[1]."

But the two poets approach their theme from opposite standpoints ; the note of the Athenian is that of triumph and exultation over his slain enemies ; that of the Englishman sorrow and sympathy for a dead friend, who lay

> " Among the slaughtered bodies of their men,
> Which the full-stomach'd sea had cast upon the sand."

Each reads his own feelings into the like action of the ceaseless element.

Thus the chief part of the poet's life was over before the wonderful development in political and artistic activity, which characterised the new Athens of Ephialtes and Pericles. Though Thespis had made his grand step, the Tragic art was still but in its cradle when Aeschylus had reached man's estate, for Phrynichus made no material innovation, and it was left for Aeschylus himself to make the next great stride by introducing the second actor and by diminishing the importance of the chorus, as well as the minor improvements of the painted masks (Fig. 13) and the buskin[2].

As Tragedy could hardly be termed an art before it had been made an organic whole by these far-reaching innovations, it is not surprising that Aristotle, as we have seen, ignored Thespis and the other pioneers, and began his historical account of the Attic stage with Aeschylus. Indeed the fact that he it was who bridged over the gulf between the old Athens and the new, as Marlowe was the link between the *Moralities* and the *Histories* and the full-blown Elizabethan drama, is the true explanation of his use of strange and monstrous forms, such as

[1] *The Atheist's Tragedy.*

[2] Hor. *Ars Poet.* 278–80 :

> "post hunc personae pallaeque repertor honestae
> Aeschylus et modicis instrauit pulpita tignis
> et docuit magnumque loqui nitique cothurno."

" Horse-Cocks " and " Goat-Stags." These were not the experi-
ments of a dramatist striving after novelties, but were rather
the survivals of those uncouth mimetic dances, of which strange
and composite forms of quadrupeds, birds and men[1] were an
essential characteristic, and which, as is proved by the material
monuments, had come down from the Bronze Age of Greece.

The last survival of the awful conceptions of a dark and
dreadful past meets us in his representation of the Erinyes,
whose terrible and monstrous aspect made pregnant women
bring forth in the theatre. We may therefore rest assured that
in his early days, as we shall presently see, and probably for long

Fig. 13.   The Masks of Tragedy and Comedy.

after, the old notions respecting the purpose of Tragic choruses
were still fresh and unblurred by time in the minds of the
Athenians.

If therefore it shall turn out that the tombs of heroes, and
offerings at these tombs, and laments for the dead, figure
prominently in almost all his extant plays, we may conclude
that these are no new inventions of the poet's fertile brain,
but merely a continuation of the traditional subjects, purposes
and performances of Cyclic or Tragic Choruses.

The Persae.   Although the *Persae* belongs to the poet's
middle period and was performed in B.C. 472, seven years after
the flight of the Persians from Greece never more to return, and

[1] Cf. Pollux, IV, 103, ὁ δὲ μορφασμὸς παντοδαπῶν ζώων ἦν μίμησις κτλ.

though, as will shortly be seen, a tomb plays a prominent part in his earliest surviving drama, yet as the *Persae* furnishes not only an admirable example of a tomb on the stage, but also of the worship of dead heroes, we shall take it first in order.

The *Persae* is no true drama; it is rather a glorious epinician poem infinitely superior to those in which Pindar celebrated, albeit with marvellous art, the victories of chariots, of horses, and of heavy-armed men or naked athletes at Olympia or Pytho. For the *Persae* recounts no mere mimicry of battle or contest. Aeschylus sang of the victory of the Greek spear over the Asiatic bow in the grim moil of war,—the triumph of free states over the despot of Asia. It stands to the Attic Drama much as does Shakespeare's *Henry V* to the Elizabethan. Just as the latter was adapted by Shakespeare from the older play of *The Famous Victories of King Henry the Fifth*, so it is held that Aeschylus in writing the *Persae* drew somewhat upon the *Phoenissae* of Phrynichus. But there is this important difference between the Greek and the English play. The latter is a dramatic representation without any plot of a series of victories over the French before an English audience who are exulting in the spectacular representation of the overthrow of their hereditary enemies at Harfleur and Agincourt. No note save that of triumph is heard throughout, only one slight glimpse of the French standpoint is given in the scene between Henry and Katherine of France. The *Persae* might indeed be well termed "The Famous Victories of the Athenians," but instead of the pictures of the victories being presented to the audience by Athenian *dramatis personae*, the grim joy of the Athenians at their great deliverance is enhanced by the spectacle wherein the *dramatis personae* are the heads of the Persian empire, who recite their own overthrow and the triumphs of the Greeks. But it was not merely to give a keener zest to the exultation of the Athenians over their foes that Aeschylus constructed his great poem from this peculiar standpoint. If it was to be a tragedy at all and to conform to the conventional type, sorrow of some sort must form a chief feature. Yet this must not be a sorrow that would cause anguish or even a sense of discomfort to any Athenian heart. Phrynichus had composed a tragedy like that of Aeschylus, in so far as it was on a recent historical event. His *Capture of Miletus* was as tragic in all its circumstances as could be desired, but the Athenians fined him for placing the miseries of their kindred before them and thus reminding them of their misfortunes. By his treatment of the *Persae* Aeschylus both avoided the fate of Phrynichus and at the same time placed on the stage a truly tragic situation, and besides he was able to introduce on the scene the immemorial centre-piece of Tragic choruses, a hero's tomb, lamentations for and propitiatory offerings to the dead.

The scene opens before the palace at Persepolis. In the centre lies the tomb of Darius. Around it slowly march the chorus composed of twelve of the greatest Persian nobles left behind to administer the Empire during the absence of Xerxes. They are full of apprehension, for no tidings have come, not even a single horseman with news of the great host that had passed into Europe. The tomb of Darius almost certainly forms the *thymele*, as scholars have long held. This in itself is a startling confirmation of the doctrine of the origin of the *thymele* given above (p. 39). Presently the elders propose to enter the hall of the palace to hold council. Next enters Atossa, daughter of Cyrus, the widow of Darius and mother of Xerxes. The elders salute her as wife of the god of the Persians and as mother of a god. The queen then tells them why she has come forth from the marriage chamber of herself and Darius. First, ascribing the prosperity of her consort to the care of some god, she declares that the eye of the house is the presence of its master. Ever since Xerxes marched away she has been haunted by visions in the night season, but on the night just passed she had had a far more manifest vision than any heretofore. She beheld two women of surpassing beauty, sisters in origin, the one in Persian, the other in Dorian garments; the one had been allotted Hellas, the other Asia. Then they began to quarrel, and Xerxes sought to quell their strife by placing collar-straps on their necks and yoking them to a car. One was docile and took the bit freely; the other proved restive and finally broke the pole. Darius standing by beheld his son's disaster. Then Xerxes perceiving his father present and viewing his catastrophe, rent his raiment. When morning came, the queen, to rid her of the evil presage of her vision, washed her hands in running water, and taking incense prayed to the averting gods. But to her dismay an eagle pursued by a kite took refuge at the altar of Phoebus. Finally she reminds the elders that if Xerxes be victorious, he will be a hero; but should he meet defeat, he is not accountable to the State, and it will make no difference provided he himself returns home safe.

The chorus of elders urge her to pray first to the averting gods, then to pour out libations to Earth, and to the spirits of them that be departed, and lastly to supplicate her husband Darius, whom she had seen in her dreams the previous night, to send blessings on herself and on her son from the world below, and to keep all evil in darkness beneath the earth, shrouded in infernal gloom. In reply Atossa declares that as soon as she goes back to the palace she will carry out their requests. After some further parley between the queen and the chorus, the former says that she will first pray to the gods, next she will take drink-offerings from her house to present to Earth and to the spirits of them which be dead; and these accomplished, she will return to them. Soon comes the messenger with the dread tidings of all that had happened at Salamis. The chorus then makes lament for those whose corpses are tossing in the tide and are being devoured by "the dumb children of the Undefiled," and they predict the anarchy that will fill the Empire. Just then Atossa returns from the palace bringing to Darius such libations and offerings as may have power to appease the dead. She bids them to ingeminate their appeals to Darius, now a spirit of power in Hades. "I myself," says she, "will head the procession and carry these earth-poured offerings in honour of the gods below."

They then pray to the gods of the nether world to be propitious and to send up the soul of Darius to the light. "Their dear departed king," they declare, "is equal in power to the *daemones*," and they beseech the Chthonian spirits to convey to him through Earth their request "even though it be in a barbarous tongue." "Does he hear me down below? But do thou, O Earth, and ye mighty rulers of the dead, allow to pass out from your abodes a mighty prince of the ghosts, the

Susa-born lord, the king of the Persians, and send up to us such a one as the Persian land hath never before covered with its sod. Dear was the man, dear is his tomb." " Aidoneus, Guide of the dead to the world above, send up to us the spirit of Darius. Oh, what a king was he! Divine truly was he, for he ruled his people prosperously. O ancient king, come visit us! Come to the surface of thy grave-howe, uplifting to our view thy saffron-dyed shoes, and revealing the crest of the royal tiara. Darius, come forth." Then from the tomb arises Darius in spectral form (φάσμα). At first he seems drowsy and but half awake, as though after life's fitful fever he had indeed slept well. He begins to address them slowly, and from the lines that follow we learn clearly the doctrine of the Athenians respecting the normal condition of the dead. They know not what is passing on the earth above, unless their spirits be vivified by offerings of blood or other kinds of libations and be invoked with special prayers. If this be done, they awake to consciousness, and they can sympathise with, and best of all they can aid, their kindred and nation. Darius knows nothing of the great events which have been happening to his Empire until he comes to the surface of his grave. Seeing the Persian magnificoes and his wife standing near, he addresses them: "Trustiest of councillors, comrades of my youth, what affliction oppresses the city? The broad earth groans as if furrowed with chariot-wheels. Dread comes o'er me as I see my spouse standing near my tomb, and right willingly I accepted her libation. Ye make lament here at my barrow and with shrill wailings to bring forth my soul ye summoned me. Yet it is not easy to pass forth, since the gods beneath are more ready to take than to restore. Yet, as I hold some place of state amongst them, I am come. But haste ye, that I be blamed not for excessive stay. What is this fresh and heavy blow that hath fallen on the Persians?" The chorus are afraid to tell him, and then, turning to Atossa, he asks her what has happened. " Is it pestilence or a revolt?" Then Atossa tells him the whole story, how Xerxes had bridged the Hellespont and marched into Greece, and how the Persian host had perished near Athens. On hearing her story Darius declares that Zeus has accomplished certain oracles: Xerxes has brought all this on himself for his arrogance in binding with chains like a slave the sacred Hellespont, thus staying the stream of the gods, and thinking to master even Poseidon himself. He then recounts the story of the building of the Empire, and its successive sovereigns. But the chorus are not satisfied with the barren recital of the past. "We want to know," say they, "how Persia is to fare better in time to come." Darius replies: "Make no expeditions against the Hellenes, for the land itself is their ally since it kills by famine those who march with great hosts." Though at first the ghost of Darius seems to know little of current events he gradually gains a clearer vision and he predicts the battle of Plataea and its disastrous result, declaring that as the Persians had destroyed temples and thrown down altars, the gods would now take them to task. The day of reckoning has come. "Zeus is ever ready to punish pride and is at hand to exact a heavy reckoning." Then Darius turns to Atossa, bids her prepare to meet Xerxes and to have fresh apparel at hand for him. "But I must depart into the darkness below. Farewell, ye elders, take such pleasures as the day affords, for the dead have no joy of wealth."

From this summary it will be clear that all the action of the play centres round the tomb of Darius, which stands in front of the royal palace just as the graves of the ancient rulers of Mycenae lay within the Acropolis, as the tombs of the kings of Cyrene lay opposite their palace in the Agora, and as the heroum of Adrastus stood in the Agora at Sicyon. Though the scene is laid in the Persian capital, and though the characters are Persians, we may rest assured that they represent for us faithfully the doctrines respecting the dead held by the Greeks of the fifth century B.C. So, though Shakespeare may lay the scenes of his tragedies in Denmark or Venice and bring before us Danish princes or Moorish captains, the thought and sentiment of his plays is not a whit less English. Aeschylus represents the spirit of the great dead king as invoked to come to the aid of his family and people, and he regards Darius as having the same powers as the old Greek heroes, such as Scephrus, who were supposed to influence the spirits beneath the earth and thus produce barrenness or plenty. In no extant passage is the attitude of the Athenians of the fifth century B.C. towards the spirits of the dead, and their view of the unseen world set out for us with clearer definition. But if we have still any doubt that Aeschylus in the *Persae* is presenting current Athenian doctrines respecting the dead, these will be at once dispelled when we turn to the *Choephori*.

The Choephori. It was not merely in his middle period that Aeschylus employed a tomb and a ghost as the central point, or at least as a very important feature, in the structure of his plays. Both occur in the *Oresteia*, which was produced in B.C. 458, just two years before its author's death. In the *Choephori*, the middle play of that great trilogy, the action centres round the tomb of Agamemnon. The play opens with the presence of Orestes and Pylades before the tomb. Orestes has come to offer a long-nurtured lock of hair to his father's spirit by laying it on his grave. He invokes the aid of Hermes, whose image stands hard by, to aid him in bringing up from the world below the spirit of his father. Meantime a band of slave-women, probably Trojan captives, headed by Electra comes forth from the palace bearing libations to assuage and propitiate the soul of Agamemnon. This they are doing by order of his guilty consort Clytemnestra, who on the previous night had had a fearsome vision, dreaming that the soul of her murdered lord beneath the earth was intent on vengeance, and by the advice of the soothsayers she is now sending these propitiatory offerings. Electra is in doubt how to discharge her mother's errand. Shall she entreat Agamemnon to be meek and gentle with his butchers, or shall she urge him to avenge his wrongs? Or again, shall she simply pour down the libation into the earth (doubtless into a *bothros*) and depart as if she were but casting forth foul water? The chorus counsel her to pray to her father to requite those who have sent the offerings. They declare that they reverence Agamemnon's tomb as a real altar[1] (Fig. 14), and they will speak since Electra asks their advice.

This expression on the part of the chorus admirably illustrates the transition from tomb to altar for which I have argued

---

[1] 198: αἰδουμένη σοι βωμὸν ὡς τύμβον πατρός.

in the case of the *thymele* (p. 39). Electra then pours the libation into the ground, for she speaks of it as "earth-drunk." While doing so, she notices a lock of hair upon the grave, which she sees to be like her own, that is, blonde[1]. She also observes footprints, which resemble in their contour, not in their size, her own feet. Some years ago I explained[2] the difficulty so long felt by scholars. The recognition (ἀναγνώρισις) of brother and sister (Fig. 14) thus naturally arises from the worship of the dead, though actually effected by the similarity in colour of the hair and the shape of the feet of the brother and sister, who are both of the blonde Achean race from the north, and thus differ essentially from the dark aboriginal population of Argolis, whilst the identity of Orestes is finally put beyond all doubt by a piece of embroidery worn by him, which had been wrought by Electra herself.

Next Orestes and Electra pray to Zeus to save the brood of the great eagle their sire, but the chorus warn them to beware lest gossip may report their proceedings to the palace. Orestes next tells his sister that the oracle of Apollo had warned him to beware of the wrath of his father's spirit beneath the earth if he did not avenge his murder. Then follows the invocation of the soul of Agamemnon by the brother and sister. But although this prayer affords a very close parallel to that offered to Darius in the *Persae* (p. 117), yet when we scrutinise it more closely, we find that Aeschylus looks at each case from a very different standpoint. There can be no doubt that the ancient Persians, like their brethren the Aryans of the Rig-Veda, had once burned their dead, although by the time of Herodotus they had probably dropped this practice to a considerable extent, for the historian tells us[3], " It is said that the body of a male Persian is never buried until it has been torn either by a dog or a bird of prey. That the Magi have this

---

[1] 158: γαπότους χοάς, cf. 89: γάποτον χύσιν, cf. *Persae*, 623: γαπότους τιμάς.

[2] In the *Early Age of Greece*, vol. I, p. 284, and in the *Introd.* to Dr Verrall's edition of the *Choephori* (1893), pp. vii, xxxiii sqq., li sq., I have given this explanation of the famous passage and it has been adopted by Prof. Tucker in his edition of that play (1901), pp. lxvi–lxix, but without any acknowledgment.

[3] I, 140.

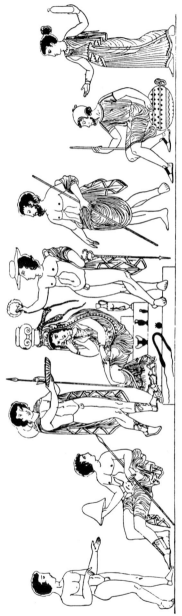

Fig. 14. Orestes and Electra at the tomb of Agamemnon.

custom is beyond a doubt, for they practise it without any concealment. The dead bodies of the ordinary Persians are covered
with wax and then buried in the ground." Cicero[1] also states
that the Persians bury their dead, and that the Magi had the
practice (still cherished by the Parsis) "non inhumare corpora
suorum nisi a feris sint ante laniata." The extreme dread of
polluting the earth with a corpse, which is so marked a feature
of the *Avesta* is really peculiar to Magism, for the ordinary
Persian buried his dead, as we have seen. According to the
Avesta, Angra Mainyu created "a sin for which there is no
atonement, the burying of the dead." For in the earth lived
a goddess Spenta Armaiti, and no corpse ought to defile her
sacred breast. Hence for inhumation there was no atonement.
Just as dreadful was it to defile fire by the contamination of a
dead body. Thus when Cambyses had the mummy of Amasis,
the Egyptian king, burned, "this," says Herodotus[2], "was truly
an impious command to give, for the Persians hold fire to be a
god and never by any chance burn their dead, since they deem
it wrong to give the corpse of a man to a god."

Yet it would appear that the Persians had burned their
dead down to the time of Cyrus[3]. Certainly they had no
scruple in burning the living, as is proved by the story of
Croesus. It is said that it was in consequence of Zeus
hurling a thunderbolt to save that monarch from being burned
to death that "thenceforth the Persians began to observe the
law of Zoroaster which forbade the burning of dead bodies or
any other pollution of the element of fire; and so the ancient
ordinance that had been neglected was established among them."
The *Avesta* in its opening chapter denounces those people who
either burn or bury their dead, and these denunciations fully bear
out the belief that the true Persians like the Vedic Aryans
had once practised cremation. Yet in spite of the ban of
the *Avesta* against inhumation, the Achaemenean kings were
all entombed, if not buried in the earth, as we know from
classical writers and modern discoveries both at Meshed-i-

---

[1] *Tusc. Disp.* I, 44. 108.   [2] III, 16.

[3] Ridgeway, *Early Age of Greece*, pp. 485 *sqq.*, and 542 *sqq.* ("Inhumation,
Cremation and the Soul").

Murghab (Pasargadae ?) and at Persepolis. The royal tombs
at Meshed-i-Murghab are older, and they are assigned to Cyrus
and Cambyses, whilst those at Persepolis are probably those of
Darius Hystaspes and his successors. We know from Strabo[1]
that Cyrus was buried at Pasargadae. Alexander visited the
tomb, which was a small tower standing in a park amid a grove
of trees. The lower part of the tower was solid but above there
was one story and a shrine with a very narrow opening. Aris-
tobulus says that by Alexander's command he entered through
this aperture and decorated the tomb. Inside he beheld a golden
couch, a table with cups, a golden coffin (πύελος), many garments,
and dresses garnished with precious stones. These he saw on
the first occasion, but on a second visit he found that the tomb
had been robbed, and everything had been removed except the
couch and the coffin, which had been only broken. The dead
body had been removed from its place. The shrine was guarded
by Magi who for maintenance received a sheep daily and every
month a horse for sacrifice to Cyrus[2].

Theophrastus[3] says that Darius was laid in an alabaster
sarcophagus. There can be little doubt that the practice of
giving the dead to wild beasts was not Persian, but the custom
of the aboriginal races which they conquered, and whose priests,
the Magi, they tolerated, just as the Celts in Gaul treated with
respect the Druids and the ancient religion of the subject
population.

Though the Persians had once cremated their dead as did
the Vedic Aryans in the belief that fire purified the soul from
the contamination of the body, they had reverted to inhumation
when the reverence for fire had increased to such an extent that
they no longer held that it had any lower phase, such as the
Hindus believe to be the case with Agni. When neither the
pure element of fire nor the Earth-goddess herself nor water
must be defiled by a dead body, there was no course left but to
leave the dead to be devoured by the beasts of the field and the

---

[1] vii, 29.   [2] Arrian, *Anab.* vi, 29.

[3] *Lap.* 6: καὶ ὁ τῷ ἐλέφαντι ὅμοιος ὁ χερνίτης καλούμενος ἐν ᾗ πυέλῳ φασὶ καὶ
Δαρεῖον κεῖσθαι. For an account of the modern condition of the royal tombs, see
Perrot and Chipiez, *Art in Persia*, pp. 196 *sqq.*

fowls of the air. Nature's mysterious chemistry would thus transmute the rotting carcase into the bodies of living creatures and thus neither earth nor fire nor water would be outraged. But it cannot be maintained that this was a new practice invented by the Magi, as a means of escaping from grave theological difficulties. The same practice still prevails amongst the Tartars, Samoyedes, and Tibetans, as it did in ancient times not only among the Hyrcanians but also among the very barbarous tribes who dwelt on the shore of the Indian Ocean south and east of Persia. The Magi then, who, be it remembered, were recruited from Media, seem simply to have clung to the ancient practice of the indigenous peoples of a large part of Asia, and continually tried to force it upon the Persian conquerors. Indo-Persian respect for the Fire-god supplied them with a lever, and the Magi did not find it difficult to put an end to cremation. But with inhumation it was different, and it seems very doubtful if they ever succeeded in constraining the mass of the Persians to abandon this practice[1].

It is even possible that in days when cremation was generally followed by the Persians, the kings were buried. The Persians, like the ancient Swedes and modern Burmese, may have held that it was very important for the weal of the land that the king's spirit should remain among his people and not depart to another region, as it certainly would, if the body were consumed by fire. From the furniture in the tomb of Cyrus and the monthly sacrifice there offered, it is clear that the soul of the great conqueror was supposed to dwell therein. The king thus continued to watch over his people (p. 30). There is no doubt that the body of Darius lay in his sarcophagus within his tomb at Persepolis, and we may reasonably believe that his spirit was honoured with periodical sacrifices like those given to Cyrus. Aeschylus was well aware of this, and he had no doubt that the spirit of Darius, though in the earth beneath, was within easy reach of those who prayed to him.

Let us now return to Greece and the *Choephori*. In Homer the bodies of the dead are always burned and as soon as the body has been consumed, the soul passes away to the unseen

[1] Ridgeway, *Early Age of Greece*, pp. 544–5.

region lying by Ocean in the West, never more to return. In the opening lines of the *Choephori*, Orestes prays Hermes to summon his father " to hear and to give heed to his (Orestes') prayer, at this very mound of his tomb." The maidens from the palace, at the bidding of Clytemnestra, are bearing offerings to Agamemnon, such as are used for propitiating the powers below (cf. Fig. 14). Electra's speech likewise shows the belief that the dead man in the tomb could hear the words addressed to him when the libations were poured down. All this is the ordinary doctrine respecting one whose unburnt remains lie in the tomb, for the spirit keeps near its tenement. But it is assumed in the *Choephori* that Agamemnon has been burned, and therefore according to Homer his spirit would be far away in the land of the dead, nor could it be consulted save by one who voyaged thither in a dark ship as did Odysseus. It is evident then that by the time of Aeschylus an eclectic doctrine had been evolved. The Homeric belief in a separate abode for disembodied spirits was adopted by some, but at the same time the ancient Athenian doctrine of the constant presence of the soul in the grave of its body was retained, the gulf between both doctrines being bridged over by the theory that even though the body was burned the soul could return to its ashes in the grave and could comprehend the prayer addressed to it. That this was a new tenet in the time of Aeschylus is shown by the fact that Orestes is made to express himself as if there was no certainty that his prayer would be heard by his father, as the latter was afar off: " Father, ill-starred father, what can I say or do to waft to you from afar to that place, where you repose with the dead, light equal to your present darkness ? " To this doubt the chorus gives an encouraging reply: " My son, the conscious-ness of the dead one is not subdued by the fierce consuming flame of the fire, but he shows his feelings even after it[1]." Then Orestes and Electra raise their lament at the grave and presently the chorus announce that " by this time there is an ally being set in motion for them in the world below, and things will favour the children." This ally is of course the soul of Agamemnon,

---

[1] *ll.* 324 *sqq.*

which, as it is far away in the Under-world, takes some time to reach the tomb where it is being invoked.

The Homeric abode of the dead, as I have pointed out[1], is not an Under-world, or Inferno, and we may therefore conclude that the common Greek and Italian belief in an infernal region was an element derived from the older race in each peninsula, just as the modern Hindu doctrine of twenty-one hells has been added to the Vedic abode of the dead with Yama and the fathers. It is probable that this new doctrine of the soul had arisen at Athens by the sixth century B.C., for cremation was then coming into use, and its introduction would be greatly facilitated by the new doctrine which removed the great difficulties presented by the pure Achean or Homeric view.

This gains confirmation from a new practice respecting the bodies of worthies. In early days the bodies of heroes had to be watched with care for fear of their falling into the hands of enemies. The best known instance is the story of the bones of Orestes told by Herodotus[2]. It would have been always easy to guard against this risk by cremating the hero, but then his guardianship was lost to his people, as his spirit would have perished or departed to Hades. It was to the policy of Solon that Athens owed Salamis, and who but Solon could keep Salamis sure for Athens ? Accordingly the body of the sage statesman was burned and his ashes sown over that island[3]. By the new doctrine the fire did not subdue the dead man's thought, and while on the one hand it was impossible for the Salaminians to cast his body out of the land, or to use witchcraft to control his spirit, so his soul would be ever present to keep the island safe for Athens. At a later period the body of Phalanthus the founder of Tarentum was treated in like fashion. We are told that it was taken up and burned and its ashes scattered over the market-place of that city[4]. No one henceforth could carry the bones away and use them against Tarentum, as the Spartans had done with those of Orestes, to the bane of Tegea.

Thus in the *Choephori* Aeschylus is expounding the new doctrine of the soul. But it is not only with respect to this

---

[1] Ridgeway, *Early Age of Greece*, vol. I, p. 550.
[2] I, 67–8.   [3] Plut. *Sol.* 32.   [4] Justin, II, 4. 13.

great doctrine that we shall find him an innovator, and not a conservative, as he has been commonly regarded.

The Suppliants. It may of course be said that since the two instances of tombs and hero worship which I have cited belong to the middle and later periods in the poet's life, they may not represent any continuity of a primitive phase of tragedy, but are really to be regarded as a distinctly new conception of the dramatist who saw in the tombs an opportunity for the exercise of his art. This objection will be quickly disposed of when we turn to his earliest extant play, the *Suppliants*, which may with some probability be placed shortly before B.C. 490.

The *Supplices* formed probably the first play in a trilogy of which the second was either called the *Egyptians* or the *Thalamopoei*, whilst the third was certainly the *Danaides*. The year of its performance is unknown, but there is now a general consensus amongst scholars that it is the earliest of the extant plays of its author. As the evidence for its chronology is wholly internal, attempts have been made to fix the date of the trilogy from supposed allusions in the *Suppliants* to contemporary political events. Thus Boeckh and other scholars, such as Kruse and Carl Ottfried Müller, assigned it to the year B.C. 461—that is, only three years before the *Oresteia*, on the ground that in that year Athens had formed an alliance with Argos and had a fleet engaged in Egypt. But the Athenian fleet was then aiding Egypt against Persia, whereas in the play all is hostility to Egypt, as Prof. Tucker[1] has pointed out, whilst it is not at all likely that Aeschylus would have shaped a trilogy simply for the purpose of commending Argos to his country. On the other hand Prof. Tucker thinks that we may suppose Egypt to stand for everything that is Oriental, and he accordingly sees in the play an allusion to the threatened attack on Attica by the Persians which eventuated in the battle of Marathon (B.C. 490). He would accordingly place the trilogy in B.C. 492-1, when the Persian invasion was anticipated, whilst he thinks that the prayer for Argos—that she may never be emptied of men—may refer to the disastrous defeat suffered by that city at the hands of the Spartans in B.C. 494, by which,

---

[1] Edition of the *Supplices* (Introd.).

to use the words of Herodotus[1], "she had been widowed of her men."

But we must rather rely on the evidence from style for the early date of the play. Aristotle, as we have seen above (p. 112), tells us that "Aeschylus first introduced a second actor, diminished the importance of the chorus, and assigned the leading part to the dialogue." Now as the chief features of the *Suppliants* are the great prominence of the chorus throughout, the very subordinate part played by the *rheseis* of the actors, and the faintness of the character-painting of the personages not members of the chorus, we are led to conclude that the play must have been composed by Aeschylus not very long after he had made his first great step—that of adding a second actor, and thereby creating a true dialogue. The prominence given to the chorus over the actor points to a period when as yet the drama had advanced but little from the stage in which Aeschylus took it over from Thespis, Pratinas and Phrynichus. Thus it is the chorus which parleys with the king of Argos, although their father Danaus is present at the same time, who might naturally have been expected to act as their spokesman. Moreover, the whole plot centres not on one of the actors, but upon the fate of the chorus of the fifty Danaids. All these considerations inevitably lead to the conclusion that the play must have been many years earlier than the great trilogy of the *Oresteia*, and must be placed considerably earlier than any of the other extant plays of the poet.

The scene, which remains unchanged throughout the play, lies near the coast south of Argos. In the middle of the stage is seen a great mound[2], almost certainly a great sepulchre, probably once sacred only to the dead that lay within, but later shared by the gods who preside over contests, of whom Zeus,

---

[1] vi, 83.

[2] *ll.* 23 *sqq.*:   ὦ πόλις, ὦ γῆ, καὶ λευκὸν ὕδωρ.
ὕπατοί τε θεοὶ καὶ βαρύτιμοι
χθόνιοι θήκας κατέχοντες
καὶ Ζεὺς Σωτὴρ τρίτος κ.τ.λ.

A curious parallel is offered by the tomb of Augustus in the Campus Martius: ὑπὸ δὲ τῷ χώματι θῆκαί εἰσιν αὐτοῦ καὶ τῶν συγγενῶν καὶ οἰκείων (Strabo, 197–9, ed. Didot).

Apollo, Poseidon, and Hermes[1] are directly named. On the mound are *xoana* or wooden images of these gods. But it is important to note that Dionysus is not mentioned either here or elsewhere in the play, although an altar, which serves as the *thymele*, stands at the foot of the mound. This fact, like the tombs in the *Persae* and *Choephori*, certainly favours the views advanced in the first part of this work—that Dionysus had originally nothing to do with the first beginnings of tragic choruses. The chorus of the fifty daughters of Danaus in Oriental attire with finely-wrought robes, forehead bands and veils, enter bearing in their hands fresh-plucked olive branches, wreathed with wool, the mark of suppliants. They recite their woes and the cause of their flight and invoke the aid of Argos, Earth and Water, the gods above, and the spirits of the dead, heavy in exacting vengeance, that are in their graves within the barrow, and finally they pray Zeus to receive the Suppliants and side with them against vice and violence. Then Danaus, who meantime has mounted the tumulus, cries to his daughters to be on their guard, as he sees the dust of a host approaching and he urges them to take sanctuary on the mound. The maidens immediately ascend the barrow invoking the chief gods whose images they behold. When the king of Argos comes, he asks why they have sought asylum on the mound. The king on hearing their tale sends Danaus to plead their cause in the city and bids the maidens descend from their sanctuary, but to leave on it their suppliant boughs and to descend into the *alsos*. Danaus comes back with the good news of his favourable reception. He once more mounts the barrow and gazing seawards espies the Egyptians approaching. Soon arrive the herald and the mariners from the Nile and once more the maidens take refuge on the mound and cling to the statues. The Egyptians have no respect for the inviolability of the place and lay hands on the girls to drag them away. But at this juncture the king of Argos once more arrives and the Egyptians depart uttering threats of future vengeance, and the maidens proceed to the city where hospitable homes await them. It is thus clear that this reverend mound, with its ancient dead each in his narrow

[1] *ll.* 193–6.

cell within and with images of the gods superadded, plays an important part thoughout the whole action of the play. It thus proves that the great importance of the tomb of Darius in the *Persae* was no mere chance invention of the poet in his mature years, but rather a clinging to the great primitive principle out of which Tragedy had sprung. This sepulchre of the mighty dead on which were placed images of the heavenly deities affords an admirable parallel for what we suppose to have taken place at the heroum of Adrastus in Sicyon, when the worship of Dionysus was superimposed upon the tomb of the hero. Furthermore it is important to note that though Dionysus is not mentioned amongst the gods whose images stand upon the barrow, nevertheless the altar at the foot of this mound, which almost certainly must belong to the gods enumerated, serves as the *thymele* around which the chorus solemnly move. Plainly Aeschylus did not consider it imperative in a tragedy that the altar round which his chorus circled should be dedicated to Dionysus. In the *Persae* and the *Choephori* the chorus move simply round a dead chieftain's grave, but here in the *Supplices* is the next step, when cults of gods are superimposed on those of the dead and an altar or table of offerings (p. 42) is added to the ancient barrow.

Now why should the gods whose images stand upon this barrow be termed *Presidents of Contests* (ἀγώνιοι)? We saw above that one of the regular ways in which the mighty dead were honoured was by *contests* (ἀγῶνες), whether of athletes or of horses. Such contests took place round or alongside of the barrows which covered the remains of the great departed (p. 36). When the worship of gods was added to that of the heroes, as was the case at Sicyon and at Tegea, that of Dionysus in the one case, that of Apollo in the other, it was but natural to regard these gods as presiding over the contests which took place close by the barrow, and thus they obtained the epithet "presiding at contests." In a later section I shall deal with the question of *Sanctuaries*, under which this particular mound in the *Supplices* distinctly falls, and the arguments there adduced will confirm the conclusion at which we have already arrived, that this great mound in the *Supplices* was certainly sepulchral.

Yet it may be said that although the graves and worship of heroes play a very important *rôle* in the dramas of Aeschylus because he was a conservative and clung to the ancient beliefs of his race, it does not follow that this doctrine had any intimate connection with the origin and evolution of the tragic art, but was quite independent of it. To this there is a ready answer. It can be shown that his two younger contemporaries, Sophocles and Euripides, continued to the last to give great prominence to the doctrine of ancestor worship and the potent influence exercised on human affairs by the spirits of the dead, though with the former the purely artistic side of Tragedy reached its zenith, while the latter was deeply saturated by the new doctrines of Anaxagoras and the Sophists.

Let us first turn to Sophocles. This man, the greatest dramatic artist of the ancient world, if not of all time, was the son of Sophilus, probably a middle-class Athenian. About B.C. 496–5 he was born not far from Athens, at that "white Colonus" which he loved so well, and which, with its golden crocus, its purple ivy, its green olive-tree and its nightingales, he has glorified for ever in the famous chorus of his *Oedipus at Colonus*. He was only a stripling and incapable of bearing arms at the time of the Persian invasion, but he was chosen for his personal beauty, and probably also from his charm of disposition, to lead the solemn chorus that formed part of the public thanksgiving for the great deliverance of Salamis. Thus his young imagination must have been fired and ennobled by the great events through which he had lived. He studied music under Lamprus, the rival of Pindar and Pratinas. In B.C. 468, when not yet twenty-eight years of age, he competed against Aeschylus and defeated the great master. Henceforward, his life was one of unceasing literary activity until he died, full of years, beloved and honoured of all, shortly before B.C. 405. He composed at least seventy tragedies and eighteen Satyric dramas, though, according to Suidas[1], his dramatic works numbered no less than one hundred and twenty-three whilst besides these he wrote elegies and paeans and is also said to have written a prose treatise on the Chorus.

[1] s.v. Σοφοκλῆς.

The actual dates of only two of his plays are known. The *Antigone*, produced shortly before the Athenian expedition to Samos in B.C. 440, secured his election by the democracy as one of the Ten Generals, but he does not seem to have had any military qualifications, since Pericles remarked of him that he was a good poet, but a poor commander. As the *Antigone* is said to have been his thirty-second play, it must be regarded as a work of his mature genius. The *Philoctetes*, produced in B.C. 409, is considered to be the last of his works by those critics who hold that the *Oedipus Coloneus*, though not produced till after his death, was nevertheless written many years before. Both the *Antigone* and the *Philoctetes* won the first prize; their author not unfrequently was second, but he was never third.

His contributions to the evolution of the Tragic Art were the introduction of the Third Actor or Tritagonist (sometimes even a Fourth), and the use of painted scenery; whilst according to Suidas he was the first to compete with single dramas instead of with tetralogies after the fashion of Aeschylus. In this, however, he probably only reverted to the practice of Phrynichus and the other early playwrights.

Sophocles stands to Aeschylus in much the same relation as Shakespeare does to Marlowe. The young Cambridge scholar before he was twenty-nine had not only shaken off the crudities of the *Moralities* and the *Histories*, but had forged that "mighty line" which became the grand instrument of dramatic expression for Shakespeare and the rest. In like fashion Aeschylus had not only freed himself from the narrow trammels and uncouth imagery of the elder age, but he had also discovered once for all the true metre and diction for Tragic expression. Sophocles had only to perfect the instrument which Aeschylus had placed in his hands, and when in B.C. 468 he defeated his master, the eagle was smitten with an arrow feathered from his own wing.

We cannot indeed point to any one of his extant plays in which a tomb actually appears on the stage, yet the burial rites of the dead and the extraordinary value attached to the possession of the bones of heroes form a leading feature in at least three of them.

Ajax. It is a commonplace with scholars that the whole
interest of the *Ajax* flags after the self-slaughter of that hero,
for the rest of the play is taken up with wranglings as to whether
the body of the hero shall receive due sepulture or not. It is
only when we moderns place ourselves at the standpoint of the
ancients and comprehend, dimly though it may be at best, the
extraordinary importance attached by them to the due performance of burial rites, that we can even faintly conceive how that
tragedy could move an Athenian audience.

Antigone. The same holds true in a large degree of the
Antigone. The play centres round the question—Is Polynices,
who has led an army against Thebes his native city, and who
has fallen in mortal combat with Eteocles, each brother having
slain the other, to be allowed the rites of sepulture or shall he
be left to birds and beasts of prey ? This theme would not
excite much emotion in a modern audience, were it not supplemented by elements that never fail to rouse the sympathy and
pity of every human heart,—the devotion of Antigone to her
dead brother, her courage in withstanding Creon, the romantic
love of Haemon for the heroine, her immurement in a living
tomb by the merciless behest of Creon, Haemon's suicide when
he finds that he is too late to rescue his betrothed from self-
inflicted death, and finally Creon's belated repentance and
agony, when he learns of his son's suicide.

It is important to notice that the tomb, in which Antigone
was buried alive and in which she strangled herself to escape
the lingering misery devised for her by Creon, plays a very
prominent part in the drama, although it does not actually
appear on the scene.

Oedipus Coloneus. But when we turn to the *Oedipus at
Colonus* we find a tomb playing a still more important part,
although it likewise does not appear on the stage. *Oedipus the
King* ends with a terrible storm of anguish, shame and despair,
when the proud monarch at last realises that he himself and no
other is the source of the pollution which is destroying Thebes
and the Cadmeans, that he has been the murderer of his father,
and the consort of his own mother, and that his sons and
daughters are his own brothers and sisters. In the *Oedipus*

Coloneus the old storm-battered craft has at last reached the harbour's mouth, and is coming into its last haven, Colonus in the land of Attica. Here the blind world-worn hero is granted an asylum by Theseus and the men of Colonus, and he promises to them a guerdon for their hospitality. When the divine token comes to Oedipus that the closing scene is now at hand, he sends to the city for Theseus, and when the king arrives tells him that his end is near. Blind as he is, he will now lead the way to the sacred spot where he is to lie in death, that no one save Theseus himself shall know the exact place. When death approaches that hero, he is to reveal the site of the grave to the best of his sons, and he in turn to his successor. Thus secured from all risk of being carried off by the Thebans or any other enemies of Athens, the bones of Oedipus, with his spirit in close attendance on them, will be for Athens an ally through all time " worth many shielded hoplites and mercenary spearmen[1]." Then the blind old man steps forth unguided by any hand, Theseus alone attending him. Soon the thunder of Zeus is heard by those who stayed behind, and presently Theseus returns and informs them that all is over. The old hulk so long tossed by the storms of calamity has found a safe mooring for ever. In return Oedipus will be to Attica an invincible guardian for all time.

Thus then in the closing years of the fifth century B.C., when Socrates had been teaching for more than twenty years, when the Hylacists of Ionia, and the clever rhetoricians of Sicily had been long disintegrating old beliefs, when the stress from plague and war had shaken men's faith in the gods, the worship of the dead and reliance on the beneficial results therefrom were as strong as ever in the Athenian mind. Moreover it is not the more advanced doctrine, such as that held by Aeschylus respecting the detachability of the soul from the body, and the harmlessness of fire to the soul that is preached by Sophocles, but the crude ancient doctrine that every care must be taken to preserve the body or bones of the hero from destruction and to guard them from the depredations of those who would work Athens ill.

[1] *O.C.* 1524–5.

If Tragedy arose from the worship of the dead and was in the Greek mind closely bound up with it, we can now fully understand why such a consummate artist as Sophocles gave such prominence to the proper veneration and security of the tombs of the mighty ones departed, why he makes the due sepulture of the dead the pivot on which hangs the dramatic movement of the *Antigone*, and why he actually devotes to the same theme a great part of the *Ajax*.

It may be said that as the grave of Oedipus was concealed with almost as much care as that of Moses, there could be no dramatic celebrations around that hero's resting-place, and that accordingly it may be inferred that there was really no connection between the worship of the dead and dramatic performances. But to this the answer is not far to seek. The case of Oedipus is exactly parallel to that of Orestes[1]. Each is buried in a land of strangers, far from his own city and his own kindred, and the safe-keeping of the bones of both is essential for the weal of the alien land in which each lies. But it was not merely of dramatic performances that these heroes were deprived. No offerings of any kind were made at their graves. Yet it would be absurd to argue that because in their cases no offerings were made at stated seasons, therefore there was no real connection between the dead and the offerings ordinarily made at graves. The cases of such differ essentially from those of indigenous heroes, who lie in the Agora or Prytaneum of their own city, secure from all danger of being carried off by the enemies of their land and race. These heroes, their families, clansmen, and citizens honour with rich offerings, solemn songs, and dramatic performances, as the years revolve. But to the friendless alien dead who lie in that same land and whose spirits are, as it were, in servitude, bound to render aid to the people who have the control of their remains, no one makes the offerings customary for the dead. They have no kindred, no clansmen. There is no one impelled by love or duty or family ties to make oblation to them, or to organise in their honour sacred dances and dramatic contests.

Euripides. Although Sophocles might have clung to ancient

---

[1] Herod. i, 67–8.

beliefs or at least reverted to them in his extreme old age, it might naturally have been anticipated that Euripides, who was so greatly influenced by the new ideas from Ionia, would have paid but little heed to such mouldering beliefs and would have disdained to use them for dramatic purposes. The son of Mnesarchus or Mnesarchides and Clito, the poet was born in Salamis in the year—some said even on the very day—of the great battle in B.C. 480. His parents appear to have been in good circumstances. Of his father's calling nothing certain is known, though by some he is called a retail merchant. The Comic poets never tired of jesting at his mother Clito as a "greengrocer" (λαχανόπωλις), though a good ancient authority denies the truth of this allegation. He is said to have been trained as an athlete, but seems to have had little fancy for such pursuits. He became a painter, and in later times pictures ascribed to him were shown at Megara. But the most important part of his education was the study of rhetoric under the famous sophist Prodicus of Ceos, and to this circumstance we may attribute in part at least the love of dialectic in his plays. Later on he was greatly influenced by Anaxagoras of Clazomenae and also by Socrates.

If Sophocles was called the "bee" on account of the sweetness of his character, Euripides on the other hand had the reputation of being morose and unsociable, and doubtless his temper was not improved by the unhappiness of both his marriages. His first competition, which was also his first victory, was with the *Peliades* in B.C. 455, the year after the death of Aeschylus. He is said to have written some seventy-five dramas, according to others ninety-two. His earliest extant play is the *Alcestis* (p. 54). In his later life he left Athens and went to the court of Archelaus, king of Macedon, who treated him with great distinction. The poet composed there plays on local topics, such as the *Archelaus* and the *Bacchae*. The king's favour, however, cost him his life in B.C. 406. Two rival poets, Arrhidaeus, a Macedonian, and Crateuas, a Thessalian, jealous of his success, by a bribe of ten minae induced Lysimachus, the master of the royal kennel, to set the hounds at him and he was torn to pieces. Archelaus had his bones placed in a costly tomb at Pella, whilst a cenotaph for him was erected at Athens[1].

His chief innovations in Tragedy on the formal side were the introduction of the melodrama in which "nobody is killed by anybody" and the use of set prologue-speakers. If then it should turn out that in some dozen of this poet's extant plays either a tomb is the centre of dramatic action, whether represented on the stage or not, or the worship of the dead or a funeral procession plays a leading part, we shall be forced to the conclusion that there must have been some principle of primary importance to bind tragedy so closely to the worship of the dead, that even the sceptic and innovator could not shake himself free from its bonds. This inference will be confirmed if we find that not merely in the forepart of his career before he might have been supposed to have shaken off the trammels of his early training, but even in his latest period, he places on the stage a tomb and makes it the centre round which pivots all the chief action of the play.

Helena.   In B.C. 412 he produced his *Helena*. Though the famous heroine had so often been reviled by the misogynous poet in his earlier plays, as a worthless woman who had run away from her husband, we find him in his later years adopting the view of Helen's conduct first put forward by Stesichorus.

In one of his earlier poems—probably *The Destruction of Troy*—that poet had treated Helen in the conventional way as the guilty wife. When at a later time blindness befell him, convinced that the deified heroine had sent this affliction upon him as a punishment, he composed his famous *Recantation*, in which he declared that the Helen who had been seen in Troy and for whom Acheans and Trojans fought so hard and long, was a mere wraith (φάσμα, εἴδωλον), whilst the true Helen had never fled from Greece with Alexander overseas.

Although Euripides borrowed the main idea of Stesichorus, and represented Helen in the play named after her as the model wife, he departed from the Stesichorean prototype in one very important particular. The plot is as follows: The true Helen was not carried off to Troy, but Hermes, by the direction

---

[1] Suidas, s.v. Εὐριπίδης.

of Hera, transported her to Egypt and handed her over to the
safe-keeping of king Proteus, who dwelt in Pharos. When the
play opens, the old monarch is dead, and his son Theoclymenus
wants to marry Helen. She rejects his offer and to avoid the
violent prosecution of his suit takes refuge at the tomb of
Proteus, which stands in front of the palace. There can be no
doubt that the tomb of Proteus was represented on the stage.
When Menelaus on his way home from Troy lands in Egypt
arrives at the palace and asks who lives there, the old porteress
at the door replies "Proteus lives here, and the land is Egypt[1]."
A few lines later on Menelaus asks the name of the lord of the
palace, and she answers: "Yon is his tomb; his son now rules
the land."

It is at this tomb that Menelaus first finds Helen seated as
a suppliant and accosts her: "O thou who hast by a desperate
struggle reached the curbstone and fire-wrought railings of this
tomb[2]." In another passage Helen says to Menelaus: "Thou

---

[1] *Hel.* 466 *sqq.*

[2] *Hel.* 546 *sqq.*:   σὲ τὴν ὄρεγμα δεινὸν ἠμιλλημένην

τύμβου 'πὶ κρηπῖδ' ἐμπύρους τ' ὀρθοστάτας,

μεῖνον.

Paley (*ad loc.*) infers that because the tomb of Proteus has a *krepis*, it was
not a mere barrow or tumulus but had architectural features. But there is
ample evidence that a stone curb or retaining wall was a regular feature round
ancient Greek barrows, as I have shown (*Early Age of Greece*, vol. I, p. 119).
Thus the famous tomb of Aepytus mentioned by Homer (*Il.* 603–4) is described
by Pausanias (VIII, 16, 3) ἔστι μὲν οὖν γῆς χῶμα οὐ μέγα λίθου κρηπῖδι ἐν κύκλῳ
περιεχόμενον. Compare the tomb of Phocus in Aegina (Paus. II, 29. 9), that of
Oenomaus near Olympia (*id.* VI, 21. 3), that of Areithous at Phoezon (*id.* VIII,
11. 4). All these tombs were mere barrows. The famous ring of stones on the
Acropolis of Mycenae, which Schliemann took for the seats of the Agora, is
better explained by Dr Tsountas as a retaining wall for the mound of earth
raised over the graves. Without such a retaining curb barrows inevitably
spread out at the base. Accordingly the two great Irish barrows at New Grange
and Dowth in the Boyne valley show each such a retaining wall.

The words ἐμπύρους τ' ὀρθοστάτας have hitherto not been properly explained.
Liddell and Scott, s.v. ὀρθοστάτης, explain it as "a kind of cake used in funeral
oblations," citing Pollux VI, 73 and a gloss of Hesychius: ὀρθοστάδη· εἶδος
πέμματος, whilst s.v. ἔμπυρος, in reference to the same passage, they explain
ἐμπύρους as "of or for a burnt offering." Let us deal with the last point first.
This explanation assumes that burnt sacrifices were offered to the dead, which
of course is a fundamental error, since fireless offerings (τὰ ἄπυρα ἱερά) were
offered to heroes. With reference to the word ὀρθοστάτας they are not more

seest me sitting as a wretched suppliant at this tomb (τάφος). Here I implore escape from marriage[1]." Menelaus asks : "Is it through lack of an altar or in conformity with foreign usage ?" To this she answers: "This doth protect me as well as would the temples of the gods." It is again at this tomb that the *Recognition* takes place between husband and wife, when Helen has returned thither after learning from Theonoe

happy. In the first place Pollux in the passage to which they refer, does not mention the word at all, but is only referring to πέλανοι, the usual offerings of the dead, whilst it is most unscientific to explain the meaning of ὀρθοστάτας in this passage from a word of different form in Hesychius, when there is every possibility of explaining it from the use of the word in other passages of the poet's plays. Thus the posts of a great tent erected at Delphi (*Ion* 1134, ὀρθοστάταις ἱδρύεθ' ἡλίου φλόγα καλῶς φυλάξας) are termed ὀρθοστάται, whilst the same term is applied (*Herc. Fur.* 980) there to "stone uprights" of some kind:

> ὁ δ' ἐξελίσσων παῖδα κίονος κύκλῳ
> πόρευμα δεινὸν ποδός, ἐναντίον σταθεὶς
> βάλλει πρὸς ἧπαρ· ὕπτιος δὲ λαΐνους
> ὀρθοστάτας ἔδευσεν ἐκπνέων βίον.

In each of these cases the word refers plainly to an upright post either of wood or stone. The same meaning gives an easy and rational explanation for the passage in the *Helena*. The very order of the words τύμβου 'πὶ κρηπῖδ', ἐμπύρους τ' ὀρθοστάτας suggests that κρηπῖδ' and ὀρθοστάτας go closely together and refer to the structure of the tomb. In other words the tomb has a stone curb or base on which stand railings or pillars. How then are we to explain ἔμπυρος? It simply means "wrought in the fire," i.e. made of metal, and thus the whole phrase may be taken as "bronze railings." ἔμπυρος is regularly applied to metal work. Thus Plato, *Legg.* 679 A, speaks of σκεύη ἔμπυρα, "implements wrought in the fire," as opposed to τὰ ἄπυρα. In *Protag.* 321 E he terms the smith's craft ἡ ἔμπυρος τέχνη. It would then appear that the tomb had a stone curb like the barrows already cited, and that it was surmounted by a metal railing. Such railings made of bronze and set on a stone curb or sill are well known in Greek temples which date back to the time of Euripides. Thus in the temple of Apollo at Bassae (built by Ictinus, the architect of the Parthenon, about B.C. 420), between the columns of the façade still remains a marble sill with the traces of the metal railings which closed up the opening between the columns and the *antae*. I cannot point to any clear instance of the use of such railings round a tomb at the same period, but as there was but little difference between the grave of a hero and a temple, there is a fair probability that such graves sometimes had railings. According to Strabo 196, 11 (Didot), the spot in the Campus Martius where the body of Augustus was cremated, was enclosed by a stone curb and an iron railing: ἐν μέσῳ δὲ τῷ πεδίῳ ὁ τῆς καύστρας αὐτοῦ περίβολος, καὶ οὗτος λίθου λευκοῦ κύκλῳ μὲν περικείμενον ἔχων σιδηροῦν περίφραγμα, ἐντὸς δ' αἰγείροις κατάφυτος.

[1] 797 *sqq.*

that the tale of the shipwreck and death of Menelaus brought by Teucer is false[1]. Thus the tomb of Proteus is the scene of the chief dramatic features of the play. But this is not all. It is not merely a convenient meeting-place : but a sanctuary as mighty as an altar where the weak and helpless can find asylum, and it is a shrine at which Menelaus prays to the spirit of the ancient king within : " O aged man, who dwellest in this tomb of stone, restore, I implore, to me that wife whom Zeus sent hither to you to safeguard for me[2]."

Just then as the Persian queen and nobles pray to the soul of Darius, and as Orestes and Electra invoke that of their dead sire to aid them in the hour of distress, so Euripides makes his hero rely in time of peril, not upon any god, but on the spirit of the ancient king, which still has vital force within the tomb before his palace gate. Thus then in the closing years of his life Euripides so far from scorning as outworn the ancient creed of his race, represents his hero and heroine not only as having resource to the protection of the old king within his grave, but what is still more significant, not disappointed in their hopes of a deliverance to be wrought by him.

Hecuba. Some twelve or fourteen years before the appearance of the *Helena,* the poet in the *Hecuba,* one of the most famous of his plays, had made a tomb the central point of a drama. This play had certainly been brought out before B.C. 423, for in that year it was ridiculed by Aristophanes in his *Clouds,* and not improbably still earlier, if a supposed allusion in the play itself (l. 649) really refers to the catastrophe suffered by the Spartans at Pylus in B.C. 425. The actual scene is laid in the Thracian Chersonese, whither the Acheans on their homeward voyage after the fall of Troy had put in with Hecuba and the other Trojan captives. But the real interest of the play centres round the tomb of Achilles at Sigeum, on which Polyxena, the youngest daughter of Priam and Hecuba, is sacrificed to the ghost of that hero. But of this sacrifice we shall treat at greater length below (p. 160).

The number of extant Greek tragedies in which a tomb plays a prominent part is proportionately so large, that we are

---

[1] *loc. cit.*   [2] 961 *sqq.*

justified in the inference that the tomb and the worship of the dead must have been closely bound up with tragedy in its first beginnings. This comes out with special prominence if we recall how rarely a sepulchre is used by the Elizabethan dramatists. Even when a tomb or a grave is placed before us, as in *Romeo and Juliet* or in *Hamlet*, it is not for the glorification of the heroic dead, but as in the Morality of *Everyman*, it serves to tell us that

> Life's but a walking shadow, a poor player
> That struts and frets his hour upon the stage
> And then is heard no more.

THE KOMMOS.

Although in many tragedies no tomb is actually represented on the stage, nevertheless a brief examination will show that in its place there are often other elements intimately bound up with the honouring and worshipping of the dead. In every land under the sun throughout the ages goes up the endless wail of the living over the loved one, from whom life has just parted for ever:

> Ingemisco, ingemisco,
> Is ever a lament begun
> By any mourner under sun
> Which, ere it endeth, suits but one?

The anguish of the human heart finds vent and relief in tears and cries of sorrow, though this outward manifestation of grief is less demonstrative in our northern lands, where from of old *honestum est feminis lugere, viris meminisse.* Moreover when the dead is carried forth to the grave, and the closing scene is at hand, fresh onsets of grief seek outward expression in the beating of breasts, and in the rending of garments, commingled with cries and broken utterances—sorrow for themselves, praise for the dead and the last lingering sad adieu.

The Greeks were no exception to this general law of mankind, and with them lamentation, wailing, beating of breasts, and rending of garments were the due meed of the dead[1]. To be

---

[1] Aesch. *Ch.* 415 *sqq.*

unwept was little better than to be denied the rites of burial. Nor did such tokens of grief cease with the burial of the lost ones. Year by year when the customary solemn offerings were made at the sepulchre, lamentations and cries of sorrow formed part of the rites that were to please and propitiate the spirits of the departed. For as the living like not to be forgotten, so too is it with the dead.

The *threnos* or lament for the dead we have already seen in Homer. Such a lament accompanied by the beating of the breast (κόπτεσθαι) was termed by the Greeks of classical times a *Kommos*, which in Attic tragedy technically meant a lament sung alternately by one or more of the chief characters and the chorus[1]. If then tragedy arose in the propitiation and honouring of the dead, the extant Greek tragedies ought to furnish us with examples of this method of showing respect to the departed. Of these there is no lack. All of them with one exception are found in plays where no tomb is present on the stage. Aeschylus supplies us with examples both of the *kommos* over him who has just died and who is being borne to the tomb, and also of what may be termed the commemorative *kommos*, sung over his grave when many years have elapsed since his burial.

Of the former kind the *Seven against Thebes* furnishes us with an admirable illustration, in the *kommos* sung by Antigone and Ismene over the body of Eteocles as it is borne back from the fatal combat with his brother Polynices to be buried with all honour in the Thebes which he had saved[2]. Antigone says "Thou smotest and wert smitten." Ism. "Thou slewest and wert slain. With the spear thou hast killed, with the spear thou wert killed." Antig. "Sorrow thou wroughtest!" Ism. "Sorrow thou sufferedst!" Antig. "Let wailing arise!" Ism. "Let the tear well forth!" Antig. "There thou liest low!" Ism. "Thou laidst thy foe low." Antig. "Alas, alas, my brain is maddened with laments." Ism. "My heart within me makes moan." Finally the body of Eteocles is carried off the stage to the grave, but the tomb is not seen.

No doubt in the years that were to come periodical

[1] Arist. *Poet.* 12 : κομμὸς δὲ θρῆνος κοινὸς χοροῦ καὶ ἀπὸ σκηνῆς.
[2] 951 *sqq.*

offerings would be made at his tomb, dirges sung recounting how he had died for Thebes, athletic contests held in his honour as they were for Iolaus, or a tragic chorus would represent his feats of arms and his victorious death. Of such a celebration we have a famous example in the *kommos* sung by Orestes and Electra over the grave of Agamemnon in the *Choephorae*[1]. From these two typical cases we can perfectly understand the nature and characteristics of such lamentations in the real life of every-day Athens. As the *kommos* is then clearly a portion and parcel of the worship of the dead, it was but natural that as Tragedy became more developed, in order to avoid the monotony of always having a tomb as the centre of action, the poet dispensed with it, but retained in its stead the lament for the dead in some form or other. In the plays of Euripides there are various examples of the *kommos*. Thus in the *Suppliants*[2], when Creon denies rites of sepulture to the champions slain before Thebes, Adrastus goes with their wives and mothers to the altar of Demeter at Eleusis, and seeks the help of Theseus. When the latter succeeds in his efforts and brings back the bodies of the dead chieftains, they are brought on the stage to the accompaniment of a great *kommos*, sung by the chorus, which consists of the seven wives of the slain and their seven handmaids. Again in the *Andromache*[3], though there is no tomb seen, there is a great *kommos* when the body of Neoptolemus, who has been murdered at Delphi, is brought on the stage, Peleus and the chorus making lament.

Again in the *Phoenissae*, though the tomb does not appear, the play ends with the bringing upon the stage of the bodies of Eteocles and Polynices, and a great *threnos* uttered by Antigone over them. In the *Alcestis* the lament of the household as the queen departs to death may be regarded as a *kommos*, whilst the speech of Theseus, now repentant and agonised, over his dead son performs a similar part in the *Hippolytus*. Again in the *Troades*[4] we have a characteristic example in the lament of Hecuba over the body of the little Astyanax, laid out for burial in his father's shield, which is

---

[1] 307 *sqq.*   [2] 1165 *sqq.*
[3] 1173 *sqq.*   [4] 1166 *sqq.*

followed by a *kommos* between her and the chorus of Trojan captives.

All are familiar with the Greek practice of erecting cenotaphs in honour of those who were lost at sea, or who for some other cause, as in the case of Euripides, had not received the due rites of sepulture at the hands of their kindred. Euripides instead of showing a tomb makes use of this custom in the *Iphigenia in Tauris*. Iphigenia has had a dream about Orestes, which has filled her with alarm. She is convinced that he must be dead, and accordingly she prepares, with the help of the chorus of Greek captives and her handmaids, to offer funeral libations accompanied with a *threnos* to propitiate his spirit in Hades.

In view of these facts we may safely conclude that in the *kommoi* and *threnoi* of the Greek plays we have not only an important element in the honouring of the dead and of the worship at the tombs of heroes, but also one of the indigenous and at the same time one of the most primitive elements in Greek Tragedy. The *threnos* or dirge for the dead is familiar in Homer, and we know that in the hands of Pindar and other poets these *threnoi* or coronachs were elevated into a form of literature. Amongst the fragments of the Theban poet are the remains of several of his *threnoi*. In the *kommoi* of the tragic poets we have simply such laments utilised for dramatic purposes. But the *threnoi* of Pindar and the *kommoi* of the tragic poets merely expressed in nobler language and more elaborate diction those emotions of the human heart which had found utterance in the spontaneous rude laments of the untutored men and women of primeval Greece. But as these lamentations for the dead had rung out through the day and through the night for countless generations before Dionysus had ever come from Thrace, or before his cult had been established even in Thrace itself, the *kommos* cannot be regarded as an element of tragedy unknown in Greece until introduced in the ritual of the Thracian god.

Tragedies especially suited for acting at the festivals of Heroes. If it could be shown that there are certain extant plays which seem especially fitted for performance at shrines

of ancient heroes, these would lend further support to our
general view of the origin of tragedy. But such dramas are
not far to seek.

Hippolytus. The *Hippolytus* will at once occur to
students of the Greek drama. The play was brought out
at Athens in B.C. 428. The author of the Greek argument
states that it was the second play of that name, and that it
was an improvement on a former one. The older was known
as the *Hippolytus* Καλυπτόμενος because at the close of the
play the hero was brought in covered with a cloth. The extant
play was entitled by way of distinction *Hippolytus* Στεφανίας
or Στεφανηφόρος because the hero offers garlands to Artemis[1].
These plays seem simply to have been first and second editions
of the same piece, and not separate plays in a Trilogy.

The scene is laid at Troezen. Hippolytus, son of Theseus
by the Amazon Hippolyte, has been brought up by his great-
grandfather Pittheus at Troezen. A model of chastity he
scorns Aphrodite and devotes himself to the worship of the
virgin huntress Artemis, by whom he is honoured with intimate,
though invisible communion. Determined to punish Hippolytus
for boasting superiority to the ordinary emotions of love,
Aphrodite makes his stepmother Phaedra, daughter of Minos,
fall in love with him. Theseus had retired from Athens to
Troezen for a year's span in consequence of the slaying of
Pallas and his sons, and his queen accompanied him. She
had previously seen Hippolytus at Athens as he was going
to Eleusis. At Troezen she now gives way to secret passion
for him. Her nurse at last extracts from her the cause of her
pining, and as a last hope of restoring her mistress to health
and happiness she reveals to the young hero under an oath
of secrecy his stepmother's love. Horrified at the disclosure
Hippolytus withdraws from Troezen. Phaedra, on finding that
her love has been revealed, hangs herself, but leaves behind
a letter in which she charges Hippolytus with having made
dishonourable overtures to her. Theseus on his return reads
the letter and is infuriated at his son's supposed baseness and
hypocrisy. He expends on his son one of the three curses

[1] 673.

which his father Poseidon has declared should be fulfilled, and
banishes him for life. In deep sorrow Hippolytus turns his
back for ever on Troezen, his dear home, and drives in his
chariot along by the sea-shore. Suddenly Poseidon sends from
out a great tidal wave a tauriform monster to affright the
horses. They upset the chariot on the rocks and leave the
young hero dying. Theseus on hearing the fatal news is filled
with mixed feelings of sorrow and satisfaction, until Artemis
appears and reveals the truth. Then follows the reconciliation
between the dying youth and his penitent and distracted sire.
Hippolytus expires, but Artemis confers on him a festival at
Troezen for all time.

At this town in classical and post-classical days many
memorials of Hippolytus and Phaedra were shown. There
was a stadium called after him. His tomb, says Pausanias[1],
" is a mound of earth not far from the myrtle tree," which was
popularly believed to date from the time of Phaedra. Close
to it was the grave of that unhappy queen. But far more
important was the precinct of great renown consecrated to
Hippolytus, son of Theseus. " It contains a temple and an
ancient image. They say that these were made by Diomede,
and that he was also the first to sacrifice to Hippolytus. There
is a priest of Hippolytus at Troezen, who holds office for life,
and there are annual sacrifices. Further, they observe the
following custom :—every maiden before marriage shears a lock
of her hair for Hippolytus and takes the shorn lock and
dedicates it in the temple[2]." According to Pausanias the
Athenians likewise had honoured the hero, since in front of
the temple of Themis was " a barrow erected in memory of
Hippolytus[3]."

Although we are not told by Pausanias that any ceremonies
were performed in his time at the cenotaph of Hippolytus in
Athens, it is probable that in earlier days sacrifices were
annually offered, and although in a later age there may have
been no dramatic performance or " tragic chorus " at the festival
of the hero at Troezen, such probably formed part of the great

---

[1] ii, 32, 4.   [2] *Id.* ii, 32, 1–4.   [3] *Id.* i, 22, 1.

ceremonials at his shrine in the classical period. Euripides [1] himself is our witness, since in the closing lines of the play he makes
Artemis declare that she will establish for Hippolytus in the
city of Troezen the "highest honours." "Unyoked maidens
on the eve of their marriage shall shear their locks for him,
and his sad story shall ever be a theme for poets." As the
rite of shearing the hair was still observed by the Troezenian
virgins in the days of Pausanias, Euripides beyond all doubt
referred to an actual contemporary practice when he alludes
to this ceremony. When therefore he speaks of poetical compositions on the story of Hippolytus and Phaedra, he is almost
certainly referring also to some form of dramatic representations
or *threnoi* at the festival of the hero. The poet knew well that
the highest honours at Troezen, as at Sicyon in the case of
Adrastus, included dramatic representations which kept in
continual remembrance the young hero's noble life and tragic
fate. Nay, we may even go further and believe that Euripides
wrote his play from the standpoint of one who was composing
a drama to honour and propitiate the illustrious dead.

Rhesus. Nor does the *Hippolytus* stand alone in this
respect amongst the plays ascribed to Euripides. If the
Rhesus be a genuine composition of that poet, as was held
by all the Alexandrian critics, its conclusion offers a striking
parallel to that of the *Hippolytus*. We know from tradition
that Euripides did write a play called the *Rhesus*, but the
majority of modern critics whilst admitting this historical fact,
hold that the true play was lost, and that the drama which has
come down to us is only a spurious imitation composed in
a later age. The arguments urged by the critics are practically
all subjective, each condemning the play for faults, which it is
assumed that Euripides could not have committed, even in his
earliest period—that to which the ancient critics and the
moderns who believe in its genuineness, assign the play. We
need not too hastily reject the extant play as spurious.
Euripides has been singularly fortunate in having had so many

---

[1] *Hipp.* 1424-6 : τιμὰς μεγίστας ἐν πόλει Τροιζηνίᾳ
δώσω· κόραι γὰρ ἄζυγες γάμων πάρος
κόμας κεροῦνταί σοι κτλ.

of his plays handed down to posterity, a fact in no small degree
due, as has long been recognised, to his popularity in Graeco-
Roman and Roman times.   His sententious utterances and his
keen dialectic delighted philosophers and rhetoricians, and thus
his plays were regularly used as texts in the schools.   As his
genuine writings thus continued to be so popular and well
known, it is difficult to see how his real *Rhesus* could have been
replaced in the many manuscripts of his works by an inferior
and spurious play on the same subject.   Bacon[1] in a famous
passage argues that only the less valuable creations of the
ancient world have come down to us: "For the truth is," says
he, "that time seemeth to be of the nature of a river or stream
which carrieth down to us that which is light and blown up,
and sinketh and drowneth that which is weighty and solid."
But this argument has been refuted by the discoveries of the
works of authors hitherto unknown or lost writings of others
whose⌠masterpieces had come down to us from antiquity.

No matter how meritorious are the results of the labours
of archaeologists and papyrographers, it must be confessed that
neither the *Polity of the Athenians* nor the recently discovered
work of an historian of the fourth century B.C., although
valuable as historical documents, has much claim to literary
merit.   Bacchylides has proved very disappointing, and the
recently discovered remains of Menander still more so, while the
new fragments of Pindar have only furnished us with examples of
his work far inferior to those great Epinician Odes that have
made the Theban eagle famous through the ages.   Of Herodas
it may be said that if his writings were again lost, Greek
literature would not be much the poorer.   The verdict of men
of culture, arrived at in the long lapse of time, has been pro-
foundly just.   Not only is it the truly great writers—Homer,
Aeschylus, Sophocles, Euripides, Pindar, Herodotus, Thucydides—that have come down to us, but the best productions
of these authors, as is clearly seen in the case of the recently
discovered fragments of Pindar.   In view of these facts it is
hardly credible that in the manuscripts of Euripides, which
preserved the best of the poet's writings down to our own day,

[1] *The Advancement of Learning*, I, 5, 3.

the true *Rhesus* could have been supplanted by a spurious and inferior work of a later age.

The subject of the play is Rhesus, the Thracian king, son of Eioneus and a Muse, or according to others, son of the river Strymon and the Muse. The plot follows the story told in the *Iliad*, Book x, of the coming of the Thracian hero. The Trojans have long looked for the arrival of Rhesus, as an oracle had declared that if he came the Greeks would be vanquished. After various incidents,—the capture of Dolon, the entry of Odysseus and Diomede into the Thracian camp, the slaying of Rhesus, and the escape of the two Achean chiefs by giving the true watchword obtained from Dolon,— the play ends with the lamentation of the Muse, the mother of Rhesus. She upbraids Athena, whose city of Athens the Muses had ever honoured, for ingratitude in instigating the deed. Finally she confers on her son Rhesus for all time the divine honours of a hero amongst the Thracians. It seems highly probable that there was some cult of Rhesus amongst the Edonians or other Thracians of the Strymonian region to which the poet is referring. As in the *Hippolytus* he makes Artemis allude to a festival and ritual in honour of the hero of that play which most certainly did exist at Troezen, we are justified in thinking that when in the *Rhesus* he puts in the mouth of the Muse the statement that she will set up a cult of her son amongst the Thracians, the poet is referring to some well-known worship of such a hero amongst the Thracians of his own day. Nor would there be any difficulty in his having knowledge of such a shrine. The subject of the play brings it into the same category as the *Archelaus* and the *Bacchae*. But even if it were written before he took up his residence at Pella, and of this we have no certainty, those who maintain the genuineness of the play have long pointed out that its subject may have been suggested to the poet by the great developments of Athenian commerce and colonisation in Thrace, which were taking place in the poet's early days, and in consequence of this they have dated the play about 440 B.C. But it must be confessed that this argument, combined with the supposed youthful style of the play, for placing it early rather than late is not sufficient to countervail that for assigning it to his last period when he was certainly devoting himself to native Macedonian themes to be acted on the spot. It seems more probable that Euripides was influenced by this in the choice of a subject, although he might well have heard of some *heroum* in honour of Rhesus from one or other of the many Athenians who had commercial relations with Thrace, and who had lived there.

Finally, the parallel between the conclusion of this play and that of Hippolytus is in favour of the genuineness of the *Rhesus*. If our theory of the origin of tragedy is true, we can understand the introduction of the reference to the establishment of a cult of a hero which has seemed so out of place to the critics. But if the play is the work of a far later age, it is not at all so likely that the playwright would have introduced such a conclusion, rather than one more in accordance with the conventional ideas of a later period. As it stands the play is admirably adapted for an age when it was still generally felt that the true object of such works was the propitiation of heroes at their shrines. No more fitting piece than the *Rhesus* could be found for the glorification and propitiation of the spirit of Rhesus at his shrine in Thrace.

GHOSTS.

Since the tomb played so prominent a part in many of the tragedies of the three great dramatists, it would be indeed strange if the ghosts of departed heroes and of others did not form an element in dramatic representations, especially as the Greeks had no hesitation in representing in any form of art the shadowy forms of the departed, provided this was done with due limitations, to which we shall presently refer.

Three extant tragedies present us with examples of ghosts introduced as part of the dramatic machinery, though the rôles played by them in the several plays differ widely in importance. The three plays are the *Persae* and the *Eumenides* of Aeschylus and the *Hecuba* of Euripides. How Sophocles treated ghosts dramatically we have no means of judging, for no spectral personage appears in any of his extant works.

The Persae. As we have already seen (pp. 113–9), the whole action of this play, as far as it can be said to have any, centres round the tomb of Darius. But the grave does not form a mere pivot for the dramatic movement, it has a far greater importance. From it rises up the ghostly presence of the great monarch who had organised the Persian empire. His queen and the Persian elders in their perplexity and sorrow have invoked his aid, and it is his soul, revivified for the time by the drink-offerings poured into his tomb, which plays the leading rôle in the concluding part of the drama by its recital of the building of the empire, by its prediction of the disaster that the Persians are to sustain at Plataea, and finally by its directing the queen and the magnificoes to follow a policy by which Persia may avoid similar catastrophes in the future.

The Eumenides. In the *Persae* the poet employs the ghost to aid the dramatic action, but the ghost is in no wise detached from the grave where the remains of its carnal tabernacle are entombed. In the *Eumenides* he introduces the ghost of Clytemnestra with awful effect, as the spectral shape of the murdered mother, herself a murderess, appears from above the scene to hound on the Erinyes and to upbraid them for their slackness in the pursuit of Orestes. Though Clytemnestra's body lies far away in Argolis, the poet does not hesitate to detach her ghost from close attendance on her mortal remains and to represent it as coming to Athens to see that vengeance is wreaked upon her son.

The Hecuba. In the *Eumenides* the treatment of the ghost is very different from that of the spectral form of Darius in the *Persae*. Euripides goes still further in dealing with the ghost of Polydorus in the *Hecuba*, for the spectre of the ill-fated prince plays neither a leading rôle, as does that of Darius, nor is it introduced to heighten dramatic effect, as is that of Clytemnestra. The phantom of the murdered youth is only one of the puppet-speakers of the Euripidean prologues, so bitterly satirised by Aristophanes in the *Frogs* through the mouth of Aeschylus.

The Acheans on their departure from Troy had put into the Thracian Chersonese carrying with them Hecuba and the other captive Trojan women. The ghost of Polydorus appears hovering over the tent of Agamemnon, in which is his mother; he details how he, the youngest son of Priam and Hecuba, too young to take part in the defence of Troy, had been sent by his father across to his guest-friend Polymnestor, the chief of the Thracian Chersonese, and that with him was secretly despatched a great store of gold, in order that if things went ill with Troy, Priam's surviving children might not want. The boy was kindly treated so long as Troy held out, but as soon as Hector fell and all was lost, the guest-friend changed. Thirsting for the Trojan gold he scrupled not to murder his young ward and to cast his body without funeral rites into the sea. For a long time it has now been tossing to and fro in the currents of the Hellespont. For the last three days the Acheans have been encamped on the Thracian shore, stayed in their homeward course by the phantom of Achilles, which had appeared from his tomb and demanded, as his share of the spoil, that Polyxena, Hecuba's youngest daughter, should be sacrificed on his grave. Polydorus has been hovering over the tent of Agamemnon, but he will now show himself to his mother that his body may at last receive due burial rites.

It might be held by a superficial student that in these three plays we can trace the gradual extension of the use for artistic purposes of such unearthly adjuncts. It might be urged that whilst in the *Persae* the poet, in conformity to the ancient belief, employs the ghost to aid the dramatic movement without detaching it from the grave, wherein rest its material relics, in the latter part of his life he had advanced far beyond the limits of the crude old doctrine that the ghost keeps close to the spot where the body lies, and that this is clearly shown by the *Eumenides*. In that play the ghost of Clytemnestra appears far away from her grave in Argolis, revivified by no libations or prayers of invocation, like that of Darius, but fired into living force by a fierce wrath against her son. Finally it might be said that Euripides, under the disintegrating causes which were destroying ancient beliefs, had abandoned all the old conventional notions respecting disembodied spirits, and that he had therefore no hesitation in using the ghost of

Polydorus as a mere piece of mechanism to supply the audience with what corresponded to a modern programme of the play.

But the use made of the ghost in each play is not purely arbitrary, for in each case the dramatist has not overstepped the strict limits imposed by the popular beliefs respecting the spirits of the dead. In the case of Darius it would have been impossible for Aeschylus to represent his spirit as coming to Athens far away from the last resting-place of his body, or hovering, like the ghost of Polydorus over the tent of Agamemnon in the *Hecuba*. The great and good king has been gathered to his fathers full of years and honour in the due course of nature. The last rites had been paid to his remains, and the full meed of ceremonial pomp had been offered at the closing scene. Thus his soul had been enabled without let or hindrance to find entrance into the Spirit-land beyond the tomb, there to be honoured amongst the dead. His parting words indeed, as his spirit returns to the abode of disembodied souls, are pitched in the same sad note as those addressed by the shade of Achilles to Odysseus, when the latter had fared in his black ship to the asphodel mead away in the shadowy West beside the Ocean stream. "Speak not comfortably to me of death, O glorious Odysseus! Thrice rather would I be a hireling and toil for a lackland, hard-pinched wight than be king of all the dead![1]" Though Darius refers to his existence in the other world in the same joyless tone as Achilles, yet when all is said and done, the Persian king enjoys the best that can fall to human souls beneath the earth, for he himself declares that he is held in honour and treated as a prince. To have represented the soul of such a hero as capable of being detached from its mortal relics and as wandering at will through space, would have been blasphemous in the eyes of the Greeks, for this was the fate of those who had lived evil lives and died in their sins.

Plato in the *Phaedo* gives us what was probably in the main the ordinary theory of ghosts, although at the same time he engrafts on it the Theory of Ideas. Philosophy, says he, partially liberates the soul even in a man's lifetime, purifying

----

[1] *Od.* xi, 488 *sqq.*

his mind. This is evidently no new idea of Plato himself, for he compares the action of Philosophy to that of the Orphic mysteries, which purged the mind from the contagion of body and sense. If such purification has been fully achieved, the mind of the philosopher is at the moment of death thoroughly severed from the body, and passes clean away by itself into commerce with the ideas. On the contrary the soul of the ordinary man, which has undergone no purification and remains in close implication with the body, cannot get completely separated even at the moment of death, but remains encrusted and weighed down by bodily accompaniments, so as to be unfit for those regions to which mind itself naturally belongs. Such impure souls are the ghosts or shades which wallow round tombs and graves, and which are visible because they have not departed in a state of purity, but are rather charged full of the material and corporeal. They are thus not fit for separate existence, and return into fresh bodies of different species of men or animals.

The Hindus of to-day practically have the same belief, for they hold that the souls of those who die in a state of impurity or by violent deaths become *bhuts,* or malevolent demons. Such a soul reaches an additional grade of malignity, if it has been denied proper funeral ceremonies after death.

Identical with this is the mediaeval and modern European belief that ghosts are the spirits of those who have been murdered or otherwise cut off suddenly in their sins. The agonised complaint of Hamlet's father testifies to this:

> "Cut off even in the blossoms of my sin,
> Unhousel'd, disappointed, unaneal'd;
> No reckoning made, but sent to my account
> With all my imperfections on my head;
> O, horrible! O, horrible! most horrible![1]"

In the Clytemnestra of the *Eumenides* Aeschylus has given us what is in some respects a parallel to the ghost in *Hamlet.* The murderess, who up to the moment of her death had continued to live with her blood-stained paramour, had certainly

---

[1] *Hamlet*, Act i, Sc. 5.

been cut off in the blossoms of her sin, with all her imperfections on her head. Moreover, criminal as she was, she herself had met the bitter doom of death from the son that she had borne and carried at her breast. According to the belief of the Tegeatans the spirit of Scephrus, when slain by his brother Limon, could not rest but became a malignant demon bringing blight and barrenness on the land, until vengeance was taken on his brother and peculiar honours recalling his own murder and the punishment of the murderer were annually paid. Thus every Athenian present in the theatre believed that there was good reason why the spirit of Clytemnestra could not rest, but wandered far from the last abode of her body as a malignant spirit thirsting for vengeance on her son.

Accordingly when Aeschylus thus detached the ghost of Clytemnestra from her place of sepulture and introduced it with splendid effect in his drama, he was not merely following the bent of his genius and working a great artistic idea, but at the same time he was also keeping within the strict bounds of the orthodox doctrine respecting the spirits of those who had wrought great crimes and had been cut off in their sins.

We have now had examples of two types of ghosts—that of the great man, who had died in the odour of sanctity, full of years and honour: and that of a great sinner, who had met in a violent death at the hands of her own son the due reward of her crimes. In the remaining example we have a third type—that of the ghost of an innocent victim of a base crime, whose body has been denied due rites of sepulture, flung out to the winds and waves "without lament, without a grave,"—in Shakespearean language, "unhousel'd, disappointed, unaneal'd." It is thus debarred from sinking to rest once for all in the abode of spirits, never to reappear except in response to the prayers of those it loved, as in the case of Darius. Until due rites of burial shall have been given, his ghost will keep wandering as it lists to and fro detached from the festering corpse that still lies in the surge of the Thracian sea. Thus Euripides when he introduces the ghost of Polydorus as a prologue-speaker, makes the ghost only do what, according to popular belief, was quite within the bounds of possibility.

In the cases of Clytemnestra and Polydorus the ghosts are represented as appearing over the top of the scene. But if the spectre of Darius had appeared in the same quarter, as is held by some and thought possible by all writers on the Greek tragedy, and not as rising out of his tomb in answer to the libations and evocative prayers of his wife and the Persian lords, it would have been an outrage on the most sacred beliefs of the time respecting the condition of the noble army of the holy dead.

In the extant Greek tragedies there is a fourth ghost—that of Achilles in the *Hecuba* of Euripides—which appears like that of Darius from the top of the tomb. But though it plays a leading part in the development of the plot, it does not appear on the stage, and therefore it will be more appropriately treated in the section on Human Sacrifice (p. 160).

The Appeasing of the Ghost.

Libations. We have seen incidentally that the ordinary fashion in which the living sought to honour and please the dead, more especially the mighty dead, was by pouring drink offerings (πέλανος, μειλίγματα, χοαί) into a hole beside or actually communicating with the interior of the tomb. Of references by the tragedians to this practice we have already had good examples in the *Choephori* and the *Persae*, whilst Sophocles[1] and Euripides[2] frequently allude to such offerings made to the dead. For example, Eurystheus in the *Heracleidae* is made to say: "Suffer them not to let libations of blood trickle into my grave." Perhaps the most familiar form of such propitiatory drink offerings is the Athenian practice of pouring oil upon the grave-stones of their relations and others. Another method of honouring more especially the illustrious dead was by contests of naked athletes and horses near to or around the

---

[1] *Antig.* 431, 902 ; *El.* 440 etc.

[2] *Heracl.* 1040 *sqq.* ; cf. *Troad.* 381 *sqq.*; *El.* 90 ; *Or.* 96, 113 etc.; *Ph.* 940; *Iph. T.* 61, 160 ; *Alc.* 854 etc.

tomb, as in the case of Iolaus at Thebes.   To this practice
there seems to be a reference in at least one extant tragedy.
In the *Troades*[1] of Euripides, Astyanax, Hector's son, has by
a common resolve of the Greeks before they fired Troy been
flung from the battlements of that city over which, under
happier fates, he might have ruled.   His mother, Andromache,
has already been carried off to Thessaly by Neoptolemus.   But
the innocent's mangled body is handed over to his grand-
mother and the other Trojan women to receive the last
rites.   As he lies in his father's shield Hecuba utters over
him a touching speech: "'Grandam,' thou used to say, 'In
sooth I shall cut off in your honour a great lock from my curls,
and I shall bring a band of my comrades to visit your grave.'"

But in four of the extant dramas of Euripides, goddesses
and heroes cannot be appeased with ordinary offerings, but
demand the living blood of a human victim.

The Iphigenia in Tauris.   In the Tauric Chersonese
it was the custom to sacrifice all strangers at the shrine of
a heroine or goddess, whom the Greeks identified with their
own Artemis.   Orestes and Pylades went to that land in search
of Iphigenia.   They were captured and doomed to be sacrificed
and that too by the very hand of Iphigenia herself, who as
priestess of the goddess has to carry out her hideous rites.
Brother and sister are made known to each other, and instead
of sacrificing Orestes and his faithful friend, she aids them
to escape and herself accompanies them.   There is thus nothing
to harass the mind of the spectator, but the other three dramas
in which human sacrifice is a principal feature are not mere
melodramas, for in two of them at least the horrible sacrifice is
offered to the dark being that cries out for human blood, whilst
in all three cases the victim is a helpless, hapless maiden.

The Heracleidae.   In this play, the date of which is
unknown but placed by some as late as 418 B.C., though
regarded by others as amongst Euripides' earlier productions,
the sacrifice of Macaria, daughter of Heracles, to Demeter is
the turning-point in the play.

On the death of Heracles, Eurystheus had not only banished

----

[1] 1182-3.

the hero's children from Argolis, but by threats and superior power had brought about their exclusion from all the various petty states of Greece in which they had sought refuge. Iolaus, the nephew and comrade of Heracles, brings the persecuted family to Athens, imploring the aid of Demophon, the son of Theseus, who then reigned there. The herald of Eurystheus arrives to claim the refugees, but the Athenian king refuses to surrender them, in spite of the threats of war. The Argive host soon appears on the borders of Attica, and Demophon prepares to meet it. But he finds it laid down by an oracle as a condition of success that he must sacrifice to Demeter the best-born maiden. Thereupon Macaria, daughter of Heracles, offers herself as a willing victim. The armies meet, and the Argives are defeated. Eurystheus is captured and brought before Alcmena, Heracles' mother, to receive his doom. The horror of this sacrifice is in some degree mitigated by the spontaneous self-devotion of Macaria. But this element is lacking in the two remaining cases.

Iphigenia at Aulis. This play was brought out after the author's death. It opens with the detention by contrary winds of the Greek fleet at Aulis. The seer, Chalcas, has declared that Iphigenia must be sacrificed to Artemis in fulfilment of Agamemnon's vow, that he would offer to that goddess the most beautiful thing which the year of Iphigenia's birth had produced. Menelaus persuades the reluctant father, and Agamemnon sends a letter to Clytemnestra bidding her come with Iphigenia in order that the latter may be married to Achilles. But the father soon repents and sends another letter revoking the former, but this second letter is intercepted by Menelaus, who upbraids his brother with his weakness. The brothers part in anger. At this juncture Clytemnestra and her daughter suddenly arrive. At the sight of the maid Menelaus is softened, but Agamemnon points out to him that the host cannot be so easily put off, since with Chalcas and Odysseus at their head they are clamouring for the sacrifice, and he himself may fall a victim to the unreasoning fury of the commonalty.

Agamemnon then has a meeting with Clytemnestra and

Iphigenia, and urges his wife to return to Argos, but she refuses. At this moment Achilles, all unconscious of the pretended marriage, enters to inform Agamemnon of the discontent of the army at the long delay; his own Myrmidons are getting out of hand. To his astonishment Clytemnestra accosts him as her son-in-law, and thereupon explanations ensue. The old servant from whom Menelaus had taken the second letter now reveals the truth, and Achilles promises to do his best to save the maiden. At this juncture Agamemnon comes in and Clytemnestra tells him that she herself is aware of his real object. Iphigenia now knows all and implores her father to spare her, carrying in her arms her infant brother Orestes. But Agamemnon relents not. Necessity knows no law. Achilles arrives flying from his enraged followers who are resolved to have the maiden's blood. Iphigenia now resolves to devote herself, and avows her resolution to die, in order that it may be said, "This woman saved Hellas." A procession is formed to the altar of Artemis. The epilogue as it now stands describes the miraculous substitution of a deer by Artemis as a victim and the translation of Iphigenia to the Tauric Chersonese. In this play there is a partial mitigation of the horror by the final self-devotion of Iphigenia, though not to such an extent as in the *Heracleidae*.

There can be little doubt that the play was composed at the close of the poet's life. But as it was not brought out till after his death, the epilogue may have been the work of some later hand, who wished to give the play a happy ending, a fate which befell *King Lear* at the hands of Nahum Tate. But even if it be granted that the epilogue as it stands was written at a later date, it may very well embody the poet's idea. To have given the play a happy ending would have been quite in keeping with his love of melodrama, as evidenced by the *Alcestis* and the *Helena*. As in the later period of his life he abandoned the time-honoured form of the story of Helen and adopted that of Stesichorus, so in the same period he may have wished to retain the chief part of the story, but to strip it of its cruel traditional ending, as it was known to Aeschylus and the rest of antiquity. We shall soon see that although

in the first part of the fourth century B.C. there were not
wanting those in Greece, even amongst her noblest, who were
ready to resort in times of stress to human sacrifice, there were
nevertheless others openly ready to withstand such attempts
and to denounce them as hateful to the All-Father.

The Hecuba. In this play, which was certainly composed
before 423 B.C. (in which year it was ridiculed in the *Clouds*),
the tomb of Achilles though not actually seen on the stage is
the central point of the tragic interest. But this grave was no
mere figment of Euripides or any other poet. The Greeks of
all periods believed that a great barrow which stood close by
the sea near Sigeum was the veritable tomb of the Achean
hero[1]. This great sepulchre by the sea is celebrated in a
picturesque little poem in the Greek Anthology[2]:

> "'Tis brave Achilles' barrow ; th' Acheans reared it high.
> For Trojans yet unborn a terror ever nigh ;
> It looketh toward the shingle that still the moaning surge
> For sea-sprung Thetis' scion shall sing a glorious dirge."

Whether Achilles lay within or not, tradition had long
identified it with that hero. At the time when Alexander
marched to the conquest of the East it was the practice to
honour the great Achean by foot-races and offerings also.
The visit of the great Emathian conqueror to the spot is not
the least picturesque incident in his wonderful career. When
the army, destined to subdue all Asia as far as the Indus, had
been assembled at Pella and made its way to Sestos, leaving
Parmenio to superintend the embarkation, Alexander himself
went down to Elaeus at the southern end of the Thracian
Chersonese. Here stood the chapel and sacred precinct of
the hero Protesilaus, who according to legend was the first of
the Greeks to leap on Trojan soil, where he straightway met his
fate at the hands of Hector. Alexander made offerings to the
hero, praying that his own disembarkation might have a happier
issue. He then sailed across in the admiral's trireme, steering
with his own hand, to the landing-place near Ilium, called the
Harbour of the Acheans. In mid-channel he sacrificed a bull

---

[1] It was explored by Schliemann in 1879 (*Troja*), pp. 244 *sqq.*
[2] VII, 142.

with libations out of a golden goblet to Poseidon and the Nereids. Himself too in full armour was the first, like Protesilaus, to leap on the strand of Asia, but no Hector was there. Thence he mounted "wind-swept Ilium," and sacrificed to Athena, dedicating in her shrine his own panoply and taking in exchange some of the arms said to have been worn by the heroes of the Trojan War. These he caused to be carried along with him by his guards in his subsequent battles. He visited the supposed palace of Priam and the altar of Zeus Herceius, at which that unhappy old king was slain by Neoptolemus. As the latter was his own ancestor, Alexander felt himself to be the object of Priam's unappeased wrath, and accordingly made offering to his spirit at the same altar for the purpose of expiation and reconciliation. But what is much more important for our immediate purpose, the pupil of Aristotle next proceeded to the great barrow of Achilles and anointed with oil the pillar upon it, and with his companions all naked, as was the custom, he raced up to it and crowned it with a chaplet, exclaiming how blest was Achilles, who in life had a most faithful friend and in death had his exploits sung by a mighty bard[1].

The Acheans after the fall of Troy on their homeward voyage put into the Chersonese with their captives, Hecuba and the other Trojan women. The afflicted queen and mother had not yet drunk the cup of woe to the dregs, some bitter drops still remained. The *Hecuba* opens with the announcement of a new sorrow. The ghost of Achilles had appeared from his barrow at Sigeum and stayed the home-bound host of the Acheans, demanding as his share of the spoil of Troy Polyxena, the virgin daughter of Priam and Hecuba. After debate it has been resolved by the Achean host that the demand of the wraith must be gratified, and Polyxena slaughtered at the "high barrow" of the hero by his son Neoptolemus. Odysseus comes to announce the decision to the distracted mother, and Polyxena is torn from her arms. The ghastly offering to the dead must be made, and the damsel is led away to be slaughtered on the grave.

Of course the dreadful scene was not represented on

[1] Plut. *Alex.* 15; Arrian, *Anab.* I, 11; Justin, XI, 5.

the stage, any more than the actual murder of her children by Medea. But nevertheless the chief pathos of the play centres round the tomb. The herald Talthybius, when all the horror is over, comes to bid her mother give burial rites to her daughter, whose warm pure blood has been poured upon Achilles' tomb. The herald details the terrible scene. In front of the barrow stood the Achean host. Neoptolemus took the noble maiden by the hand and led her to the summit of the howe, and with him went none but the chieftains, the herald himself and some chosen youths, whose horrid task. was to restrain the struggles of the victim. The herald proclaimed silence to the host, and then Neoptolemus raised on high a golden cup and prayed to his father that he would receive the propitiatory libation and " come to drink the dark fresh blood of the maiden "; that his wrath may thus be assuaged, and that he will permit the Acheans to loose from their moorings and fare homeward. As he prayed, the whole of that great host repeated the response. Then he drew from its scabbard a gold-mounted sword, and made a sign to the chosen youths to seize the maid. She saw the sign and said: "O ye Argives, that have destroyed my native land, willingly I die. Let no one touch me, for with good courage I will lay bare my neck. In heaven's name leave me free that thus in freedom I may die, for a king's daughter I am. It shames me to be called a slave amongst the dead." The hosts murmured in assent and king Agamemnon bade the young men loose her. As soon as she heard the order, she rent her vest and laid bare her neck and breast, beautiful as though wrought in marble, and invited Neoptolemus to deal the fatal blow. He, though faltering for pity of the maid, dealt her the death stroke.

It may be possible to see in the treatment of human sacrifice in these three plays a gradual movement in the poet's mind, which perhaps was the reflection of the general tendency of the day. In the *Hecuba*, which may very well be the earliest of the three, there is little or no mitigation of the horror. Polyxena indeed is not slaughtered before the audience, but Talthybius gives a minute and graphic picture of the dreadful spectacle. As has been well remarked, it is only in the willing resignation and noble resolution with which Polyxena meets her fate that we have any alleviation of the pain which we feel in common with Hecuba.

In the *Heracleidae*, which may very possibly be some years later than the *Hecuba*, the pity and horror excited in the audience is mitigated by the spontaneous self-devotion of Macaria, who in order to save her brothers and sisters offers herself, all unprompted, as a willing victim.

In the *Iphigenia*, which is beyond all doubt the latest of the three, if the epilogue was either composed by Euripides himself, or, though written at a later date, embodied his own ending, we have not merely a substantial mitigation of the horror, but in the happy ending find a tragedy turned into a melodrama. The feelings of the audience have indeed been harried by the vain pleading of the maiden for pity, and they have seen her depart in the procession to be the victim on the altar of Artemis. But there is no description of the closing scene. On the contrary, instead of a messenger coming and describing her sacrifice, the epilogue gives instant relief to the high-wrought feelings of the spectators by announcing that the goddess has at the last moment found a deer as a substitute, as Jehovah supplied a ram in the story of Abraham and Isaac.

It may be urged that although human sacrifices had been commonly offered in all parts of Greece by them of old time to angry deities and to the spirits of the savage dead, yet at the date when Euripides introduced such themes into his plays, he was only reviving for dramatic purposes the shadowy traditions of a long vanished past. But was this really so? It is easy to show that human sacrifices, such as those dramatised by Euripides, were actually performed within historic times in Greece. Thus in the First Messenian War, Aristodemus, the Messenian hero, offered his daughter in sacrifice, as did Agamemnon in the *Iphigenia*. Again Aristomenes, the bulwark of Messenia in her second struggle against Sparta, is said to have sacrificed five hundred prisoners to the deity of Mount Ithome, whom the Greeks of a later age designated as Zeus. But it may be said that these occurred at a period which can hardly be called classical. Yet down to the second century after Christ the

Lycaean Mount in Arcadia was year by year the scene of a horrid rite, the foundation of which was ascribed to the ancient king Lycaon. To propitiate the dark spirit of the spot he sacrificed to it a human babe on the altar, which in later times was termed that of Lycaean Zeus. "And they say that immediately after the sacrifice Lycaon was turned into a wolf[1]."

"On the topmost peak of the mountain," says Pausanias[2], "is the altar of Lycaean Zeus in the shape of a mound of earth. On this they offer secret sacrifices to Lycaean Zeus, but I did not care to pry into the details of the sacrifice. Be it as it is and as it has been from the beginning." But it may be urged that although in wild and savage Arcadia and in Messenia human sacrifice might be practised, yet in the more advanced communities of Hellas—Athens, Thebes or Sparta—such awful rites had ceased from a remote age. Yet we must sorrowfully confess that the facts of history are against this idea. Of all the great names connected with the story of the glorious rise of Athens, that of Themistocles stands first. It was he who foresaw the possibility of a naval dominion for Athens, and that the time was not far distant when she might have to depend for safety on her "wooden walls," and it was his wisdom and eloquence that persuaded the Athenians to expend on the building of a navy the silver of the mines of Laurium, hitherto squandered in popular doles. When the stress and panic of Xerxes' invasion fell upon the Greeks, it was he who counselled them to meet the Persian fleet at Artemisium, and it was his energy and surpassing ability that induced the allied squadrons to make that stand in the narrow strait of Salamis that wrought the salvation of Greece. Yet on the very eve of that great day this man, the foremost of his age, brave in battle as wise in council, offered three Persian captives to Dionysus the Cannibal[3]. But it was not merely the highest minds of the first part of the fifth century B.C. that were ready to resort to human sacrifice in seasons of danger and anxiety. On the eve of the battle of Leuctra in B.C. 371 the Spartan and

---

[1] Paus. VIII, 2, 3.   [2] VIII, 38, 7.

[3] Plut. *Pelop.* 20 *sq.*: τοὺς ὑπὸ Θεμιστοκλέους σφαγιασθέντας ὠμηστῇ Διονύσῳ πρὸ τῆς ἐν Σαλαμῖνι ναυμαχίας.

Theban armies lay right opposite each other. In the plain of
Leuctra were the graves of the daughters of Scedasus, who were
called the Maids of Leuctra, for on that spot they had been
outraged and done to death by Spartan strangers, and there
too were they buried. Their father went to Sparta demanding
retribution, but failed to get any atonement for this atrocious
crime. He returned home and calling down curses upon the
Spartans, he slew himself upon his daughters' grave. Oracles
and old saws had warned the Spartans to beware of the wrath
of the Maidens of Leuctra, though there was a doubt as to what
place was meant, since there was a little seaside village of that
name in Laconia, and a large town in Arcadia. It was many a
year before the battle of Leuctra that the outrage was perpe-
trated. On the night before that decisive struggle, Pelopidas[1],
the liberator of Thebes, and one of the loftiest spirits of ancient
Greece, was sore troubled by a vision. He dreamed that he
saw the daughters of Scedasus wailing round their graves and
hurling malisons against the Spartans, and that Scedasus called
upon him for the sacrifice of a fair-haired virgin ($\pi\alpha\rho\theta\acute{\epsilon}\nu\sigma\nu$
$\xi\alpha\nu\theta\acute{\eta}\nu$) to his daughters, if he wished for victory on the
morrow. Perturbed by this strange and unrighteous behest,
he arose and told his vision to the soothsayers and his fellow
generals. Some held that he must not disregard it, and
adduced precedents from olden time, such as the sacrifice of
Menoeceus, the son of Creon, and of Macaria, the daughter of
Heracles, and in modern times that of Pherecydes the
philosopher, put to death by the Spartans, and whose skin
in obedience to an oracle was carefully kept by the Spartan
kings. They pointed out also how Leonidas had sacrificed himself to save Hellas. Moreover, said they, Themistocles offered
human victims to the Cannibal Dionysus before the battle of
Salamis. In all these cases, they asserted, success had justified
the deed. On the other hand there was the case of Agesilaus,
who when starting like Agamemnon from Aulis to Asia, though
the goddess claimed his daughter as a victim, had refused to
offer her up. His tender-heartedness eventuated in the disgrace
and defeat of his expedition. But others sought to dissuade

---

[1] Plut. *Pelop.* 21 *sqq.*

Pelopidas from this course, urging that no celestial being desired so barbarous and revolting a sacrifice. "The world," cried they, "is not ruled by Giants and Titans, but by the Father of all, both gods and men. Just as foolish was it to suppose that the spirits (δαίμονες) took delight in human blood and gore. If there are such, we must disregard them as being impotent, for it is in consequence of the feebleness and wretchedness of their souls that such outrageous and savage desires are implanted and abide in them." As the captains were thus disputing and Pelopidas was sore perplexed, a filly from a troop of horses came galloping through the army, and halted right before the chiefs. Her bright yellow mane and tail, her fine action, her high spirit, and her bold whinnying were manifest to all. Theocritus the prophet took all in at a glance, and cried to Pelopidas, "Here is the victim that thou wantest. Why wait for another virgin? Take thou and use God's gift." In a trice they seized the poor filly, led her to the maidens' barrow, recited over her the prayer of consecration, crowned her with a garland, and cut her in pieces. With a deep sense of relief, they spread through the camp the news of Pelopidas' dream and how they had offered the sacrifice.

We abhor all animal sacrifice as we think of the beautiful chestnut[1] filly, at one moment exulting in her youth and freedom, next seized by a grim band of high-wrought men, and slaughtered on the maidens' grave. But all honour to the good seer Theocritus, whose righteous heart and quick wit in pointing out a substitute, beyond all doubt averted the sacrifice of some noble yellow-haired Theban maiden. Had he not pointed to the filly, a deed as dreadful as the legendary immolation of Iphigenia by the fear-ridden kings at Aulis would have been wrought. The poor filly by her untimely death redeemed from slaughter a more precious life, as in the epilogue of the *Iphigenia* that heroine was saved by the miraculous substitution of a deer. No wonder that Lucretius burst into fierce denunciations against the ancient creed which manifested itself in such deeds as these:

quod contra saepius illa
religio peperit scelerosa atque impia facta.

[1] Ridgeway, *Origin and Influence of the Thoroughbred Horse*, p. 300.

Aulide quo pacto Triveai uirginis aram
Iphianassai turparunt sanguine foede
ductores Danaum delecti prima uirorum[1].

From the evidence just adduced there can be no doubt that
even in the fifth and fourth centuries before Christ, the foremost
minds in the leading states of Greece were ready to resort to
human sacrifice in times of exceptional anxiety and peril.
Accordingly when Aeschylus referred to the sacrifice of
Iphigenia, Sophocles to that of Menoeceus, and Euripides
made such offerings the leading theme in three of his extant
plays, they were not alluding to or utilizing for mere dramatic
effect a practice from which the Greek conscience had long
revolted and which only survived in old wives' legends.
Aeschylus himself had fought on the ship of his brave
brother Ameinias in the great battle in the Strait, and like
every other in the fleet he knew well that Themistocles had
sacrificed three human victims to a god. In that same year
Sophocles, a youth of sixteen summers, had formed one of the
chorus of Ephebi that danced round the altar in celebration of
the great deliverance, and there was not one of those that
danced, or of that great multitude who looked on and
rejoiced, who was not well aware of the horrid prelude to
the great victory. On the day of the battle the parents of
Euripides in the isle of Salamis itself watched anxiously the
issue. There they, like many another Athenian, had sought
refuge from the Persian, and there too. that same year was
Euripides born. As he grew up to boyhood, and listened while
men and women talked of the dark days when the Persians
occupied Athens, of the awful suspense of the night before the
battle, and told their children the story of the great naval
triumph, the sacrifice to Dionysus must have been a familiar
theme.

Thus to all the great dramatists human sacrifice was
no mere misty legend, but a grim and dreadful reality. And
if this was so with the authors, no less was it with their
audience. Every one in the theatre who listened to the
recital of the sacrifice of Polyxena knew that human sacrifice

[1] I, 82–6.

was a living practice. At Athens indeed it might only be resorted to in times of peculiar peril, but they well knew that
in many parts of Greece, in Arcadia, Chios, Tenedos, Cyprus,
year by year human victims were offered to gods or heroes.
For each one then in that great audience the story of the
slaying of Polyxena had a realism impossible for the modern.
In the *Heracleidae*, as we have seen, the horror is mitigated
by the voluntary self-devotion of Macaria for the deliverance of
her own family, whilst in the *Iphigenia at Aulis*, though the
horror is intensified by the girl's pleading for her life, yet there
is some little mitigation in her final resolve to die willingly for
Greece, but much more in the epilogue by which the play is
turned into a melodrama, all ending happily by the substitution
of a deer as the victim. In each of these two plays the audience
was not harrowed by any recital of the act of sacrifice, but this
we have to the full in the *Hecuba*. If the poet in the two
former plays was careful not to exhibit or describe through the
mouth of an eye-witness the closing scene of the horrid rite,
why had he less scruple in the case of Polyxena? But to the
average Athenian of the fifth century B.C. the case of Polyxena
differed essentially from those of the other two heroines. The
latter were free maidens offered to appease an angry deity on
behalf of their own kin. But in an age of universal slavery,
when the captive purchased from the slave-dealer was as much
a chattel as any sheep or goat, the sacrifice of a slave-girl to
propitiate a mighty Greek warrior excited no great repugnance
in the audience. The difference between slave and free is
brought out clearly in Polyxena's entreaty that she be left
unbound and permitted to die free, and not in bonds. But
though the fate of Polyxena and her noble bearing may have
excited pity and fear in the Athenian mind, the fact that she
was an alien and a captive moderated the horror which the
story of Talthybius might have otherwise roused. When we
once place ourselves at the standpoint of the Athenian
audience, we can understand why Euripides did not hesitate
to give in all fulness of detail the sacrifice of Polyxena, and
why that audience were not harrowed at its recital. Themistocles
had offered Persian captives to Dionysus, and why should not

the Acheans have sacrificed a captive Trojan to the mighty son
of Thetis?

By the time of Euripides and certainly by the first part of
the following century, there were many in Greece who abhorred
such rites. But no real change in the moral attitude towards
this dreadful practice could be effected while animal sacrifice
in any form survived. So long as the slaying of cattle and
sheep continued to be an essential part of the religious life,
there lurked in the hearts of the masses, as at this present hour
in West Africa and in many parts of Asia, an ineradicable belief
that of all sacrifices to appease an angry spirit a human life was
the most effectual. In the forepart of the first century of our
era the Galilean had commenced his career of conquest over
cruelty—the cruelty of man who too often ascribed a cruelty
like or worse than his own to his god—that cruelty which by
the daily slaughter of oxen and sheep still made the courts of
Jehovah reek like the shambles. Yet centuries earlier some
Psalmist had sung, "Thinkest thou that I will eat bulls' flesh
or drink the blood of goats?" The Hebrews had as a whole
ceased from passing their sons and their daughters through the
fire, and from giving the "seed of their bodies for the sin of their
souls." But more than a century after the death of Christ, year
by year as the seasons revolved, some helpless babe, snatched
from a wretched mother's breast, warmed with its young life-
blood the altar of the Arcadian Moloch. Such hideous rites
were only to disappear from Greece when Christianity had
abolished for ever all animal sacrifice by the far-reaching
doctrine that its Founder's blood had once for all appeased
the anger of the All-Father. But the deep-rooted belief in
the efficacy of human blood still lingers in Christianity, though
robbed of its cruelty, it is true. Spiritualised and etherialised,
it still rings out in the last agony of despairing Faustus.

> See where Christ's blood streams in the firmament!
> One drop of blood will save me.

THE SANCTUARY.

In certain Greek tragedies, where a tomb is represented
on the stage, there are no libations offered nor *kommoi* sung.

Nevertheless the sepulchre plays a very important part. In the *Helena* of Euripides, as we have already seen (p. 137), that heroine, in order to escape from the importunities of Theoclymenus, son of king Proteus, takes refuge at the tomb of that old king which stood in front of his palace. When Menelaus arrives, he finds Helen seated at or, far less likely, within the tomb of Proteus[1]. They do not as yet recognise each other, but Menelaus asks her why she is seated at the railing of the tomb. Later on when the *Recognition* takes place, Helen says to him: "This tomb protects as though it were a temple of the gods[2]." Afterwards[3] Menelaus prays to Proteus: "O aged one, inhabiter of this sepulchre of stone, restore to me my spouse whom Zeus sent hither for thee to hold in ward."

Though Aristophanes in his *Thesmophoriazusae*[4] ridicules Euripides for this passage and makes one of the women reproach him for speaking of a tomb as though it were an altar of the gods, we cannot doubt that Euripides made no innovation by making his heroine take sanctuary at the grave of Proteus. He simply adapted for dramatic purposes the immemorial doctrine and practice of his race. In this matter at least Aeschylus is most certainly with him, since in the *Choephori*[5] the Chorus declare that they reverence the tomb of Agamemnon as if it were an altar.

There can be no doubt that the principle of the sanctuary which has played so important a part in a certain stage of legal institutions—Christian as well as Greek and Hebrew—had its root in the primitive veneration and fear of the wrath of the dead man in his tomb; for it was a supreme matter of belief that the spirits of the departed within their graves were cognisant of and took a concern in the affairs of their families and people, and that in times of danger they could and would assist their kin if properly approached. It followed that if in the hour of extreme peril man or woman took refuge

[1] 547.   [2] 797.   [3] 961 *sqq.*
[4] 887:   κακῶς ἄρ' ἐξόλοιο κἀξολεῖ γ' ἔτι,
           ὅστις γε τολμᾶς σῆμα τὸν βωμὸν καλεῖν.
[5] 104.

at the tomb of some one who had been great and powerful in life, his spirit would protect them and wreak vengeance on the pursuer, should he seek to slay the suppliant at the grave or drag him thence to perpetrate the deed elsewhere.

We have already seen in the *Suppliants* of Aeschylus, that the daughters of Danaus and their father on their arrival in Argolis take sanctuary on a great tumulus which stands in the forefront of the scene. On this barrow are *xoana* of Zeus, Apollo, Poseidon and Hermes, and in front of it is an altar. As before pointed out Dionysus is not included amongst these deities "who preside over contests," and accordingly the *thymele* in this play is not his altar. The Danaides invoke first the aid of the gods above, secondly that of the dead beneath in the earth lying in their graves, as exactors of heavy retribution; and finally they call upon Zeus the Saviour. Here as in the *Helena* a sepulchre is regarded as an inviolable sanctuary, but in this case the cults and images of various gods have been superimposed upon the barrow and on the worship of the dead within. Here we have the transition from the simple sanctuary consisting of a chieftain's grave, such as that of Proteus, to that formed by some shrine or temple of the heavenly gods. It is easy to show that Euripides and Aeschylus are faithfully reproducing the belief and practice of their time. It is needless to adduce fresh parallels for worship at the grave of a hero and for the belief in his power to exact heavy vengeance, for that has been already amply shown in the case of Scephrus at Tegea. Now in that very town was one of the most venerated sanctuaries in all Hellas, the temple of the being known as Athena Alea. "From of old," says Pausanias[1], "this sanctuary had been looked upon with awe and veneration by the whole of Peloponnese and it afforded the surest protection to all that took refuge in it. This was shown by the Lacedaemonians in the case of Pausanias and of Leotychides before him, and by the Argives in the case of Chrysis; for while these persons remained in the sanctuary, neither Lacedaemonians nor Argives would so much as demand their surrender." The goddess so dreaded was not really

[1] iii, 5, 6.

Athena, but the ancient Arcadian heroine Alea, upon whose cult that of the goddess Athena had been superimposed in later time, just as that of Zeus had overlaid that of Amphiaraus at Oropus, that of Trophonius at Lebadea, and that of Agamemnon in the Troad. In this shrine of Athena Alea we have the full absorption of the ancient heroic personage buried there into one of the great divinities, the completion of the earlier stage of which we have seen in the case of the great barrow in the *Supplices* of Aeschylus, where the images of the gods are placed on the mound, but the dead in their graves beneath are still invoked separately.

There can be no doubt that the Christian sanctuaries of mediaeval times are the lineal descendants of those of pagan days, for the saint in his shrine, be it lowly chapel or stately cathedral, is simply the old hero under a new name. The fugitive who could clutch the great knocker on the north door of Durham Cathedral had reached a haven of safety, for the pursuer who would slay him or drag him thence must reckon with the wrath of S. Cuthbert. But as in mediaeval times such sanctuaries, for example Westminster, became abused and proved the asylum of all sorts of malefactors and criminals, and thus became a real danger to the community, so was it in the Greek world also. The story of the great temple of Artemis at Ephesus and that of Apollo in Branchidae are very similar to that of Athena Alea at Tegea. It is absolutely certain that the shrine of Apollo was originally that of the hero Branchus, the eponymous hero of the clan of the Branchidae, under whose control the oracle remained, even after the Greek colonists had come and the cult of Apollo had been grafted on that of the native hero. Although we know not the name of the local heroine at Ephesus, there can be little doubt that the worship of Artemis had been imposed on the shrine of a native divinity, just as it had been on that of Orthia at Sparta and as that of Athena had overlaid the cult of Alea at Tegea. It is more than likely that the great shrine of Diana of the Ephesians owed no small part of its fame and popularity throughout all western Asia Minor to the fact that it had an asylum of a most inviolate kind. The boundaries of the

sanctuary had been gradually widened[1]. Alexander the Great
extended them to a stadion; later came Mithridates and he,
like Alexander, wishing to gain the favour of the priests,
pushed still further the limits of asylum. He shot an arrow
from an angle of the temple roof, and it was held that it flew
beyond the stade and the limit was accordingly advanced.
Mark Antony went still further and doubled the extent,
thereby including in the sacred precinct a portion of the city.
But this proved a curse for it benefited none but criminals,
and accordingly Augustus abolished this last extension.

But it is not only in the *Helena* that Euripides makes use
of a sanctuary for a heroine in distress. In the *Hercules
Furens*, when Lichas seized Thebes in the absence of that hero,
Megara, the wife of the latter, took sanctuary with her three
sons at the altar of Zeus the Saviour. So in the *Andromache*
that hapless heroine, who is still buffeted by storms of calamity,
in order to escape death at the hands of Hermione, the daughter
of Menelaus and wife of Neoptolemus, takes sanctuary at the
altar of Thetis. But when her relentless enemies learn the
place of concealment of her child and threaten to put it to
death unless she surrenders herself, she leaves the altar and
resigns herself to her fate.

The evidence which I have adduced makes it clear that
when the dramatists represent some of their characters as
flying for refuge to tombs of heroes and altars of gods, they
are inventing no new expedient, but are simply employing for
dramatic purposes a practice of peculiar and immemorial
sanctity in Greece, and which had arisen solely out of the
worship of the dead. Neglect of this fundamental element
in Greek life and its concomitants has led to a mistake respecting the true scene of the trial of Orestes in the *Eumenides*.

The scene of the second act of the Eumenides[2].
It will at once be said, What objections are there to the
traditional view—that Orestes found sanctuary on the Acropolis

---

[1] Strabo, 547, 1 *sqq.* (Didot).

[2] This section is mainly reprinted from the *Classical Review*, 1907, vol. xxi,
pp. 163–8. There is a summary in *Jour. Hell. Stud.*, 1907, vol. xxvii,
pp. 56–8.

and that his trial took place upon the Hill of Ares? The former was the most famous spot in Athens, and on it stood the Erechtheum, the oldest temple of Athena, already famous in Homeric days. Yet the difficulties of this view will be obvious as soon as they are stated. In the first place, though there were in Athens four localities all intimately associated with trials of persons charged with homicide, not one of these was situated on the Acropolis, though, it is true, weapons and other inanimate objects which had shed the blood of men or of oxen were tried in the Prytaneum, the ancient residence of the Archon Eponymus on the north slope of the Acropolis. Secondly, though in the play Orestes is represented as taking sanctuary at a shrine of Pallas, and as clasping in his arms her ancient βρέτας, there is not the slightest evidence that any image of the goddess Athena on the Acropolis, whether ancient or recent, offered an asylum to those who fled before the avenger of blood. Thirdly, in the play the goddess is always termed Pallas by the Pythian Priestess, by Apollo, and by the Furies in dialogue, though on two occasions Orestes does certainly address her as Athena, and she is so termed by the Furies twice in choral parts. Yet we know for certain, both by literary tradition and from inscriptions, that the goddess who dwelt in "the strong house of Erechtheus" on the Acropolis was never called *Pallas,* but was invariably known either as *the Polias,* or as Athena (or Athenaia) Polias[1].

On the other hand I propose to show that (1) there was a very ancient tribunal (if not the most ancient at Athens) for cases of homicide, more especially for that class of homicide to which Orestes pleaded guilty, situated outside the city wall to the south-east of the Acropolis; (2) that there was here a most ancient wooden image (ξόανον) to which those whose hands were reddened with the blood of their fellow men might fly to avoid the instant vengeance of the pursuer; and (3) that this image was never known by the name of Athena or Athenaia, but always by that of Pallas or Palladion.

Now as there were five different localities in or near Athens closely connected from of old with trials for bloodshed, it is

---

[1] Cf. Frazer's note on Paus. I, 26, 5.

most unlikely that Aeschylus would in this play lay the scene
of the trial at any spot other than one of those associated
in the popular mind from time immemorial with the trial
of homicide. This is all the more unlikely since he represents
the first tribunal for that crime as instituted to try Orestes,
whilst he also refers to the establishment on the Hill of Ares
of a great council (βουλευτήριον) which was not only to try
cases of deliberate murder, but also to keep ward and control
over the public morals[1].

Down to the time of Pausanias[2] (A.D. 180) there still
survived at Athens five tribunals for cases of bloodshed.
(1) There was the Areopagus, which sat on the famous hill
that rises on the west over against the Acropolis. Here were
tried cases of deliberate murder, wounding with malice, arson,
and poisoning. (2) To the south-east of the Acropolis, outside
the wall, lay an ancient shrine called the Palladion, so named
from a venerable image of Pallas, which tradition variously
declared to have been brought from Ilium, or to have fallen
from heaven, or else to have been set up by Athena in her
repentance for having killed her playmate Pallas. Here sat
the court known as the τὸ ἐπὶ Παλλαδίῳ, where were tried
those who had committed involuntary homicide (τοῖς ἀποκτεί-
νασιν ἀκουσίως). "Nobody denies that Demophon was the
first person tried here," but there is a difference of opinion as
to the crime for which he was tried, i.e. whether it was for
killing Argives by mistake, or for accidentally trampling
an Athenian under his horse's feet in the dark. (3) There
was the court known as the Delphinion, also situated on the
east side· of the Acropolis and outside the city wall. It
was a shrine of Apollo of Delphi, and in it were tried cases
of justifiable homicide, e.g. him who had slain an adulterer
taken in the act. "On such a plea Theseus was acquitted

---

[1] *Eum.* 684 *sqq.*:

> κλύοιτ' ἂν ἤδη θεσμόν, 'Αττικὸς λεώς,
> πρώτας δίκας κρίνοντες αἵματος χυτοῦ.
> ἔσται δὲ καὶ τὸ λοιπὸν Αἰγέως στρατῷ
> ἀεὶ δικαστῶν τοῦτο βουλευτήριον.

[2] I, 28, 8–12.

when he had slain the rebel Pallas and his sons. But the custom was in former days, before the acquittal of Theseus, that every manslayer either fled the country, or, if he stayed, was slain even as he slew." Yet it will soon be seen that the court probably owed its name to an older legend. (4) At Phreattys, on a tongue of land projecting into the sea at Zea, was held a court to try any manslayer who, during his period of exile, might have committed another crime of the same character. The judges sat on the shore, whilst the accused was literally docked in a boat moored off the beach, that he might not pollute with the miasma of his guilt the land of Attica. (5) In the Prytaneum, as already stated, were tried weapons, especially the axe with which was slain the ox at the Buphonia.

If it be said that Pausanias does not refer to the trial of Orestes as having taken place at the Palladion, and consequently that this shrine cannot be its true scene, I may at once point out that there is the same objection to the Areopagus, for Pausanias[1] says that that court was first established to try Ares for the murder of Halirrhothius, and makes no mention of the trial of Orestes at all.

Aeschylus gives us a totally different account of the establishment of the first tribunal for manslayers, but as he wrote some six centuries and a half before Pausanias, we are justified in assuming that his statement represents a far older legend than that of the later writer, and accordingly we may leave on one side the latter's account of the first cases supposed to have been tried at the Palladion, the Delphinion, and the Areopagus. Originally the judges in all these five courts for bloodshed were the ancient body called the Ephetae. The King Archon presided and probably with the fifty Ephetae made up the Fifty and One, a term by which the body was likewise known. According to Pollux[2] the Ephetae were constituted by Draco. Up to that time the Basileus had investigated and tried all cases of bloodshed, but Draco referred

---

[1] I, 28, 5.

[2] VIII, 120: for an excellent summary of the evidence relating to the Ephetae see Dr Sandys' note on Arist. *Ath. Pol.* c. 57.

such to the Fifty and One, and to this system of reference Pollux ascribes the origin of their name Ephetae. But like so many other provisions in Draco's enactments the body had only been reconstituted, having really existed from time immemorial. The fact that they were selected on the ground of high birth (ἀριστίνδην αἱρεθέντας) of itself indicates that they were a survival from oligarchic and monarchical times. It is highly probable that in the Ephetae presided over by the Archon Basileus (himself the shadow of the ancient king), we have the survival of the ancient Gerousia or Boule. This view will be found to be quite in accord with certain statements of Aeschylus.

By Solon's reforms the Ephetae were replaced on the Areopagus by a body consisting of ex-archons, though jurisdiction in the minor courts was still left to them. Aristotle [1] speaks as if they still continued to sit in these tribunals down to his day, but there is evidence that by the end of the fifth century B.C. ordinary dicasts sat in the Delphinion and Palladion, for we hear of seven hundred dicasts, a number inconsistent with the Fifty and One. Pollux [2] tells us that gradually the tribunal of the Ephetae was laughed to death.

It is clear that with the courts of Phreattys and of the Prytaneum we have nothing to do in our present inquiry. The Areopagus, the Palladion, and the Delphinion therefore remain as the three possible scenes for the asylum and trial of Orestes, unless we make the wild assumption that the dramatist laid the scene of the trial at some spot never associated either in fact or tradition with trials for homicide. It is useless to urge that the dramatists are not at all particular as to the spot in which a scene is laid. For though this may be so when an Attic dramatist is composing a play the scene of which is laid at Troy, at Argos, or at Thebes, he certainly would not expose himself to ridicule and criticism from his Attic audience when dramatising a legend which was indissolubly bound up with one of the courts established for homicide, the very origin of which was ascribed to the trial of Orestes.

Let us consider what are the conditions required for the

---

[1] *Ath. Pol.* c. 57.   [2] VIII, 125.

spot where Orestes was tried. First of all there must be a most ancient image of the goddess. Secondly, it must be an image to which manslayers actually fled as suppliants when they could plead that the act was involuntary, as urged by Orestes in his own defence, or that it was justifiable, as was pleaded on his behalf by Apollo. Thirdly, this image ought to bear the name of Pallas and not that of Athena, for Apollo at Delphi orders Orestes to " go to the city of Pallas and take your suppliant seat there embracing in your arms her ancient image. And there having judges to decide on these matters, and arguments in mitigation of your crime, we will find means to relieve you from your troubles, for it was even in obedience to me that you slew that body which gave you birth." Then Apollo tells the Eumenides that Pallas will see justice done at the trial of Orestes. Fourthly, on that spot ought to sit the most ancient tribunal for trying homicide that was known at Athens, for Athena declares that the case of Orestes is too serious for one to decide, and therefore she will institute a *thesmos* to deal with such cases, who are to be the noblest of her citizens[1]. These last words seem especially to apply to the Ephetae, who, as we have just seen, were chosen ἀριστίνδην. Moreover, when Athena says that the case of Orestes is too great for one to decide, we seem to have a direct allusion to the tradition preserved in Pollux that " in old days the king heard cases of bloodshed, but that Draco established the court of Ephetae." Furthermore, this oldest court for homicide cannot be one for deliberate murder, but only for the trials of those who could plead extenuating circumstances.

Let us examine the respective claims of all the three competitors beginning with the Delphinion. As this was the shrine of the Apollo of Delphi, it is inconceivable that there would be in it a most ancient image of Pallas, such as that at which Orestes took sanctuary and which he clasped in his arms. For assuredly the object of adoration in the Delphinion would have been a statue of Apollo and not that of the goddess. Moreover, this shrine of Apollo was not an immemorial place of veneration, as is fully shown by its name,

[1] *Eum.* 465: κρίνασα δ' ἀστῶν τῶν ἐμῶν τὰ βέλτατα.

for it represents that particular form of cult connected with Apollo at Delphi, and accordingly we must regard it as adventitious at Athens. As Apollo based his defence of Orestes on the ground that he was justified in slaying his mother to avenge his father, it would appear that trials of those who pleaded justification for their shedding of blood, such as those who had slain an adulterer taken in the act, or those who had slain others in self-defence, as in the mythical case of Theseus, were associated with this shrine, because Apollo was supposed to have first laid down at Athens in the case of Orestes the principle that intentional homicide could be justified.

Let us now turn to the court of the Palladion. (1) Here stood the most ancient image of which we have any account in Athens. According to the legend given by Pausanias[1] " after the capture of Ilion Diomede was sailing homeward, and night having fallen when they arrived off Phalerum, the Argives disembarked, as in an enemy's country, taking it in the dark for some land other than Attica. Hereupon Demophon being also unaware that the men from the ships were Argives came out against them and slew some of them, and carried off the Palladion." Another legend says that the image had fallen from heaven upon the hill of Ate, whilst still another story says that Athena slew her playmate Pallas and erected an image of her. The Palladion had closed eyes, and was a type essentially different from that of the statues of Athena.

(2) Each year the Ephebi carried the image out of its shrine to Phalerum to the sea and back again with torches and every form of pomp[2]. The Nomophylakes marshalled the procession[3]. Doubtless the image was taken down to the sea to be laved in the sea-water, in order to remove the pollution which during the previous year it might have contracted from the embraces of those who, like Orestes, had taken refuge and clasped it in their arms. That the object in bringing the

---

[1] loc. cit.

[2] C. I. A. II, 469, 10: ἐπειδὴ οἱ ἔφηβοι...ἐξήγαγον δὲ καὶ τὴν Παλλάδα κἀκεῖθεν πάλιν συνεισήγαγον μετὰ φωτός, μετὰ πάσης εὐκοσμίας (cf. C. I. A. II, 471, 11).

[3] Suidas, p. 1273: οἱ δὲ νομοφύλακες τῇ Παλλάδι τὴν πομπὴν ἐκόσμουν ὅτε κομίζοιτο τὸ ξόανον ἐπὶ τὴν θάλασσαν.

statue down to the sea was to wash it from all impurity is rendered clear by the passage in the *Iphigenia in Tauris*[1], where Iphigenia effects the escape of Orestes, Pylades and herself by telling Thoas the Tauric king that it was necessary to purify the image of Artemis from the miasma of Orestes and Pylades not by fresh water, but by sea-water, "for the sea washes away all human pollution." We need therefore have no doubt that the Palladion was used from time immemorial as a sanctuary in which those whose hands were red with human blood took refuge. (3) In it sat the Ephetae, who had once sat even on the Areopagus until Solon had replaced them by a body of ex-archons.

(4) There is not the slightest evidence that trials for deliberate murder ever took place here, for they would seem from their first institution to have been held on the Areopagus. Of course it may be said, if the trials for wilful murder were held from the first on that famous spot, then that must have been the oldest court for homicide, since deliberate murder was the most serious offence, and for it a tribunal would be first erected. But this is a complete misconception of the evolution of the law of trial for murder at Athens and in many other places. We are told by Aeschylus[2], and Pausanias (*supra*) repeats the same tradition, that in old days at Athens prevailed the stern rule, that whoso had shed man's blood, whether accidentally, justifiably, or wilfully, should be slain even as he slew.

This was exactly the same doctrine as that held by the Semites on the other side of the Mediterranean. Amongst the latter we have the clearest proof that the first step in any modification of the custom by which the avenger of blood was permitted to kill the manslayer, no matter whether the latter had slain his victim by accident or design, was the establishment of sanctuaries. Such were the six cities of Refuge enjoined by Jehovah through the mouth of Moses. "That

---

[1] Eur. *Iph. Taur.* 1193: κλύζει θάλασσα πάντα τἀνθρώπων κακά. Cf. Farnell, *Cults of Greek States*, vol. I, p. 304.

[2] *Choeph.* 305:   δράσαντι παθεῖν
    τριγέρων μῦθος τάδε φωνεῖ.

the manslayer may flee thither, which killeth any person at
unawares (ἀκουσίως). They shall be unto you cities of refuge
from the avenger; that the manslayer die not, until he stand
before the congregation in judgment[1]." If he could show that
he had shed blood unwittingly, he was spared and there he
dwelt until the death of the High Priest at Jerusalem. It
will be observed that the manslayer was tried at the asylum
where he had taken refuge, not brought somewhere else to be
tried. This was but natural, seeing that if he once quitted his
sanctuary he was liable to be slain by the avenger at any
moment. The Semitic practice gives us the clue to the various
steps in the evolution of the law of homicide at Athens. Here
as in Palestine the ancient custom was that the slayer should
be slain. As the first relaxation of this merciless rule was the
establishment of an asylum for those who had unwittingly shed
blood, so we are justified in assuming that when at Athens
we find distinct tribunals for different kinds of homicide, involuntary, justifiable, and deliberate, the first named (i.e. the
Palladion) must have been the oldest, that for deliberate
murder (the Areopagus) the last, that for justifiable (the
Delphinion), the second; but this is exactly what Aeschylus
assumes, for he represents that the first tribunal for homicide
was established for cases where extenuating circumstances were
alleged—Orestes himself pleading that he had committed the
crime under the compulsion of Apollo, and the god urging that
Orestes was justified in killing his mother to avenge his father.
In other words Aeschylus represents the first tribunal as
instituted for both the classes of homicide which in historical
times were divided between the court of the Palladion and
that of the Delphinion. But this is only what might have
been expected, for the first step in the amelioration of the
law of vengeance would be in the case of those who had killed
unawares, the second would be the feeling that a man, even
though he slew deliberately, might be justified in so doing.
Naturally those who first urged the latter plea took refuge at
the ancient sanctuary whither resorted those who had slain
a man unawares; and it would be only later that a separate

---

[1] *Numbers*, xxxv. 11-13: πᾶς ὁ πατάξας ψυχὴν ἀκουσίως (LXX).

court would be established for the second class of extenuating circumstances.

But this is completely in accordance with the statement of Aeschylus, for the court first established to try homicide was held at a sanctuary which contained a most ancient image of Pallas. But as it was at the court of the Palladion that trials for involuntary homicide were held, there can be little doubt that the court of the Palladion was older than that of the Delphinion. Moreover, as the name Delphinion shows, that shrine was of comparatively recent origin, and as its connection with justifiable homicide apparently arose from the belief that Apollo had first broached that doctrine at Athens in the case of Orestes, we must conclude that it was of more recent date than the Palladion.

Let us now turn to the remaining claimant, the Areopagus. How does it fit the conditions of the case? (1) There was there no ancient image called by the name of either Athena or Pallas, for Pausanias only mentions a statue of Athena Promachos on the Hill of Ares. (2) There is not the slightest evidence that any other form of homicide except deliberate murder was ever tried there. (3) It is only as the last step in the evolution of the law of homicide that the community steps in between the next of kin and the deliberate manslayer, and insists that a solemn inquiry into the facts of the case shall be carried out before the accused shall be put to death. Accordingly the court of the Areopagus comes latest in the process of legal evolution. That court therefore fails as completely as the Delphinion to fulfil the required conditions, whereas the Palladion, as has just been shown, is in strict accord with all the requirements of the play. For it had an immemorial *xoanon*, used as a place of sanctuary by manslayers, and this was never called by any other name than that of Pallas or Palladion, whilst in its precincts was held the court for the trial of involuntary homicide which we have just seen was the first stage in the mitigation of the pitiless rule of a life for a life.

In the first attempt to mitigate the severity of the antique law the king and his council of elders would naturally be the body who would decide whether a particular manslayer had shed blood involuntarily or justifiably. I have already pointed out that the Fifty and One consisting of the Basileus Archon and fifty others chosen for their high birth look like the survival of the ancient king and Gerontes or Boule. The Basileus laid the case before the court (εἰσάγει) as Athena does in the play. Aeschylus evidently believed that the first trial for homicide took place before the ancient Boule, for otherwise he would not have represented it as taking place in a Council chamber (βουλευτήριον)[1]. Whilst it is very likely that in ancient times the king decided all ordinary cases himself, as did the Egyptian kings, and as is perhaps implied in the tradition preserved in Pollux, yet in cases of bloodshed the king would have felt like Athena in the play, and held that such cases were too serious to be tried by any one individual, whether mortal or immortal, and accordingly he laid (εἰσήγαγε) the matter before the Boule.

If it be urged that although Orestes took sanctuary at the Palladion, nevertheless he was tried on the Areopagus, and in support of this contention it be said that the words πάγον δ' Ἄρειον τόνδ' Ἀμαζόνων ἕδραν refer to the spot where the trial is proceeding, it may be at once pointed out that τόνδε is simply used δεικτικῶς, as is so often the case ("yon Hill of Ares"), for the reference to the Areopagus is only secondary, having been introduced by Aeschylus, as is commonly held, in order to support the Areopagites against the democratic legislation of Pericles and Ephialtes.

But there are several grave objections to this view. In the first place, it has already been pointed out (supra) that it was in the very essence of an asylum that the manslayer should remain there until it had been decided whether he could plead extenuating circumstances or not. Orestes would have been exposed to the vengeance of the Furies if he had been removed from the Palladion to be tried on the Hill, as is now supposed by my friend Dr Verrall[2], who, whilst adopting my view of the place of asylum, still clings, though not very strongly, to the

---

[1] *Eum.* 540: πληρουμένου γὰρ τοῦδε βουλευτηρίου.
[2] *The Eumenides of Aeschylus* (1908), pp. 183-8.

Areopagus as the scene of the trial. Again, if the trial took place on the Areopagus, it is strange there should be no reference to the two famous unhewn stones of Anaideia and Hybris, on which stood the accuser and the accused respectively. Furthermore, at the close of the play Athena declares that she will send the Erinyes by torchlight to the cavernous recesses beneath the earth, under the conduct of her attendants who guard her *bretas*, whilst the best-born of all the land of Theseus shall come, a goodly company of maidens, married women and aged matrons. It seems very unlikely that Athenian women would be represented as present on the Areopagus during the trial, more especially as such trials took place by night, and ready to form a procession. Moreover, there is no reason why the attendants of Athena who had charge of her ancient image should be present at a spot where there was no shrine of the goddess, and no ancient image known either as Pallas or Athena. On the other hand, if the procession started from the Palladion, moving from south-east to the Areopagus, the attendants of Athena will naturally be ready to escort the Furies, now clad in scarlet like Metics (as my lamented friend, the late Dr Headlam, has cleverly shown[1]), to their future abode in the side of the Areopagus. Moreover, the words εὐφαμεῖτε δὲ, χωρῖται (989) and εὐφαμεῖτε δὲ πανδαμεί (991) have no force, if we hold that the procession is simply moving down from the top of the hill to the cavern in its side, for why should all the Athenians be present? On the other hand if the procession is passing across the lower town from the Palladion to the Areopagus, then the exhortation to the whole population to observe a religious silence is completely in place. Finally, if the procession moved from the court on the Areopagus down the hill to the cavern in its side, we ought naturally to meet some word or phrase in the marshalling of the procession, to signify that it was descending the side of the hill. But no such word as καταβαίνειν occurs, but simply the term βᾶτε, well suited to the progress through the town.

We have already compared the claims of the Erechtheum with

---

[1] 982: φοινικοβάπτοις ἐνδυτοῖς ἐσθήμασι: *Jour. Hell. Stud.*, xxvi, 268 *sqq*.

those of the three chief courts for the trial of homicide, and
we have found that the former fails to satisfy any of the
necessary conditions. But as the Areopagus and the Delphinion
also fail in all respects except that they were tribunals for
homicide, whereas the Palladion fulfils them all, we may conclude that the scene both of the asylum and trial of Orestes is to
be laid at the Palladion, that immemorial sanctuary of Athens,
and which was almost certainly the grave of an ancient heroine.

In our survey of the extant Greek tragedies we have found as
an integral part of the structure in not a few of them a *threnos*
or a *kommos*. But such a feature was already familiar in
Homeric days and we know not how long before. It can then
have no more been derived from " the grotesque Satyric form "
than tombs, the libations to the dead, human sacrifices and the
use of graves as sanctuaries, all of which figure so prominently
in a large proportion of these dramas. But as the laments for
the departed, the worship of ancestors by sacrifices and mimetic
dances and the use of tombs as places of asylum all go back on
Greek soil to a period long anterior to the introduction of the
cult of Dionysus into Attica and Peloponnesus, these practices
which are so conspicuous in our extant tragedies cannot be
survivals in such plays from Dionysus and his uncleanly cult.
We are led on the contrary to conclude that they are rather
survivals from that primaeval worship of the dead, such as we
saw in the cult of Adrastus at Sicyon, and that it was from
such that Tragedy proper originated. It may be said that in
the *Pentheus* of Thespis and the play of the same name written
by Aeschylus and in the trilogy on the misfortunes of Lycurgus
composed by Polyphradmon, there is good evidence for the
Dionysiac origin of Tragedy, because the calamities of these
heroes were visitations from the Thracian god. But it might
just as well be maintained that as the sorrows of the Labdacidae
were due to the spurning of Apollo by Laius, and as the rending
of Glaucus by his own mares was the work of Aphrodite,
Tragedy therefore must have sprung from the worship of one
or both of these divinities. In the case of the *Pentheus* and
the *Lycurgeia* it was almost certainly the hero and not the god
who was the central figure, as is indicated by the name of the

play and of the trilogy and as is undoubtedly the case in the *Oresteia*.

The result of our examination thus confirms the evidence already adduced for our belief that Tragedy arose in the worship of the dead, and that the only Dionysiac element in the Drama was the Satyric play.

CHAPTER V

THE EXPANSION OF TRAGEDY

κήρυσσε, κῆρυξ.
AESCH. *Eum.*, 536.

ALREADY under Phrynichus Tragedy had begun sometimes to turn her eyes from the heroic past and to look for
themes in contemporary events, as for instance in the *Capture
of Miletus*, which proved anything but a successful experiment
for its author, yet an example to be followed in no long time
by Aeschylus with a more fortunate result in his *Persae*. But
Aeschylus was destined to extend the sway of the Tragic art
over realms into which neither Phrynichus nor any other of
his predecessors had dared to enter. He realised to the full the
depth and breadth, the grandeur and the terror of the Tragic
art; for he not only made the Drama a mighty engine for dealing
with the great social and political problems of his day, but he
went much further, and passing the flaming bounds of time
and space, essayed to discuss the supreme problems of morals
and religion; not merely man in relation to man, but man in
relation to the Universe and to God.

The Supplices and the Eumenides. We have already
had occasion to examine briefly the plot of the *Supplices*
(p. 127), but only for the purpose of showing the important
part played throughout by the great barrow which forms the
central point in the scene. Let us now examine its structure
with greater care and try to discover the real meaning of the
play.

The trilogy deals with the story of the fifty daughters of
Danaus who, in order to escape marriage with their cousins the

fifty sons of Aegyptus, fled with their aged father to Argos. The *Supplices* deals with their arrival in Argos, their kindly reception in that state, and the repulse of the pursuers. The second play, which was either the *Aegyptii* or the *Thalamopoei*, dealt with the coming of the sons of Aegyptus in strength to Argos, the defeat of the Argives, and the capture and the forced marriages of the Danaids, and their murder of their husbands, with the sole exception of Lynceus, spared by Hypermnestra. The third play contained the trial of that heroine for disobeying her father, and her acquittal when Aphrodite herself came to plead her cause.

It has often been remarked that the *Supplices* cannot properly be termed a tragedy, for there is no catastrophe and it has a happy ending. The play certainly contains no thrilling action, nor is there anything in it to rouse the emotions of the modern playgoer except the spectacle of the fifty helpless maidens and their father. But it might as well be said that the *Eumenides* is not a tragedy. It must be remembered that Aeschylus regarded each trilogy as a whole, and as in the *Oresteia* the *Eumenides* is preceded by two plays supremely tragic, so the *Supplices* was succeeded by a drama in which a dreadful tragedy was enacted. But it may be that there are elements in the play, as in the *Ajax* of Sophocles, which do not appeal to us moderns, but would have acted powerfully upon an Athenian audience. Let us strive to find out what these elements may be.

The chorus probably consisted not of twelve or fifteen, as is often held, but rather (as Tucker has well argued) of the fifty Danaids, for as the chorus speak of themselves as the fifty daughters of Danaus, and as we may suppose that the Athenian audience could count, there would have been a grotesque incongruity between the statement of the chorus and their actual number. Fifty was the original number of the dithy-rambic chorus of Arion, and fifty it continued to be, according to Pollux, down to the time of the *Eumenides*. As the chorus enter, their leader recounts how they have fled from Egypt not because they had committed crime, but rather to escape from crime, since they had left the home of their ancestress Io in order to escape a hated union with their cousins. They pray

that Zeus may receive the suppliants, and that the gods may
side with them against vice and violence, and they declare that
human wantonness is putting forth new leaves. Then Danaus, who
has meantime mounted the grave-howe, cries to his daughters
to be prudent as he sees the dust of a host approaching from
Argos, and he urges them to take sanctuary on the mound.
The Danaids immediately leave the orchestra and ascend
the tumulus, invoking the chief gods whose images they
behold.

The king of Argos soon arrives, and demands from what
country they have come. He finds it hard to believe that
people of their complexion can be Greeks, for they are more
like Libyans, Egyptians, or Amazons. Then the Danaids
convince the king that they are really descended from Io the
Argive heroine. He asks why they have sought asylum with
the gods of the mound. They tell him that they have fled
from marriage with their cousins. Finally the king is moved
to send Danaus with suppliant boughs to plead his cause before
the people in the city. The king bids the maidens leave their
sanctuary, depositing there the boughs, and descend into
the *alsos*. Then the king departs to summon the Argive
assembly, and the chorus thereupon pray to Zeus to save them
and to destroy the Egyptians. Soon Danaus returns alone,
having moved the pity of the Argives, for the assembly was
of one mind, thanks to Zeus working through the eloquence of
the king[1]. Thereupon the chorus prays for the prosperity of
Argos. Meanwhile Danaus, who has once more ascended the
mound, is gazing seawards and sees the Egyptians approach.
Then he departs to the city to seek aid, and meantime the
chorus prays for escape from the loathed embraces of their
cousins. Soon enter the Egyptian herald and mariners, and
thereupon the Danaids take refuge once more on the mound
and cling to the statues. The herald threatens and boasts, and
finally he proceeds to lay hands upon them and drag them
away by their hair and garments. At this crisis the king of
Argos arrives, and after some altercation the Egyptians depart,
uttering threats of vengeance on their masters' part, whilst

[1] 579–603.

the maidens make their way to the city, where they will find
a home.

Let us now examine the reasons given by the chorus for
their flight and the grounds on which they claim the pity
and protection of Argos. They have left Egypt because they
abhor the union with their cousins the sons of Aegyptus[1],
whom they describe as a lewd swarm (ἑσμὸς ὑβριστής), and
pray that they may perish before they mount bridal beds from
which immemorial custom debars them[2].

Again the Coryphaeus prays, "Grant not to youthful lust
to find unrighteous consummation, but straightway spurn all
wantonness, and bring to happy pass such wedlock as is right[3],"
whilst further on she speaks of the sons of Aegyptus as "kindred
who defile their own race[4]." Finally she tells the king of
Argos that they have come "through loathing an unblessed
wedlock there in Egypt[5]." Such then are the moral grounds
urged by the chorus in their plea for sanctuary.

But surely to an Athenian audience in the time of Isaeus
a more futile plea for succour could not have been advanced.
So far from there being any objection in that period to the
intermarriage of cousins, the law permitted the marriage of
half-brothers and half-sisters provided they had not the same
mother (ὁμομήτριοι) but were sprung from the same father
(ὁμοπάτριοι). Moreover at Athens if a man left no son, his
daughter became in a certain sense his heiress (ἐπίκληρος),
but she really, as the term means, was nothing more than an
adscripta glebae, an inseparable appendage to the estate. The
next of kin could claim her in marriage, unless her father had
provided otherwise by will. The heiress was simply the medium
for conveying her father's estate to her own son, for if on her
marriage she bore two sons, the eldest would become the heir
to his father's family, whilst the second might be adopted into
that of his maternal grandfather and on coming of age, if his

[1] 9.
[2] 37 sqq.:   πρίν ποτε λέκτρων ὧν θέμις εἴργει
                 σφετεριξάμενον πατραδελφείαν
                 τήνδ' ἀεκόντων ἐπιβῆναι.
[3] 75.   [4] 220.   [5] 326.

grandfather were dead, he would succeed to the inheritance
of which his mother was the heiress.

Not only could the next of kin claim the heiress, if she was
still unmarried, but even if a woman was already married, and
she, by the death of her brother, became an heiress to the
family property, her next of kin could claim her and could
compel her husband to give her up. Again, if a man after his
marriage became next of kin to an heiress, he might put away
his wife and marry the heiress. Accordingly then the plea of
the Danaids that the marriage with their cousins was incestuous
would have excited nothing but contempt in an Attic audience
of the time of Demosthenes.

But had this law of the marriage of heiresses always been
the custom at Athens or was it but of comparatively recent
date? The fact that even in classical times when succession
was through males, the claim of a woman who had no brothers
to the family land remained paramount, points distinctly to
a time when all property descended through women.

There were distinct traditions that in old days wedlock was
unknown at Athens and that children were named after their
mothers. According to Justin[1] it was Cecrops who first
established the marriage bond, whilst according to Varro[2],
it was under this same king that the women lost their votes
in the assembly, and that the children no longer received the
mother's name. Up to that time the women sat in the assembly
along with the men. A double wonder sprang out of the earth
at the same time, in one place the olive tree, and in another
water. The king in terror sent to Delphi to ask what he should
do. The god answered that the olive tree signified Athena,
and the water Poseidon, and that the citizens must choose after
which of the two they would name their town. Cecrops called
the assembly; the men voted for Poseidon, the women for
Athena, and as there was one woman more, Athena prevailed.
Thereupon Poseidon in wrath sent the, sea over all the lands
of Attica. To appease the god, the citizens imposed a threefold
punishment on their women: they were to lose their votes,

[1] II, 6.
[2] ap. Augustine, De civitate Dei, xviii, 9.

the children were no longer to receive the mother's name, and they were no longer to be called Athenians after the goddess. As McLennan points out, this story is a tradition of a genuinely archaic state, and cannot have been the invention of a later time, for Athena in it represents Mother-right. If it be contended that Varro and Justin are but late writers, it must be remembered that both of them contain much valuable information garnered from earlier sources, and that their statements are amply corroborated by the Athenian law respecting the marriage of half-brothers and half-sisters, provided that they were not sprung from the same mother. Whilst legal conservatism would retain an ancient custom once of peculiar importance, it is most unlikely that the Athenians in later times would have introduced any such law, more especially at a time when the whole tendency was to magnify the importance of the male parent.

It is clear now that Athens once had the system of descent through women which prevails still over wide areas of the earth, and which once was the rule in a great part of Europe, for instance, with the ancient Spaniards, and amongst the ancient peoples on the south and east of the Mediterranean, of whom the Lycians are the most typical example. The latter were allied to the Greeks in blood, and with them down to very late times kinship was reckoned through women, the children being called after their mothers, and the property descending through the female line[1]. If a woman cohabited with her slave, the offspring were full citizens, but if a free man lived with a foreign woman or a concubine, even though he was the first in the state, the children had no rights of citizenship, whilst according to Nicolaus Damascenus they left their inheritances to their daughters and not to their sons.

It is then certain that at Athens there had once been a time when descent was traced and property passed through females, a fact proved by the circumstance that brothers and sisters by the same father might marry freely, whilst the union of half-brothers and half-sisters sprung from the same mother was considered incestuous. In such a condition of society,

[1] Herod. i, 173.

marriage outside the kin is the normal rule, that is what is
called Exogamy. Clearly then, when the Danaids complain
that their cousins are forcing on them an unnatural union, they
take their stand on the doctrine of exogamy, whereas at Athens,
from the end of the fifth century and after, marriage within the
kin is peculiarly favoured, or as McLennan would say, Endogamy
was the rule. But as we have just seen that descent through
women was once the rule at Athens, there must have been
a period of transition from the one system to the other, and
there is evidence to show that the older system was still fresh
in memory in the time of Aeschylus.

The *Eumenides*[1] furnishes us not only with evidence of
descent through women, but also shows that in the Athens
of the fifth century B.C., there was a clear recollection of a time
when the marriage tie can hardly be said to have existed
at all. When the Erinyes declare that their office is to drive
matricides from their homes, Apollo asks, "What if he be the
slayer of a wife who has murdered her husband?" To this
the Erinyes replies, "That would not be kindred blood shed
by the hands of kindred." "Truly," says Apollo, "ye make of
none effect the solemn pledges of Hera Teleia, and Zeus. The
Cyprian goddess too is flung aside and is dishonoured by this
argument, source as she is of the joys dearest to mortals. For
the marriage bed, ordained by Fate for husband and wife,
is a bond stronger than a mere oath, guarded as it is by
Justice." Again, when Orestes demands of the Erinyes why
they persecute him, though they did not pursue his mother
Clytemnestra in her lifetime for the murder of her husband,
they reply that "She was not of the same blood as the man
whom she slew."

As Athens once had the older system to which the Danaids
cling, there must have been a time when the archaic form
gradually gave way to that which we find fully established in
the days of the Attic orators. When did this take place?
The question of the transition to succession through males
instead of females plays a central part in the *Eumenides*. In
that play the dread goddesses, who are maintaining the

[1] 201 *sqq.*

immemorial customs of the land when indicting Orestes for the slaying of his mother, lay down that the tie between mother and child is especially sacred, in other words the doctrine embodied in the Attic law which forbade intermarriage between half-brothers and half-sisters by the same mother. On the other hand Apollo is charged by them with overthrowing primaeval ordinances and introducing strange practices, when in defence of Orestes he declares on the authority of Zeus that the tie between the father and the child is much closer. Now unless the Athenian audience in the year 458 B.C. was fully aware that succession through females had been the ancient practice at Athens, the main point on which the triumphal acquittal of Orestes depends would not have appealed to them in the slightest degree. We are therefore justified in the inference that down to the fifth century B.C. there were many survivals of a time when succession passed through the female line and when the law of exogamy was still a matter of common knowledge to the mass of Athenians.

Now if this was so in 458 B.C. when the *Oresteia* was exhibited, it must have been still more the case when the *Supplices*, supposing that we are right in considering it the earliest extant play of the poet, was composed. Accordingly the plea of the suppliants to be saved from an endogamous marriage with their cousins would probably appeal to many in the audience who first heard it. The breaking down of ancient customs cannot be effected in a few years even by a Napoleon, and in an ancient state such as Attica, with its numerous small communities rigidly conservative, the process of change must indeed have been slow and great opposition must have been roused in many quarters by the proposals to alter the time-honoured methods of tracing forms of kinship and succession.

I have already given the plea urged by the chorus against their marriage with their cousins on the ground that such was immoral. In their conversation with the king of Argos we find another objection equally strong, one not moral but material. The king asks them why they have become suppliants of the gods whose images are worshipped at the mound where they

have taken sanctuary, bearing their wool-wreathed olive boughs.
The leader replies, "In order that I may not become the
bondswoman of the sons of Aegyptus." The king asks, "Is this
merely because there is a family quarrel, or because it is
unlawful?" She avoids a direct answer by asking "Who would
purchase relations as owners?" The king, who is not at all
a sentimental statesman, replies, "It is in this way that men's
power becomes aggrandised."

The Coryphaeus declares that she does not want to become
a bondswoman to her cousins and furthermore she has a great
aversion to purchasing with her property relations who will in
reality be her owners. In this she is simply expressing the
feelings of the Athenian heiresses, who by the new legislation
were to be treated merely as appendages to the family estate,
who could not marry whom they pleased, and who, even if
already married to some other man, might, under certain
circumstances, be torn from their husbands to gratify the
cupidity of the next of kin.

That the poet is alluding to the Attic law relating to
women is rendered all the more probable by the words of the
Argive king:

"Suppose the sons of Aegyptus have authority over you
by the law of your city, alleging that they are your nearest
of kin, who would seek to withstand their right? Needs be
that you must plead according to your own country's laws, that
they have no authority over you[1]." Now as every Athenian
woman in the later classical period must have a κύριος, a man
who had control over her and managed her estate, whether
father, brother, or next of kin, the use of the term κῦρος by the
king of Argos is of great significance; it confirms the view
that the chorus are really voicing the objections made by the
party at Athens, especially women entitled to property, not
only against the innovations by which they were deprived of

---

[1] 362 *sqq.*:   εἴ τοι κρατοῦσι παῖδες Αἰγύπτου σέθεν
νόμῳ πόλεως, φάσκοντες ἐγγύτατα γένους
εἶναι, τίς ἂν τοῖσδ' ἀντιωθῆναι θέλοι;
δεῖ τοί σε φεύγειν κατὰ νόμους τοὺς οἴκοθεν,
ὡς οὐκ ἔχουσι κῦρος οὐδὲν ἀμφί σου.

managing their estate and marrying whom they pleased outside their kindred, but also against the new proposal by which the heiress was in the power of her next of kin, and thus became, in the words of the chorus, nothing more than his bondswoman.

Now let us turn to the king's reply. To the rhetorical question of the Coryphaeus, " Who would purchase relations as masters ? " the king answers, " This is the way in which men's power is aggrandised." What is the meaning of these words which the Coryphaeus does not attempt to gainsay ? They mean nothing more or less than that as soon as the rule of marriage outside the kin is broken down, the property can be kept within the kin instead of continually passing to the use of men of other families. In this way each *genos* (like the Rothschilds) can increase greatly in wealth and influence. No wonder is it that the Coryphaeus made no reply, for the truth of the king's sententious utterance can be abundantly proved from the history of Mediterranean lands. So long as a tribe is in the hunter state, the rule of exogamy leads to little trouble, for there is no property except some articles of dress, a few weapons and ornaments, and these are usually buried with the dead owners. With the acquisition of domestic animals and the first attempts at cultivation difficulties begin to arise. There is now property to inherit, and that property passes to the daughters and to the men whom the daughters choose to marry, whilst the sons seek homes for themselves with the daughters of other families, their sisters in some cases at least giving them a dowry in order to help them to obtain eligible *partes*. This for instance was the usage amongst the ancient Cantabrians in north-west Spain, where we are told by Strabo[1] that the daughters inherited the family property, but that they dowered out their brothers to the women of other families. So long as there is still much unoccupied land, no real pinch would be felt by the sons, but when the cultivable land is not of great extent, and becomes practically all under occupation, the position of the sons becomes precarious. A man may or may not secure a wife with a comfortable " matrimony." If he does not, he sees the family property pass with his sister or his female cousins to the men

[1] 137, 30 (Didot).

of other families, whilst he himself wanders where he may
as a lackland. There is only one way in which he can enjoy
the family property and that is to marry his cousin or even
his sister. Some years ago I pointed out in a public lecture
that this was the true explanation of the strange practice of
the marriage of brothers and sisters in Egypt, not only in the
royal family but also amongst all grades of the population.
These marriages were not confined to half-brothers and half-
sisters, but as is proved abundantly by documents relating to
the payment of taxes whole brothers and whole sisters sprung
from the same parents regularly contracted marriages. When
therefore the Ptolemies married their sisters, it was not through
a mere freak of depravity, but was completely in conformity
with the usage of their subjects. Thus we are told by Pausanias
that when Ptolemy Philadelphus fell in love with his full sister
Arsinoë and married her, it was contrary to the customs of the
Macedonians, but agreeable to those of the Egyptians over whom
he ruled[1].

It is now clear that in the transition from succession through
females to that through males, which we find in the time of
Isaeus and Demosthenes, there must have been a breaking
down of the principle of exogamy. It is not unreasonable to
suppose that the first attacks on an immemorial social institution
of such primary importance would arouse the strongest feeling
and would only finally succeed after long struggles.

A consideration of the law of inheritance in two other
countries of the Eastern Mediterranean will show us probably
the steps which led up to the position of women, such as we
find it to be at the end of the fifth century B.C. at Athens. In
Lycia we saw that if a free woman had a child by her slave,
it was perfectly legitimate, and if a daughter, it would inherit
the family property. At Athens the heiress was nothing more
than an appendage inseparably attached to the family inheritance.
The famous Gortyn laws may show us some of the steps by
which probably Attic law relating to heiresses advanced to the
stage at which we find it in the days of the Orators. Thus
at Gortyn, although the sons had the sole right to the town

[1] I, 7, 1.

house, its furniture, and the cattle, the daughters shared in
the rest of the inheritance, each daughter getting half as much
as a son. If a girl was an heiress ($\pi\alpha\tau\rho\omega\iota\hat{\omega}\kappa\sigma$), she might
marry whom she pleased within the limits of her tribe, if she
was content with the town house and half the remainder of the
estate, the next of kin taking the other half. If there was no
next of kin, the heiress might marry any one of her tribe who
would have her; if not, the law lays down that she may marry
whom she can. Again if a married woman became an heiress,
she was not compelled to leave her husband, although she
could do so if she pleased. If she divorced him she was not
always free to marry whom she pleased: for if she was childless
she must either marry the next of kin, or indemnify him; but
if she already had children, she might marry any member of
her tribe who would have her. So too with a widow if she
became an heiress. Though at Athens it was obligatory on the
next of kin either to marry the heiress, or to provide her with
a dower if she were poor, there was no such obligation at Gortyn,
for the next of kin was not compelled to marry the heiress if he
gave up his claim to the estate. Again whereas at Athens the
property of the heiress became the property of her son as soon
as he came of age, at Gortyn the mother had the same rights
over her property that her husband had over his, and as long
as she lived her children could not divide her property against
her wish. At her decease it was transmitted in the same way
as the estate of a man. Finally at Gortyn an heiress under
certain circumstances could marry a serf and the offspring would
be legitimate.

As the Lycians were closely connected in blood with Crete,
and in fact are said to have been emigrants from that island,
it would seem that in the Gortyn laws respecting the property
of heiresses, which show far more consideration for the rights
of women than those of Athens, we have not an outcome of
more enlightened legislation, as is held by Mr Jevons[1], but rather
the result of an attempt to advance in the same direction as
that made by the men at Athens, though in Crete the men
either did not desire or had not been able to encroach so much

[1] P. Gardner and F. B. Jevons, *Manual of Greek Antiquities*, p. 562.

on the ancient rights of the women. The Gortyn code shows us really an earlier stage in the transition from exogamy to endogamy than that seen at Athens, and we may not be wrong in holding that the first steps taken at Athens may not have been unlike what we find as the actual state of things in Crete or at least at Gortyn.

Let us return to the lines under discussion. The meaning of the answer of the king of Argos to the Danaids is now clear. "You may not," says he, "like being compelled to marry your kinsmen, but all the same it is best for the kin, for the family property will thereby be kept together, and consequently its power and influence will increase."

When once we realise that the change over from female to male kinship was a burning question at Athens in the first half of the fifth century, being still of sufficient interest to form the central feature in the third play of the great trilogy of the *Oresteia* in 458 B.C., we can readily understand that the audience which listened to the *Supplices* in the opening decades of that century found in its plot a theme for them of absorbing interest, but which would have aroused just as little feeling in the days of Demosthenes as it does in ours.

Now what was the attitude of Aeschylus himself towards these social innovations ? It has always been the fashion amongst scholars to speak of the poet as a great religious and political conservative, but I venture to think a re-consideration of the question will lead us to a different conclusion. Briefly stated the grounds for the ordinary belief are (1) his oft-repeated reverence for Zeus and the other gods, and (2) his eulogy on the Areopagus. Yet investigation will show us that the great dramatist so far from being a conservative was the great proclaimer of a new religious and social gospel. It is perfectly true that from first to last the power of Zeus and the gods is constantly reiterated in all his plays. Thus in the *Supplices* itself, probably his earliest extant work, the chorus at the very outset invokes the aid of Zeus, and elsewhere in the play Zeus is described as the helper of the helpless, as he that helps to right them that suffer wrong, as the all-seeing one, whose eyes behold all that is done upon earth, and finally as the judge of the wicked after death. Zeus, Apollo, Poseidon and Hermes, in the order given, have statues on the sacred mound where the chorus took sanctuary. From the standpoint of Aristophanes and his contemporaries Aeschylus may indeed be regarded as a conservative. But is he so when judged in relation to his own time? Were Zeus and Apollo gods of immemorial reign at Athens? The poet himself tells us explicitly in the *Prometheus Vinctus* that new gods have arisen which have upset the ancient order of things, and these new gods especially are Zeus, the overthrower of the Titan brood, and his son Apollo. In the *Eumenides* the Erinyes complain that Zeus and Apollo are upsetting the old order of things, whilst they declare that they themselves are trying to uphold the ancient customs of the land, such as kinship traced through the mother. The dramatist would never have dared to speak thus of Zeus and Apollo unless his audience were well aware that the two great deities were but new-comers into Athens. Moreover a striking confirmation of the statement of Aeschylus is furnished by an examination of the shrines of the gods at Athens. Though, as we know from Homer, Athena had her home on the Acropolis in the "strong house of Erechtheus," yet down to the latest days neither Zeus nor Apollo had a temple on that famous citadel. Though Zeus in later times had managed to annex an altar in front of the north door of the Erechtheum, down to the last he never could find entrance into the great temple itself, in which Athena and Poseidon reigned. Again the names of the temples built in honour of Zeus and Apollo in other parts of the city show clearly that they were adventitious and not indigenous deities. That of Zeus was called the Olympieum, whilst those of Apollo were termed respectively the Pythium and the Delphinium, showing that the cult of Zeus was derived from Olympus in Thessaly, whilst that of Apollo had been introduced from Delphi.

Moreover the Zeus temple was not of ancient date, for we know that it was begun by the despot Pisistratus in the plain to the south-east of the Acropolis about the middle of the sixth century B.C. So indifferent however as a whole were the Athenians to the worship of the Olympian, that in the glorious

years after the overthrow of the Persians and when great
revenues flowed in from allies and subjects, and when Pericles
was lavishing vast sums on the Parthenon, not a single stone
was added to the shrine of Zeus. Even when the Athenians
were utterly exhausted towards the close of the Peloponnesian
War, they spent a large sum on rebuilding the Erechtheum,
the home of Athena and Poseidon, yet the temple of the
Father of gods and men still lay neglected. It was only in
B.C. 174 that it was brought near to completion not by the
expenditure of Athenian money but by the munificence of
Antiochus Epiphanes. Indeed it was not finished until the
reign of Hadrian.

So far then from Aeschylus being a conservative in religion,
he is the champion of the gods Zeus and Apollo against the
dread dark beings revered in primitive Athens, which are upheld
by the Eumenides in the play named after them. The Erinyes
held that there could be no mercy for the shedding of kindred
blood, but Apollo on the authority of his father Zeus proclaims
that the sinner after due purification can meet with pardon and
forgiveness. Again in that same play though Athena is made
to declare herself altogether the child of Zeus, yet at no distant
date she had always been regarded as the daughter of Poseidon,
who continued down to the last, as we have just seen, to share
with her the Erechtheum. According to Herodotus[1] it was only
quite late that she became wroth with Poseidon, repudiated
him as her father and affiliated herself to Zeus.

Nor are we without some hint as to the time and
cause for the introduction of the new doctrines into Athens.
We have just seen that it was Pisistratus who laid the
foundations of the temple of Zeus, and it is familiar to all
scholars that it was under that same despot that the study
of the Homeric poems assumed an active form at Athens. In
these poems, though Athena may play a prominent part,
Poseidon is but of very secondary rank, whilst Zeus the All-
Father and Apollo his son are the chief divinities of the Acheans.
In these poems likewise descent was reckoned by males amongst
the Acheans, and the sanctity of the marriage tie holds a fore-

[1] iv, 180.

most place as, for instance, in the case of Penelope. Aeschylus therefore was the Apostle of a new gospel which centred round Zeus and Apollo, and their Testament was the *Iliad* and the *Odyssey*.

To Aeschylus the religious conceptions of the Homeric poems and their loftier morality came as a revelation. In the old world of which the Eumenides were the champions the worship of the mere local ancestor, out of which Tragedy sprang, was all-pervading. To the imagination of Aeschylus the Achean Zeus, the overthrower of the Titans and all the dark powers which had brooded over primaeval Athens, was a perfect illumination. Instead of narrow local fetish cults of dead heroes and heroines came the conception of the All-Father, the All-seeing one whose eyes are in every place beholding both the evil and the good, and helping them to right that suffer wrong, punishing the guilty, yet having mercy and forgiveness for the sinner. Henceforward with him although the spirits of the dead that dwell in the graves beneath the earth may be capable of wreaking dreadful vengeance, yet there was a greater power whose force and controlling influence was as wide as the firmament itself.

But the Achean gods had not merely brought into Athens a gospel of mercy and forgiveness for the sinner, but along with their cult came a social doctrine strange and repulsive to the ancient goddesses of the land. When Apollo asks the Eumenides why they had not punished Clytemnestra for murdering her husband, they reply that as he was of a different *genos* from hers, it was not a case of the shedding of kindred blood. Apollo answers, "What, are the sacred pledges of Hera Teleia and Zeus of none effect in your eyes, nor those of Aphrodite, the giver of the greatest joys to men?"

In other words Apollo is simply urging the doctrine of the sanctity of marriage as seen amongst the Acheans of Homer. On the other hand in Hesiod the marriage bond is unknown amongst the gods, but as Aristotle says that men make not merely the forms of the gods like unto their own, but also their lives, we may infer that with the people amongst whom the *Theogony* was shaped, wedlock was but lax. But as amongst

the Homeric Acheans the marriage bond is held sacred, we may
have little doubt that the ἱερὸς γάμος, the sacred rite of marriage,
celebrated between Zeus and Hera year by year at Argos, and
probably in every community in Greece, was the outcome of the
religion of Zeus. It is clear from the discussion between the
Eumenides and Apollo that the marriage tie was not held sacred
in ancient Athens, but that it was only introduced along with
the worship of Zeus and Apollo. But as succession through
males is only possible when strict wedlock has been established,
the final decision of Athena in the *Eumenides* in favour of
closer affinity of the child to the father than to the mother is
but a natural corollary to the doctrine of the sanctity of marriage.

Let us now return to the trilogy of which the *Supplices*
is held to be the first play. We saw that although the
conclusion of that drama pointed to the triumph of the ancient
doctrine of marriage outside the kin, yet in the second play
the tables were turned, for the sons of Aegyptus vanquished
the Argives and captured the daughters of Danaus. It probably
also contained the forced marriage of the maidens with their
cousins and the murder of all the husbands save Lynceus
spared by the *splendide mendax* Hypermnestra. Then came
the third play, the *Danaides*, in which the trial of Hypermnestra
for disobeying her father and sparing her young consort was
probably the central feature. We know for certain that
Aphrodite herself came forward as advocate for Hypermnestra
and triumphantly vindicated her action, on the ground that
she was completely justified by love towards her young husband.

We have just seen that Apollo in the *Eumenides* asks the
Erinys has she no regard for the sacred marriage rites of Hera
and Zeus and for Aphrodite. Here in the earlier trilogy
Aeschylus himself had already justified the breaking down
of an artificial social system by the all-conquering power of
love. There is therefore no support left for the assumption
that Aeschylus was an unbending conservative except in his
advocacy of the Senate of the Areopagus. But a man must not
be branded as unprogressive because he does not think that
every change proposed, no matter what its direction, is whole-
some and wise. In that great Council composed neither of
hereditary legislators nor yet of those directly chosen by the

masses, but of men who had been elected by the people to the
highest offices of the state, Aeschylus saw a salutary barrier to
the wild tide of democratic impulse, the very fact which marked
it out for destruction by Ephialtes ,and Pericles. But time was
to show that the instincts of the great dramatist were right.
If in the Peloponnesian War the democracy, on the proposal of a
demagogue, could pass a decree for the massacre of the whole
male population of Mitylene, and on the morrow rescind that
decree and had to despatch a swift and well-manned galley to
stay if possible the execution of their dreadful mandate, then
Aeschylus was surely right in holding that some assembly not
directly elected by the people was necessary to save it from its
own folly. But his advocacy of the Areopagus was in vain, and
according to one tradition it would seem that in consequence
of the *Eumenides* the dramatist deemed it prudent to retire to
Sicily. There some three years later he met death far from that
Athens for which he and his valiant brothers had fought and
bled at Marathon, Salamis and Plataea.

The Prometheus Vinctus. In the *Supplices* the poet
dealt with a social revolution, yet the problem which he
discussed in that play was not merely concerned with the
structure of Athenian society, but was indissolubly bound up
with great moral problems. Though indeed he did not face
the latter in the *Supplices*, we cannot be sure that he did not
treat of them in one or other of the remaining plays of the
trilogy. But be that as it may, as has just been shown, he
dealt with them fully and fearlessly in the *Eumenides*, produced
some thirty years later. In that as in all his other extant
plays, the *Persae* excepted, his thoughts are fixed on the origin
of evil and on the dark and relentless forces which beset the
life of Man, against which, no matter how the bravest and
noblest may strive, his efforts are as futile as those of the
Getae who when it thundered shot their arrows in impotent
rage towards the heaven, as futile as the resistance offered to
the demons of the sandstorm by the Libyans, and as futile as
the rash fury of the Cimbrians who when the Ocean burst
over their lands "took up their arms against a sea of troubles
and by opposing" only compassed their own destruction. How
helpless are even the best of mankind to cope with these

mysterious and resistless powers, unseen yet ever present, Aeschylus has shown us in the famous dramas founded on the tales of Thebes and Pelops' line. *The Seven against Thebes* is the last act in the long drama that opens with the folly of Laius in contemning the behest of Apollo. It was the third play in the trilogy of which the *Laius* and the *Oedipus* were the first and second. With these three dramas Aeschylus proved victorious in B.C. 467 over Polyphradmon, the son of Phrynichus, who competed with his *Lycurgeia*. The Satyric drama of the *Sphinx* completed the tetralogy of Aeschylus, and was, as its name implies, almost certainly based upon the same legend as its tragic companions. We may infer with high probability that in this trilogy Aeschylus traced the steps of that curse which, for no cause intelligible to mortal minds, dogged the house of Labdacus for three generations. Why should the son born of Laius and Jocasta have been the predestinated murderer of his father ? Why should that hapless child when rescued from death on Cithaeron by the kindly shepherd and grown to a noble manhood in the house of Polybus have been guided by a stern and mocking fate to the spot where part the ways to Delphi and to Daulis ? Why should he there have met Laius and his company, and from a quarrel, not of his own choosing, have slain unwittingly him who begat him ? Why finally should this gallant youth have come to Thebes and have saved that harassed city from the ravages of the Sphinx only to be rewarded with the hand of his own mother ?

In reply to such questions the ordinary Greek contented himself by saying " Man is but the plaything of the gods." But this was an answer far from satisfying a mind like that of Aeschylus.

As the *Laius* and the *Oedipus* have not survived, we cannot say how the dramatist worked out the story of that Ate which wrought havoc in the house of Labdacus. On the other hand by the preservation of the *Oresteia*, the only extant Greek trilogy, we are enabled to see from what standpoint the poet viewed that series of unmerciful disasters that had dogged the Pelopidae from that hour in which the fated golden lamb had first appeared in the flock—the defiling of his brother's marriage bed by Thyestes, the fearful vengeance of the injured Atreus by feasting his brother on the flesh of that brother's own offspring, the sacrifice of Iphigenia by her father, which estranged her mother's anguished heart from Agamemnon for ever and made her the more ready to become the paramour of Aegisthus; this in turn led her to the murder of her husband on his return from Troy to that home to which he brought Cassandra as his concubine. This murder must in its turn be avenged and to the innocent Orestes descends the *hereditas damnosa* of the family curse. Through no act of his own, but under the divine direction of Apollo, he incurs the most awful of all pollutions by shedding the blood of the mother that had borne him in her womb and suckled him at her breast.

Yet his doom is not to be that of Alcmaeon in the older legend, who slew his mother for compassing his father's death, though she had no justification such as that of Clytemnestra, and knew no pardon, and found no rest on this side the grave. But a new dispensation had dawned for Greece and Athens. Apollo in the *Eumenides* pronounced in the name of the Father upon the matricide an absolution full and complete. Already thirty years before, Aeschylus in the *Supplices* had described Zeus as the friend of the suppliant and as helping them to right that suffer wrong.

But this is far from being the only aspect of the All-Father which he has set forth in his plays. When we turn to the *Prometheus Vinctus* the picture of Zeus there presented is altogether different, for he is pourtrayed as a cruel and capricious tyrant in his dealings with gods and men alike. As the whole scheme of that play is the relation of Zeus to the other gods and to mankind, a brief examination of its action may enable us to discover why Aeschylus has represented the Olympian in such startling contrast to the image of the All-Father left us in his earliest and latest extant dramas.

The date of the play can be fixed within fairly definite limits. It is almost certainly later than the eruption of Aetna in Ol. 75. 2, B.C. 478, to which the poet alludes[1]. The dramatist

[1] 375 *sqq.*

was in Sicily during the years B.C. 472—68 and probably saw, if not Aetna in eruption, the ravages wrought by its lava steams. No one places the date of the play later than this period. Thucydides when speaking of another great eruption of Aetna which occurred in the spring of B.C. 425 and which destroyed the territory of the Catanians, says that according to report this had taken place fifty years after the last, i.e. the one to which Aeschylus refers. According to Thucydides[1] therefore the date of this eruption would be B.C. 475, but it is not unlikely that he is simply speaking in round numbers, and that the true date is B.C. 478. There had been an earlier eruption of Aetna, which had occurred subsequently to the settlement of the Greeks in Sicily, but Thucydides does not tell us how long anterior this was to that which occurred in his own time.

The *Prometheus Bound* ($\Delta\epsilon\sigma\mu\omega\tau\eta\varsigma$) is supposed to be the second play of a trilogy of which the *Prometheus the Fire-bearer* ($\Pi\upsilon\rho\phi\dot{o}\rho\varsigma$) was the first, and the *Release of Prometheus* ($\Lambda\upsilon\dot{o}\mu\epsilon\nu\varsigma$) was the third. The Satyric drama is unknown. It cannot have been the *Prometheus Pyrcaeus*, for that was the last of the tetralogy which included the *Persae*.

The scene is laid on a bleak cliff in the Caucasus, which Aeschylus regarded as being in the Scythian desert. The play opens with Prometheus in custody of Kratos and Bia. The first lines give us the keynote. Kratos orders Hephaestus, the divine smith, to rivet the fetters on Prometheus because such is the command of Zeus, and at the same time Hephaestus is reminded that Prometheus had stolen his fire and had bestowed it upon mankind. Prometheus is to be punished in order that he may abandon his desire to befriend the human race and that mortals may learn to bear with patience the sovereign will of Zeus. Hephaestus reluctantly obeys and only through fear of the Olympian is he willing to shackle a brother god, and justifies this reluctance by declaring that kinship and comradeship are strong bonds. Kratos answers that one may do anything except become king of the gods. The fetters of adamant are now fast fixed, and Prometheus utters his famous appeal to all Nature[2]—he calls

[1] III, 116.   [2] 88 *sqq.*

upon the divine aether, the swift winged winds, the river founts,
the multitudinous laughter of the rippling waves, on Earth the
All-Mother, and on the All-seeing Sun to behold the torments
which this new ruler of the gods has inflicted upon him.
Prometheus has prescience of what his fate will be, but not
a full foreknowledge, as we shall presently see. He knows that
he is doomed to bondage for ten thousand years, and he must
bow to 'Ανάγκη, "for the might of Necessity is irresistible[1]."
He declares that all these torments have come upon him
because of the gifts that he had bestowed upon men, more
especially the boon of the stolen fire concealed in a stalk
of fennel, which had enabled them to develop the arts of
life. At this moment he hears a rustling through the air,
and bodes some coming woe. His fear is quickly dispelled,
for the Chorus of the Daughters of Ocean and Tethys now
enter. Far away in their sea-caves they had heard the replication
of the hammer-strokes as Hephaestus riveted the gyves on
Prometheus. Prometheus adjures them to behold his misery.
They sing how a new steersman now grasps the helm of Olympus,
how Zeus is supreme ruling with new laws, and how he is
bringing to nought the mighty ones of yore. They assure
Prometheus that he has the pity of all the gods except Zeus,
who will not relent until either his wrath has been glutted
or he has been overthrown by craft. Prometheus replies that
the day shall come when Zeus will sorely need his aid, but
never will he give him the counsel that may save him until he
is released from his bonds and Zeus has made requital. The
nymphs answer that the ways of Zeus are past finding out.
"Zeus," answers Prometheus, "will yet be brought low and then
and not till then will Prometheus be ready for reconciliation."

The Chorus now ask why so grievous a punishment has
been meted out to him. Prometheus tells his story. Wrath
had broken out amongst the Titanic gods and strife ensued,
some wishing to expel Cronus and make Zeus king, others
taking the part of Cronus and urging that Zeus should never
reign[2]. Prometheus, warned by his mother Gaia, advised the
Titans to rely on craft and not on mere brute force, but they

---

[1] 105.   [2] 205 *sqq.*

set his counsel at nought. Then acting on his mother's advice, he took the side of Zeus and by his counsels that god consigned to Tartarus Cronus, the Ancient of Days, and all who took his side. Though Prometheus had done so much for Zeus, the latter requited him ill, for like all despots he distrusted his friends. Zeus assigned their duties to the various gods, but took no account of hapless mortals. It was his design to annihilate mankind and to create a new race. Prometheus interposed and saved men from the thunderbolts of Zeus and planted golden hope in the breasts of mortals. Prometheus tells the nymphs that he knew what was before him, when he helped mortals, but he did not realise that his punishment would be so grievous. It is thus clear that his prescience was limited.

At this point Oceanus himself comes on the scene, not merely as a kinsman, but as a friend. He counsels Prometheus to bow to the will of the new ruler of the world, for Zeus even though his seat be very far away, may hear his words. Ocean himself had hated the whole revolution in heaven, but he had yielded to Zeus and he advises Prometheus to do the same. Prometheus commends the wisdom of Ocean's admonitions, but yet he is unmoved. He relates the sufferings of two brother Titans, Atlas who far in the West bears upon his shoulders the pillar of the sky, and Typhon who by the strait of the sea lies crushed beneath the roots of Aetna, whence in time to come shall burst forth streams of lava. When his advice has been rejected by Prometheus, Oceanus departs riding on his griffin. The Chorus then point out to Prometheus that Zeus is ruling by laws of his own and manifesting arrogance to the gods of the older empire. Already all the earth groans aloud and sheds tears sighing for the departed glories of the grand old sway of Prometheus and his brother Titans. The races of men settled in fair Asia are moved with pity, as are the Amazons in the land of Colchis, the Scythians that dwell by Lake Maeotis and the martial host of Arabia[1].

[1] In *Trans. Cambridge Philological Soc.*, vol. II (1881–2), pp. 179–180, I defended the reading Ἀραβίας of Med. against the various conjectures of Hermann (Σαρματᾶν), of Burges (Ἀβάριες), and of Dindorf and Heimsoeth

Prometheus resumes his story[1]. He relates the miserable condition of mankind until he gave them intelligence. "Having eyes they saw not, and hearing they did not understand." They had no houses built with bricks nor knew how to work in timber, but like the frail ants they dwelt deep in the sunless recesses of caves. They knew no remedy for disease, neither salve nor drug nor potion. They had no knowledge of the stars nor had they as yet marked out the seasons; they had no domestic animals until Prometheus yoked for them the steed, obedient to the rein. He too taught them the arts of augury and divination by inspection of the entrails, and to offer burnt sacrifices. He devised for them numbers, chief of inventions, and gave them the art of writing. He instructed them in the building of ships and sea-craft, and finally he revealed to men the treasures buried in the earth—copper, iron, silver and gold. In a word all the human arts are due to Prometheus.

The Chorus suggest that by yielding to Zeus Prometheus may yet be free and be not inferior to Zeus himself. Prometheus replies that he will yet be delivered, for Art is not so mighty as Necessity. The Chorus ask who wields this Necessity. He answers, the Three Fates otherwise called the Mindful Erinyes. The Chorus ask if Zeus is weaker than these. Prometheus replies that he is, for he cannot escape what is intended for him. They ask, Why, what is destined for Zeus except to reign for ever, for his kingdom is an everlasting kingdom? To this question Prometheus makes no reply. He has his secret and by it he will escape from his pains. The Chorus then tell Prometheus that his misery is due to his own disobedience and his assertion of his right of private judgment. Gods can get no aid from weak, powerless mortals who are but

---

(Χαλκίδος), by citing Xenophon, *Cyropaedia*, VII, 4, VIII, 6, and VII, 5, as well as Plaut. *Trin.*, 933. Those passages clearly show that the Arabians meant are the people called Ἄραβες σκηνῖται inhabiting a long strip of country far north of Babylon near the upper waters of the Euphrates, and running up to the confines of Cappadocia and Armenia. They thus dwelt at no great distance from the shore of the Euxine and were easily known to the Greeks who visited the coasts of Pontus. Aeschylus was therefore not so ignorant of the geography of this region as has been generally supposed.

[1] 444 *sqq.*

the creatures of a day. By no contrivance can men overstep the eternal fitness of things established by Zeus, "this lesson I learn from looking upon your affliction, Prometheus. Very different is my present lay from that which I sang at your nuptials when you wedded Hesione my sister." With this closes the first part of the play. It ends with the keynote struck in the opening lines. The will of Zeus is supreme. All must yield to it, be they gods or men. Prometheus has saved mankind from destruction, and has taught them to sacrifice to the gods, but "to obey is better than sacrifice and to hearken than the fat of rams."

Io, daughter of Inachus, now enters. She has been metamorphosed into a cow by Hera, and though by this time the herdsman Argus of the thousand eyes has been slain by Hermes, she is still haunted by his spectre as she careers along, maddened by the gadfly. She calls upon Zeus to free her from her misery. Prometheus recognizes her as the daughter of Inachus, who had inflamed the heart of Zeus with love, and who had suffered grievously from the jealousy of Hera. She asks Prometheus who he is and requests him to recount his misfortunes, but the Ocean nymphs are curious to hear her story, and she accordingly recounts to them her sorrows.

Once she dwelt a happy maiden in the house of her father Inachus at Argos. Then came a time when nightly visitants to her virgin bower said to her, "Why live so long in maidenhood, when a high espousal is ready for thee, even the bed of Zeus himself? He is smitten with love of thee. Go forth to thy father's byres at Lerna, that Zeus may find relief from his ardent desire." She hearkened not to these monitions, but at last told them to her sire. He sent to the oracles of Pytho and Dodona, but riddling answers were returned. Finally Loxias, at the behest of Zeus, sent an oracle declaring that unless Inachus thrust her forth from his house, it would be destroyed by the thunderbolts of the Olympian. Sorely against his will her father at last turned her forth, for the bridle of Zeus constrained him, unwilling though he was. Straightway her form and mind suffered a strange change into a cow with horns. Stung by a gadfly she rushed distraught towards Lerna, but ever the herdsman Argus dogged her steps. Even when he is slain, still maddened by the gadfly she careers through land after land.

It will be noticed that Io is punished not for any unchastity on her part, but because she refused to yield to temptation, even though the tempter was Zeus. In her story therefore as in that of Prometheus unquestioning obedience to the Supreme is emphatically preached and enforced.

When Io's narrative is ended, Prometheus tells her the toils and sufferings that still lie before her, and he describes her course towards the rising sun to the Scythians, who dwell in waggons and use the bow; she will pass by the Chalybes, and reach the Amazons, who in time to come shall settle at Themiscyra by the river Thermodon; she will then come to the Cimmerian Bosphorus which will take its name from her. Prometheus points out the selfish cruelty of Zeus to this hapless maiden because he desired her love. He then adds, "Is not this ruler of the gods alike tyrannical in all things. Because he desired, god as he is, to enjoy this maiden, he hath inflicted on her these long wanderings? Alas, O maiden, a sorry suitor hast thou had." Prometheus is now about to continue his recital of the future sufferings of Io, when the latter says that it is best for her to end her misery once for all by flinging herself from the cliff. Prometheus points out that his fate is far harder than hers since death is denied to him and he must endure until Zeus shall have been expelled from his throne. Thereupon Io asks eagerly, "Is it destined for Zeus to be deposed some day?" Prometheus then tells her that Zeus is preparing to make a marriage which will cost him his throne, and bring him to nought. Io asks if this marriage of Zeus will be with a goddess or a mortal woman. He replies that this new spouse will bring forth a son more mighty than his father. Zeus will not be able to avert his misfortune unless Prometheus be released from his bonds. He that can release him against the will of Zeus shall be sprung from Io herself and he shall be the thirteenth in direct descent from her. Then Prometheus gives her the choice of either learning the rest of her own wanderings, or the name of her descendant who shall be his redeemer. The Chorus ask

him to do both. Prometheus consents, and then narrates the
rest of the wanderings of Io. She is to go south and is to beware
of the whirlwinds; then she will pass the surge of the sea, and
come to the Gorgonian plains of Cisthene, where dwell the three
daughters of Phorcys, with one eye in common and one tooth
each, on whom looks neither the sun by day nor the moon by
night. Hard by dwell their three sisters the Gorgons, feather-
clad and with snaky locks. She is to beware of the Grypes,
the pointed sharp-beaked dumb hounds of Zeus, and the one-
eyed host of the Arimaspians, riders on horseback who dwell by
the gold-washing stream of the river of Pluto. Finally she will
come to a swarthy race who are nigh neighbours to the sun, and
dwell near the river of Ethiopia. She will descend along its
banks until she reaches a cataract, whence the Nile hurls its
holy stream. Finally she will pass into the Delta, where it is
fated for her and her posterity to found a colony. At this point
Prometheus breaks off his narrative and describes her previous
journeyings to prove that he is speaking the truth about those
which still await her. He tells her how that "at Dodona that
portent passing belief, the talking oaks" had addressed her as
the destined spouse of Zeus. Then he resumes the narration
of her future fortunes. At Canopus Zeus will restore her to
her senses and human form by his divine touch, and will at the
same time impregnate her with Epaphus. In the fifth generation
from him, the Danaides shall return to Argos to avoid an
incestuous union with their cousins. They shall all slay their
husbands on the marriage night save Hypermnestra, who will
prefer the name of coward to that of murderess. From her
shall spring a race of kings of whose stock shall arise a hero
bold in archery and he shall release Prometheus from his bonds.
This prophecy had been given to him by his mother Themis or
Gaia, one of the ancient Titan brood.

But how he is to be freed he refuses to tell. Doubtless
the story of this deliverance formed the plot of *The Release
of Prometheus*. At this moment a sudden burst of frenzy
from the sting of the gadfly seizes Io. The Chorus on beholding
her misery declare "Wise was the man who framed the saw,
'marry a wife in your own rank.' An artificer must not aspire

to wed a maid from a family puffed up by wealth nor yet from one inflated with pride of birth. May ye never see me becoming a paramour of Zeus, nor wedded to one of the heavenly host. For I am filled with fear when I behold the virgin Io so grievously tormented because she rejected the advances of Zeus. Yet marriage with an equal I regard without dread." The Chorus add that they see no means of escaping the designs of Zeus, should his eye light with favour on a maiden. Prometheus here interposes with a declaration that Zeus is seeking a marriage which shall cost him his throne and shall bring him to nought. Then shall be fulfilled the malison which Cronus hurled at him in the hour of his expulsion from his immemorial seat. Zeus is arraying against himself one whose bolt shall be more mighty than the all-dreaded thunderstone and more piercing than the lightning flash. The Chorus thereupon remind him that those who pay homage to Adrasteia (Necessity) are wise. Prometheus replies that he has already known two tyrants cast out of the citadel of heaven and "a third," says he, "ye shall yet see deposed." At this moment Hermes is sent by Zeus to warn Prometheus against recalcitrancy, but Prometheus bids him go back to his master. Hermes threatens him with still worse torments from Zeus. The cliff to which he is bound shall be shivered, and its fragments will crush him; an eagle shall day by day gnaw his vitals (Fig. 15), and he shall know no respite until some god shall undertake to descend into the sunless realms of Hades and abide in the gloomy depths of Tartarus. Prometheus thereupon rails more fiercely than ever against Zeus: "Let Zeus do what he may, Prometheus can never die."

We are now in a position to form a judgment on the meaning of this drama. More than one scholar has pointed out the resemblance between its story and that of the Fall as described in *Genesis* and the Redemption of Man by the suffering and the death of Christ. It cannot indeed be denied that the play deals with the same eternal theme of the origin of Evil as set forth in the Hebrew Scriptures and the New Testament, that theme on which Milton's devils as they sat on the "specular mount"

"reasoned high
And found no end in wand'ring mazes lost."

Yet a closer examination of the *Prometheus* will show that the resemblance is merely superficial, though in each case alike the keynote is disobedience. In the first place, there is no indication in the Greek drama that mankind had fallen from

Fig. 15.   Prometheus tortured by the Eagle.

a state of primal innocence and perfection. On the contrary Aeschylus conceives man as having been originally in much the same state as his fellow animals, until Prometheus gave him superior intelligence and taught him the use of fire, the building of houses and the other arts of life, except the wearing of skins or any other form of dress.   Thus he regards man from the standpoint of the evolutionist rather than from that of the Hebrew Scriptures. In the latter Jehovah had created Adam and Eve as perfect beings and had set them in a place of unalloyed happiness and bliss. From this they are expelled and rendered liable to death and " all the ills that flesh is heir to " because in yielding to the temptation of the serpent, they had committed the arch-sin of disobedience to his distinct command. But in the legend of the *Prometheus* mankind has not been guilty of any act of disobedience, for they are but as the insensate beasts around and Zeus in the mere wantonness of a despot marked them for destruction. In the next place Prometheus is not even the son of Zeus, but belongs to an older and lower order of gods, whilst Christ on the other hand is the only begotten of the Father. Finally Prometheus saved mankind in direct opposition to the will of Zeus, whereas Jehovah is represented as himself having sent his only son into the world to redeem mankind. Christ indeed has to suffer as did Prometheus, but the Father, when his will is fulfilled by the passion and death of Christ, raised him up to his own right hand in heaven. On the other hand Prometheus will have no respite from his suffering until some one shall rescue him in direct opposition to the will of Zeus. As we have already seen, the one point in common is the doctrine that disobedience is the greatest sin in the sight of both Jehovah and Zeus. There can be no doubt that this is the lesson inculcated by the *Prometheus*. The sufferings of a god and a mortal woman—Prometheus and Io— form the whole plot of the drama. Each of these has suffered for doing what to men seems right, but each has been terribly punished by the Supreme Ruler for disobedience to his will, even when that will is being exercised contrary to all the moral notions of man. Prometheus has redeemed mankind from misery, and taught them to sacrifice to the gods and other practices of religion. But a dreadful penalty is inflicted on him to enforce the law that " to obey is better than sacrifice." The lesser gods who stand between Zeus and mankind must be taught to yield obedience as unquestioning as that demanded from mortals.

For mankind Io is made the exemplar. Hitherto she has

been regarded by scholars as not differing from the other mortal paramours of Zeus, and therefore not unnaturally persecuted by the jealous Hera. But the story of Io shows that so far from her being frail in virtue and ready to become the concubine of Zeus, her virgin chastity recoiled from his embraces, and that it was her refusal to yield to lust that brought upon her all her afflictions. Like Prometheus she will at last find deliverance, but only when in the land of the Nile, Zeus shall have had his will of her and begotten Epaphus.

But just as the utterances of Kratos and Oceanus demonstrated that the sin of Prometheus was disobedience, so those of the Chorus make it no less clear that Io's sin is the same as that of the beneficent Titan who suffered for mankind.

The Release of Prometheus has unfortunately been lost, yet from other works of Aeschylus we can clearly gather that his own doctrine respecting the sovereignty of Zeus was diametrically opposite to that put into the mouth of the rebel Prometheus. As we have seen in the *Supplices*, it is to Zeus that the helpless daughters of Danaus turn for aid, to that Zeus whose eyes are in every place, the defender of the helpless and who helpeth them to right that suffer wrong; it is to this same Zeus that the Chorus of Theban maidens turn in the dire hour when the Seven champions are thundering at the gates of their native city and when rapine and slavery are staring them in the face. In the *Eumenides*, the sequel to the troubled story of the house of Pelops, it is the doctrine of Zeus the All-Father which triumphs over that of the relentless All-Mother, that Gaia from whom Prometheus sprang. For it is the ordinance of Zeus that Apollo maintains against that of Earth in her dark and dreadful phase of the implacable Erinys.

It is not without significance that in the older world of Hellas it was to Earth or Themis, the All-Mother, that men and women looked for aid, whilst the great Fathers Uranus and Cronus are presented as mere savage monsters, gross as those that figure in many a myth of modern savages. But in the Homeric poems very different is the picture given of the lord of Olympus, the Father of gods and men. This conception of Zeus had not been evolved in Greek lands, but had been brought down into Greece by invaders from the north. Once introduced into Greece the worship of Zeus gradually spread, and though regarded as a father stern and relentless to those who broke his laws and set at nought his will, yet he was no Uranus or Cronus, for he is full of mercy for all mankind and will not that even the matricide, stained with his mother's blood, shall perish. For Orestes by his dreadful act had obeyed unquestioningly the divine command and shall therefore meet with mercy and pardon.

It is not without significance that more than once in reference to the suppression of human sacrifices as at Potniae and Phigaleia in Arcadia, an oracle sent by Apollo had ordered the substitution of an animal for a human victim. As Apollo is represented by Aeschylus as the proclaimer on behalf of his father Zeus of the new doctrine of mercy and forgiveness, so from his prophetic tripod at Delphi (assigned to him, so said the legend, by his sire) messages of mercy were sent from time to time into the dark places of Greece, putting an end for ever to human sacrifices. As is set forth clearly in the story of the dream of Pelopidas (p. 165), it was the grand conception of Zeus as the All-Father that was the chief factor in the abolition of such horrid rites in Greece.

Let us now sum up our results. Aeschylus has been universally treated as a conservative who clung to all the beliefs and institutions of the past. But viewed in the light of the evidence set forth in the preceding pages he must rather be regarded as one who whilst cleaving fast to all that was best such as the Senate of the Areopagus, in things that were old was the herald of great and far-reaching reforms, whether artistic, social or religious. No blind votary of tradition was the man who first saw that living actors were the essential and the chorus only ancillary, and thus gave the drama its true form once for all, who elevated the chorus itself by ridding it of the crude and fantastic elements which it had inherited from the mimetic dances of primaeval days; and who equipped Tragedy with a fitting metre and a grand and stately diction meet to express the noblest thoughts and ideas of the human heart and mind. No less revolutionary was he in his con-

ception of the boundless range of subjects which could be
voiced by his new and magnificent instrument, and so he
became the champion of a nobler and a purer morality, the
advocate of a more advanced and stable social system, and the
apostle of a new and loftier religion. In the evolution of
Tragedy he left for Sophocles nought save to consummate its
art and for Euripides nought save to inaugurate its decay.

Laus Deo, Pax Vibis, Requies Mortuis.

INDEX

228 INDEX

Thracians, red-haired, 10; dark-haired, 10; of Pangaeum, 11; their coins, 11; dress of, 20
Threnos, 1, 142
Thymele, 2, 38, 39 *sqq.*, 42, 46, 129, 130
Thymoetes, 75
Tibet, mystery-plays of, 95
Tiger, Red Devil, 95
Tiryns, sacrificial pit, 31
Tomb, of Agamemnon, 44, 119; of Proteus, 44; revered as an altar, 119; of Cyrus, 123; of Antigone, 132; with curb-stone and railing, 138; of Achilles, 140, 160; of Darius, 161; as altar, 170
Tombs, incorporated into worship of gods, 48; of heroes in Tragedy, 48; in Greek tragedies, 110 *sqq.*; of Aepytus, Phocus, Oenomaus and Areithous, 138; sacrifices at, 156
Totemism, 26
Tourneur, Cyril, 111-2
Tragedy, its supposed Dorian origin, 2; evolution of, 42; religious rite, 55; early history of, 56-7; writers of, 57; rise of in Greece, 67; origin of, 185; expansion of, 187 *sqq.*; trage-dies, competition in, 49; extant, very pure, 52; *see Tragoedia*
Tragic, dances, 28, 56; representing sorrows of heroes, 29; chorus, 47; contests, 49, 59; origin of name, 70
Tragikos, 91
Tragobolos, Dionysus, 80
Tragoedia, origin of name, 70
Treasures, hoard of, 33
Trial for homicide, 176 *sqq.*
Tripod, as prize, 36
Troades, 143, 157
Trochaic, tetrameter, 57; tetrameters invented by Phrynichus, 65
Troezen, memorials of Hippolytus and Phaedra, 145
Tronis, barrow at, 30
Trophonia at Lebadea, 36
Trophonius, 36
Tsountas, Prof., 138
Tucker, Prof., 120, 127, 188
Tydeus, 28
Tyndaridae, 107
Typhon, 209
Tyrtaeus, 8

Varro, 191
Vases, 44
Vedda drama, 102-7
Veddas of Ceylon, their dramas, 102
Vegetables, offerings of, 50
Verbs, unaugmented in Epic and Tragedy, 7
Vere, Aubrey de, 84
Verrall, Dr, 120, 183
Vestments, ecclesiastical, 91
Victims, substituture, 81
Virgin, sacrifice of, 165
Vishnu, incarnation of, 95
Viza, in Thrace, its carnival play, 16
Vizianos, M., describes Thracian carnival play, 16
Vollgraff, Dr, 73

Wace, Mr A. J. B., on Thessalian carnival play, 20, 50
Waddell, Col., 95
Waegmundings, 33
Waggon used in Tragedy and Comedy, 61
Walters, Mr H. B., 46
War, border, 84
Water, 191
Wedlock, 190
Westminster, sanctuary of, 172
Whale's Ness, 33
Wife of Beowulf, 34
Wigs, 91
Wine of Thrace, 24
Wolf, Lycaon turned into a, 164
Wolf-skin, 90
Women, descent through, 12, 190; lose votes, 191
Worship, of ancestors, 29; of saints, 29
Wraith, 137

Xanthippus, his grave, 30
Xanthus, 74, 75, 83
Xoana, 129

Yaku invited to partake of food, 107

Zeus, 128, 189; at Athens, 200; his aegis, 96; the Homeric, 217; Am-phiaraus, Trophonius, Agamemnon, 39; Phratrius, 77
Zoilus, 85
Zoroaster, 122